Opa Nobody

AMERICAN LIVES | *Series editor: Tobias Wolff*

UNIVERSITY OF NEBRASKA PRESS | LINCOLN AND LONDON

Opa Nobody

Sonya Huber

Huber. ꝗ Library of Congress Cataloging-in-Publica-
tion Data ꝗ Huber, Sonya, 1971– ꝗ Opa Nobody / Sonya
Huber. ꝗ p. cm. — (American lives) ꝗ Includes bibli-
ographical references. ꝗ ISBN 978-0-8032-1080-6 (cloth :
alk. paper) ꝗ 1. Buschmann family. ꝗ 2. Germany—Gene-
alogy. ꝗ 3. Germany—History—20th century. ꝗ I. Title.
ꝗ CS629.B85 2008 ꝗ 929'.10943—dc22 ꝗ 2007028312 ꝗ Set
in Quadraat and Quadraat Sans by Bob Reitz. ꝗ Designed
by R. W. Boeche.

Contents

Preface

This book is an attempt to summon my German grandfather, a socialist and anti-Nazi activist whom my mother once described as a "nobody." I came to him at a time of personal need, wanting a mentor. I sought a friend who understood the challenges of trying to make a new world while keeping a home and family together. The problem with this conversation was that my grandfather died five years before I was born.

I started this project by collecting family stories. Then I found I needed background about the history of German social movements. Ultimately, this need sent me across the Atlantic, where I waded through archives and musty file boxes. Slowly I felt I was beginning to understand the world in which my grandfather Heinrich Buschmann Jr. lived. As a writer and a granddaughter, I used this research as my scaffolding, and I used the tool of intuition to listen for my grandfather's voice. My strong desire to know about his life led me out onto a limb, which was in another sense a place I felt most comfortable as a writer: in the scenes of his life as I imagined them.

In these pages you will find a dialogue: scenes from my life, in my voice, alternating with scenes from my grandfather's life. The scenes from my grandfather's life are necessarily fiction. Each element of these scenes, however, is grounded closely either in research or in family anecdote, and at no point does the narrative veer into convenient drama merely for the sake of a story. The vast majority of the significant scenes are grounded in specific or general fact brought to me through family story or representative of a probable occurrence as suggested by historical research (with one important exception described below). I have tried to stay as true to the large story as possible with regard to my grandfather's political activity and affiliations. The details, large and small, come from reality, and I have noted as best as I could in the text what is known and unknown. The act of inhabiting another period would have been even more arrogant an assumption, I believe, had I not taken great pains to read everything I could get my hands on about my subject. Still, I am sure only of one thing: that inaccuracies remain, and that the best term for this form may be a "nonfiction novel."

I wish to highlight a major departure into fiction in the text, which I hope I have also made clear in the text itself: I have no idea about the specific actions of my great-uncle Josef "Jupp" Buschmann during the war. He was a member of the Waffen-ss, Hitler's elite guard, but I have no proof that he committed any act of violence or that he aided in the destruction of life or in an eastward shipment of human beings. On the other hand, mere membership in the ss is shocking enough, and it would be naïve of me to assume that he was not involved in these crimes. Re-creating Jupp's consciousness in these pages is the fiction I am least comfortable with, because I fear I may have gotten him completely wrong. I don't know enough about him to understand his choice to shift from left-wing socialist to Waffen-ss guard. I fear I have "underimagined" the horrors this man, described to me as genial and amiable, may have committed, but I will probably never know the truth. Similarly, I have absolutely no evidence that my grandfather Heina Buschmann presided over the title transfer of the homes of Jewish residents of Marl and Recklinghausen. I fictionalized these scenes because the truth will probably never be known. But to pretend my family was innocent would be a far worse fiction, in my opinion—and one that is too often seen as acceptable in our discourse about current and past events, where the disclaimer of "We didn't know" is seen as subtle absolution.

Because of the ethical black hole presented by the Nazi regime, the choice to fabricate conversations and internal dialogue in this "nonfiction novel" may seem to the reader to be a dangerous or questionable choice for representing an era in which facts and truth must be indelibly protected, lest we forget. But for the same reasons, I felt drawn to inhabit these scenes with as much closeness as possible. My aim was not to create fiction for entertainment's sake but to draw the reader into a world that would produce the sense of a lived experience—in short, to make it *feel* real. When reading history of the Third Reich, I felt tempted to dissociate from the perpetrators because in one sense of "fact" I am not one of them. However, in many other senses, this is my own history to unravel. And the logic of separation, of "I didn't do it," has also sometimes been used by subsequent generations of Germans, and the children of perpetrators of other acts of genocide, to separate themselves emotionally from the history and actions of their families and their people.

Some Germans and some families employ silence masterfully. At places where history stops and the record fades, it would be entirely possible for me to write, "And here the story ends," and let this vagueness be my escape, a shoulder shrug. But the historical record gave me an entry point, a doorway, and also a challenge. In this book I am seeking a form that allows me to follow the thread of history in order to imagine the events that had an impact on the changing consciousness of my grandfather. Without writing his life in scenes, that consciousness would have been much less available to me.

I believe my grandfather's consciousness to be one small piece of a puzzle: how is it that any human can endure repression and make small and large decisions during a period of political tyranny and fascism? Memoirs and personal accounts of those living at the time were invaluable to me during the research for this project, yet I found myself wanting a deeper understanding of the daily choices made in a normal life during a horrifyingly abnormal time.

A bit of historical background: when I researched the period of my grandfather's childhood, I was shocked to discover a rich socialist universe in Germany that existed both before and after World War I. My grandfather grew up in revolutionary times. Bavaria at one point declared itself a socialist Soviet-style republic, and the northwestern industrial Ruhr area of Germany was an autonomous socialist zone later invaded by the German government. The upheaval and the sense of community ownership of the political process are both almost unimaginable today. For this reason as well I wanted to allow the reader and myself the chance to step into this world and to feel this alternate existence. Within this world, too, are the seeds of the Nazi era; I wanted to wrestle with, if not understand, some of the causes of the Nazi horrors. My research showed me that socialism came to Germany first, and National Socialism (Nazism) was a parasite of this movement. The Nazis used socialist language and terminology because they were speaking to an audience for whom these ideas were essential. This was also the root of much exploitation and confusion of workers, some of whom were drawn to the populism of Nazi rhetoric without seeing the movement's true aims of division and destruction.

Herr Heinrich Eppe of the Archiv der Arbeiterjugendbewegung (the Archive of the Worker-Youth Movement) in Oer-Erkenschwick was absolutely essential in helping me to understand the world of my grandfather. Herr Eppe explained the importance of former socialist working-class youth in the reformation of Germany's democracy after World War II. "No one studies this subject now," he said. "Not even in Germany." At the time he was compiling a database to track the numbers of those in leadership positions who had been members of the Arbeiterjugend, or Worker-Youth. In some ways, he argued, the ability of the country to reemerge from Nazism had much to do with the prewar socialist youth movement. Herr Eppe helped me trace my grandfather through the archive's collections of activist newspapers, none of which were searchable electronically. He also connected me with Herr Gustav Hackenberg, who gave me what would be the last day of his life to tell me stories about my grandfather.

Historian Detlev Peukert's *Ruhrarbeiter Gegen den Faschismus* (Ruhr Workers against Fascism) was essential in my research. This book presents an amazing array of details about the anti-Nazi resistance in the Ruhr. I wish also to thank the staff of the Archiv der sozialen Demokratie der Friedrich-Ebert Stiftung (the Archive of social Democracy of the Friedrich Ebert Institute) in Bonn, where I was able to look at many flyers and pamphlets related to my grandfather's political work. Through the Stadtarchiv Marl (City Archive of Marl) I found evidence of my great-grandfather's and great-grandmother's political roles, their campaigns for public office, and their involvement in the local socialist Weimar government. Staff members at the Kreisarchiv (County Archive) Recklinghausen were also very helpful in providing information about my grandfather's work life.

The International Institute of Social History in Amsterdam has a wealth of materials, both online and in its collections, tracing the existence of social democracy in Germany. Its materials allowed me to hold in my hands flyers and newsletters made by Nazi resistors during World War II. This archive's collection of postwar labor materials in Germany was also very useful. I am tremendously grateful to the PEO Foundation and the American Council on Germany, both of which provided funding for travel and for the year and a half of research prior to my trip. Professor Alan Beyerchen of the Department of History at Ohio State University allowed me to take his survey course on modern German history as a graduate student, met with me individually, and made valuable suggestions for planning my research trip. The Ohio State University MFA program in creative writing provided me with a wonderfully supportive environment in which to grow as a writer.

My family, of course, receives the lion's share of thanks for giving me stories about my grandfather. My uncle Klaus Buschmann unearthed stunning documents in his cellar and patiently carted me around the Ruhr. Klaus set up interviews and generously gave of his time and affection. My aunt Christa Buschmann translated documents and combed her memories. Oliver and Katrin Buschmann and Christiane and Udo Krolcyzk provided levity and hospitality during this research trip. Thanks also to many others who took the time to speak with me and share their memories. Evidence about my family's activities during the Third Reich was difficult to come by. My grandfather's massive personnel file was essential in piecing together the outline of his activity, but efforts to find information about my grandfather and about his brother during the Third Reich through visits to the Berlin Document Center, which contains an archive of Nazi Party activity, were unproductive; these documents are just now becoming more widely accessible.

Thanks to my husband, Donny Humes, for his support and understanding, and deep thanks to my son, Ivan, who makes all of my questions more necessary and urgent. Deep thanks also to Lee Martin, mentor and friend, whose confidence in me made any outlandish project seem reasonable. Sincere thanks also to Jenny Young, Kathy Bohley, Trish Houston, Monica Kieser, Brooke Davis, Bill Roorbach, Jovan Karcic, the staff of the University of Nebraska Press, and all the organizers for their constant support and encouragement.

Above all, I want to thank my mother, Gerhild Heidi Huber, who told me the first stories, the family stories that change shape over time and transform into something multifaceted and yet still true. She mined her memory for every scrap of family history and made long-distance phone calls to hunt down recollections and rumors. She examined photos with a magnifying glass, sat through long interviews, read several versions of this manuscript, and gave generous comments. Ultimately, her most wonderful gift was that she surrendered her opinion of her father and allowed her relationship with him to change and grow as she let me into the circle of his love.

And thank you in advance to the reader for coming along on the journey to imagine my grandfather through this perilous terrain.

Acronyms of Political Parties

These acronyms, listed chronologically by year of formation, include many of the left-wing political parties in Germany up until World War II. Only about half of these acronyms are mentioned in the text, but the various splinterings of the parties and groups are mentioned as a backdrop to the political action of the text.

SDAP (1869) Sozialdemokratischen Arbeiterpartei, or Social Democratic Workers' Party

SPD (1890) Sozialdemokratische Partei Deutschlands, or Social Democratic Party of Germany (reformation and name change)

AJ (1908) Arbeiterjugend, or Worker Youth, organized under SPD

SAG (1916) Sozialdemokratische Arbeitsgemeinschaft, or Social Democratic Working Group, an independent group to the left of the SPD, which became the USPD

USPD (1917) Unabhängige Sozialdemokratische Partei Deutschlands, or the Independent Social Democratic Party of Germany, with the youth group Freie Sozialistiche Jugend (FSJ), or Free Socialist Youth

KPD (1918) Kommunistischen Partei Deutschlands, or Communist Party of Germany, with the youth group Communist Youth Union of Germany (KJVD)

SPJ (1919–22) Sozialistische Proletarierjugend, or Socialist Proletarian Youth, connected to the USPD

VAJV (1919–22) Verband der Arbeiterjugendvereine
Deutschlands, or Worker-Youth Union

SAJ (1922–32) The SPJ and the Verband der Arbeiterjugendvereine came together to form the Socialistische
Arbeiter-Jugend, or Socialist Worker-Youth (SAJ)

SAPD (1931) Socialistische Arbeiterpartei Deutschlands,
or Socialist Workers' Party of Germany, a left-wing
organization formed to oppose the SPD, with youth
group Sozialistiche Jugendverband (SJV), or Socialist
Youth Union

The Intuition of History

Why try to change the world?

Dear Opa, Grandfather, Heina Buschmann: I knelt down in the reference section of a midwestern American library, beat-tired, already late for another damn political meeting at a cheap Chinese restaurant. I tried to conjure you from a volume on German history. Come on, socialist, anti-Nazi, German, man I'd never met. Appear and tell me how to live without fear. "Life-long activist" reads so cool in the history books. But the family hardly mentions your name now, so bitter toward the man with the agendas and the pamphlets stuffed in his pockets, the distracted look on his round, sleepy face. You were no inspiration to me as I grew up in a Republican small town, a south side Chicago mallrat turned shaved-head anarchist. I didn't even know your stories, but then I seemed to turn weird and angry as if an underground tide pulled my blood in that direction. But we don't believe in those blood stories, do we, Opa?

There is no answer. I know a few stories: where they lived, the

coal mines, the organizing, the coal dust, the sickness, and the
political turmoil. And so I imagine his beginnings, the seed of
him.

Heina, you may have opened your mouth to cry, but your chest
folded up like a wad of paper and wouldn't release. Heina let out
a thin noise between his teeth. His mother, Lina, bent over her
pregnant belly and reached for Heina in the cotton blankets. She
sat down heavily as she felt his forehead. The child's face was red
and flushed.

"Verdammte," she said. Damn it, damn it all. She wiped the
mucus from Heina's nose and saw in the handkerchief the green
of wild infection, flecked with the black dust that coated their
lungs, their apartment, and their lives, the coal dust that lined
the window sills, grayed the wash, and powdered their skin. No
wonder the babies died.

My great-grandmother Lina, a fiery woman with black hair
and dark eyes, takes the name "the Dragon" in family lore, der
Drache, repeated with a solemn shiver. At the time of her birth in
1880 the newly formed country of Germany had outlawed socialism. In 1898, not even twenty, she fled her home (fled why? What
drew her and what chased her?) and moved three hundred miles
from Germany's southeast to the northwestern city of Köln, a
bold step for a working-class girl. She found work as a maid with
a colonel in the Reich military. In that household she met my
great-grandfather Heinrich Sr., a young stable hand who had already launched his grand career of rabble-rousing and getting
fired.

I can taste this much from the intuition of history: Lina ran,
the way we dark-haired, nervous, stunned, and skittish women
of our clan do, and she found a man with the sun in his eyes and
the laughing confidence that revolution and a better life were

right around the corner. She married Heinrich Sr. on October 25, 1900, in a cloud of disapproval, a Lutheran girl marrying a Catholic, a runaway marrying a socialist wild man. No one from her family attended the wedding. Two young miners, twenty-four-year-old Karl Ermshaus and twenty-three-year-old August Rehm, stood as witnesses.

The year after their wedding, Lina's strong man went down in the mines, which exploded and flooded and smashed men's hands and feet and took their lives and didn't pay nearly enough. The miners stood shouting on the picket lines, and strikes spread like brush fires from one mine to the next—in 1872, '89, '90, '91, '93. Heinrich Sr. learned the trade of riling up a crowd as he dug black hunks of coal. As a child I knew none of this, had been told only that he could bounce knives by their points on his biceps and that he ate raw onions. I had imagined him as a weird German clown, standing up at Thanksgiving to grab the carving knives and marching around the table in a tank top with muscles bulging like Popeye, an onion in his mouth and eyes streaming happy tears.

Then Lina was pregnant, and I am sure there were moments of sunlight and the springtime smell of red heather as the couple went riding with the socialist workers' bicycle club through the paths of the Haard nature preserve. A century later, my uncle Klaus carefully handed me a thick red bundle of cloth, tinged with the warm glow of age. I unwrapped it to see that it was a red flag, embroidered with an ornate yellow S for *Sozialismus* surrounded with the spokes of a bicycle wheel and the logo for the Marl-Hüls chapter of the biking club. I imagined the revolution proceeding forward joyfully with every push of the workers' pedals. This flag and other signs told me that my grandfather Heina was born into a Red universe. There were workers' stamp clubs, drama clubs, hiking clubs, chess clubs, first-aid societies, women's clubs, and gymnastic clubs; there were socialist newspapers, cooperative grocery stores, and bars. After the Kaiser outlawed socialism in the mid-1880s, the movement's roots went underground, stretched deeply and broadly into the German soil.

In a Red universe Lina and Heinrich Sr. must have lain in bed and shared the pillow talk of strategy and political arguments, whispering about possibilities as if exploring a grand hall with windows and doors waiting to be forced open. Oh, those horizontal political meetings, filled with the drug of being loved for your body and your mind, your instincts and your skills, all tinged with sweat and pheromones and hope.

I knew those meetings. Lying on the floor of a dorm room at an organizers' training in Washington DC, I wondered how to drop my Boston activist fiancé because I'd fallen for the organizer sleeping next to me. I moved with organizer number two to Chicago and pushed him to propose marriage so we could get the future going. I left chaos in my wake as I sketched an action plan and a campaign for my personal revolution. When I failed I simply chose a new short-term target. I fell in love with organizer number three, whose eyes snapped with light as he talked about anarchism and the Chicago radical labor insurgency. We stood on a street corner, arguing about how I wanted to have a baby but couldn't sketch a viable strategy while working fifty hours a week for a nonprofit and barely getting by. He did not kiss me then; he gave me a speech about allegiance to the working class.

In this Chicago winter, with my personal life in ruins of my own creation, I began to wonder if anyone could successfully love both politics and a partner. That was when I first heard the rumor that Heina's father, Heinrich Sr., was a raging rebel.

Mom brought the sentences from a visit to Germany: "Heinrich Sr. hung a red flag on a mountainside. Uncle Klaus told me he organized a union."

I held onto the phone. My must-do, what-now life dipped into a moment of complete stillness.

I was exhausted; changing the world had stopped being fun. I fell easily into another century, seeking some imagined comfort. I could picture the romantic scarlet flap of a red banner in the breeze, but I could not imagine the feeling of having one's father hang that flag. Having an organizer rebel for a daddy, I imagined, would provide a source of guidance, a North Star. I gradually submerged myself in family history, collecting stories and asking questions. I learned that Heina's mama, Lina, was a sharp woman torn between misery and elation; I paired timelines to life stories and felt the knife-edges of deprivation that must have accompanied the glorious and simple story of rebellion. I learned that a lung infection almost killed young Heina at the same time that coal miners' strikes tore through Germany. And if I wanted my grandfather, my new rebel family, I had to start with that two-year-old, who reached for a pained, distracted Mama and a Papa aflame with change.

Lina's rage sparked from ordinary flint and steel. Maybe Heinrich Sr. worked a night shift down in Auguste Viktoria shaft number 1, and Lina curled her body around her baby son Heina and her belly, pregnant with a second son. Tonight she didn't want to hear any of Heinrich's stories about handing out the pamphlets from the miners' union, tacking up the posters in the miners' washroom, or treading that fine line with the bosses.

Heina felt his mother's hand on his chest and believed the terrible pinch in his lung would fade away any minute now. He drifted into sleep and dreamed of a black dog biting him in the side and shaking him like a toy. Heina rolled in the thistles of heat, cut by the dog's teeth. He didn't hear himself described in his father's speeches as Papa cursed the mine owners who didn't pay the miners enough to feed their families. Heina felt bright lights and dreamed he was in the mine shaft under his father's lamp, but didn't see the scalpel the doctor used to cut through his pink two-year-old skin, the metal fishing like a hot stab into the delicate envelope of the lung through an ooze of warm blood and then tearing the flesh-paper, letting out that hateful green bile as infection drained into a metal bowl.

Days or weeks later, footsteps scuffed on the stairs up to the third-floor apartment, and Lina glanced at the breadboard to estimate how much she could spare for dinner. Heinrich Sr. slammed open the door, and four men with mussed hair and wild eyes crowded in. They had scrubbed at the mine washstands, but without much soap the dust became a paste that stained their hands and etched black lines into their wrinkled faces.

"Heinrich," Lina whispered, jutting her chin to the corner crib where Heina slept. "I can't feed these men. All I have is soup and bread. And they're so loud."

Heinrich grabbed her forearms. "Lina, don't worry about the bread," he said, his pale blue eyes wild and tinged with red. "You're going to remember November 28, 1904. The next strike's coming—I can feel it!" Heinrich narrowed his eyes, trying to catch a thread of excitement in his wife's look. Why wouldn't she cheer him on like last year at the picket line?

During the early strikes I imagine Lina stood with Heinrich. Wild girl, you had your heart in your throat. There might have been smoke in the air from a bonfire but also the eerie calm of the mines at rest. Oh, those lovely picket-line jitters, history itself and power, too, giving off an electric charge. You took your place on the line in a phalanx of miners' wives. I read how the women used their children in carriages as decoys to ward off police, smuggling illegal pro-labor pamphlets during a strike, or even filling the carriages not with children but with stones to hurl at the scabs and the cops.

These stories about revolutionary baby carriages held a strangely familiar echo. When I was young, Mom told me a story: she said adult Heina had pushed a baby carriage containing anti-Nazi literature hidden under a baby. As an adult I had never asked about this tale, and I think I held back because I sensed pain there as murky as truth. The anti-Nazi pamphlet story wasn't told with pride; Mom's voice pinched with resentment and fear.

The story became a nugget of history suspended like an insect trapped in amber. Nothing to know. And if you tried to know your way into it, you had to shatter the shiny bead to get at the truth. It remained a sentence in the back of my mind, a marker for all the things I could not ask. That shallow locket of my inheritance held a hinged and two-part tale with a mirror image that pulled me to Germany. I rubbed the story until it shone, my hard proof that Heina risked his life to stand up to the Nazis. It made me want to know the man who would do such a brave or stupid thing.

I imagine Heina in my mother's story—a slight man, short, with forward-thrust shoulders—tightening his grip on the handle of a baby carriage, feeling the smooth wood slide under his fingers as he pushed the buggy down a sidewalk in Marl. The carriage held my uncle Klaus, a sickly baby with an ever-present smile who didn't know World War II had exploded all around him. The baby's body and the blankets in the carriage hid a stack of crudely printed anti-Nazi flyers, most likely smuggled in from Holland. In my vision of the story Heina pushed the carriage down the sidewalk past the mine entrance, passing women who strolled along the curved street to the bakeries.

Klaus coughed and spit up a thin line of white drool. Heina leaned into the carriage and patted his pockets for a handkerchief. He'd left the house without one. He mopped the spit with the corner of the blanket, then reached under the baby and slid the sheaf of papers down toward the foot-end of the carriage. You wouldn't want to have two or three couriers risk their lives only to ruin the batch of flyers with baby vomit.

All Heina had to do was to leave this stack of flyers in the phone booth at the pharmacy. The flyers were disguised with a wrapper that said, "Sale on Potatoes for German Health." Someone—for his own safety he did not know who—would take the stack tonight and walk quickly up and down the streets of this neighborhood, shoving the flyers into mailboxes.

Frau Schmiede, his wife's friend, stepped out of the bakery doorway as they passed. Klaus cooed. Frau Schmiede leaned into the carriage, reached her hand toward Klaus's cheek.

"He's cold, Heina," she said. She looked up, blue eyes kind but piercing under her taupe hat. "What were you thinking to bring a baby out in this weather? There's more coal dust than air today."

Heina nodded, caught his breath in his throat, said something about taking the child out to give his mother a break. Frau Schmiede's hand curled, grabbed the blankets, and tucked them firmly under the child.

The story, repeated and repeated, grows like a pearl around a grain of sand. I read books and wrote grant proposals to find out more. A few years into the search, I sat at my uncle Klaus's dining room table and struggled to string German words together. *Kinderwagen*, baby carriage. I repeated the story about Heina and the anti-Nazi baby carriage, opening my palm to surrender my treasure to the light of day.

Klaus looked at me strangely, dark eyes mulling over my words, mechanic's hands curled on the doilied table. He stuck out his lip, considering how to tell me the truth.

"Nein, dat war die Oma Lina!" No, Klaus explained, Oma Lina pushed the carriage, with her son Heina as a baby inside. We traced and retraced each word. I had fallen in love with my opa based on a misunderstanding and a mirror image.

My books confirmed that Lina had most likely ferried pro-union flyers in the baby carriage. The truth is buried way back in these years, wrapped in rough cotton. Lina stashed a stack of flyers, tucked a blanket on top, and then added her baby boy, firstborn Heina, who might have peered over the edge of the carriage, absorbing the blurred shapes of a crowd, a many-headed beast, the muffled sounds of shouting and rhythmic chants.

I want to see this Dragon who makes the family shudder even decades after her death.

One of the other men, desperately thin and probably sick with worms, pulled out a chair. "What can we do but strike?" he asked.

Heinrich turned to Lina and said, "They just posted notice today: longer shifts down in the holes at the Bruchstraße mine, and no increase in pay." The third man at the table, chewing a slice of bread, shook his head and grunted in anger. "So we'll be next. We won't take it."

Lina sighed, sick for the moment of the union and the heartbreak it brought. "It's the Poles, though, who are working for nothing, driving down your pay," she muttered. Lina turned back to the soup, angry at the Poles and at the whole world, overfilled with anger and want. Acrid bitterness sloshed up over the sides of her soul.

The dark Poles, the dirty Polish with their shifty eyes . . . Lina, I hear over and over that there was hatred and fear in you, and I am only guessing it had partly to do with bloodlines. Your little boy Heina will grow up to marry a half-Polish girl, and you'll treat her so cruelly. I will get that Polish girl's face, the dark almond eyes, olive skin, and the cheekbones that make people ask, "Greek? Cherokee? Turk? Lebanese?" The face that made the kids at the midwestern grade school yell out, "Jew!" But I am German, a stew of your cruelty and its object.

Heinrich caught Lina's arm. "The Poles are on the front lines, over a hundred of them working down in Bruchstraße. You don't work with them, you don't know," he said.

Her nostrils flared and the heat rose in her throat. "I read it in the *Miner's Paper*, everyone says it's so. They're starving us."

Lina and Heinrich glared at each other, fire-black eyes meeting ice-blue stones of resolve. "Lina," he said, "you're wrong." She was never afraid to have her own opinions, and Heinrich had loved this about her from the start, but she wouldn't listen or think before she spoke. Ahh, but that—even in the midst of fierce disagreement—was love, a new kind of revolutionary love where a woman could open her mouth like that and have no fear of getting slapped.

He tucked his lips together, considering her, then shook his head and sat down with the men, who began their clipped and earnest planning, guessing, figuring. They wondered what the union would do, whether it would stand with them or cut them off at the knees. Heinrich never minded the fight. He seemed to open his steel-colored eyes every morning with new energy to give and to work. That red-hearted hope was exactly what she'd fallen in love with, and now she wanted to beat him, to drive that stupid hope right out of him before it killed her.

Lina felt the spasm of a headache coming on and rubbed her temple. The baby shifted inside her, a roiling fish. She turned back to the stove to check the thin soup, and with her face turned safely away from the men she fought back tears. Fever seemed to be creeping up the back of her own neck, and she tightened her grip on the spoon. She had a flash of nightmarish visions: turning the soup on herself, scalding her own face, blinding herself to this horrible small apartment, to the late nights and the cold meetings and the sick children and the waiting and wanting. It was unbelievable, that this horrid small room was her life, that Heinrich came home and coughed up black chunks, coagulated dust flecked with red, and that she was bringing another child into this hell.

Does that rage dissipate? Two generations later, my mother's heart rose and fell on an echoing ripple of that fear. I see her turning toward the stainless steel sink in her 1970s midwestern subdivision tract home, stomach churning. Despite the refrigerator and indoor plumbing, she felt the familiar money panic, the pitch of the earth about to give way. She had succeeded in leaving Heina and home by moving across the ocean to the promised land of America, but I know her dark eyes flashed, in the way that a person who has come from one version of hell can flash her eyes. The whole world seemed to depend on a thin veneer of normalcy and moderate stability (the first real home, a little bit of money) that could crumble and disappear with the grease down the drain.

Mom ran water in the sink, washed the coat of grease off her thick, strong fingers, sighing at the way dirt seemed to collect in the pocket underneath the diamond of her wedding ring. Dad nursed another golden can of Miller Lite, the Champagne of Beers, his face splashed in the flickering TV light of a black-and-white horror movie, Dracula's disembodied hand creeping between the slats of a cemetery fence. Dad had done every kind of job imaginable: butcher, cotton-picker and potato-grader, pill-grinder at a pharmacy firm, salesman of fancy cookware. He'd stitched up bodies on operating tables as a surgeon's helper and worked his way through college on the geriatrics ward. He wanted to go to medical school but couldn't afford it, so he got into the burgeoning nuclear safety business. Mom and Dad started a fledging business, with an office in the basement packed with files and papers. Dad went to make sure radiation stayed where it was supposed to, and later he began to clean it up when it had escaped, the twentieth-century version of my great-grandfather Heinrich Sr.'s job, taming the heat from the bowels of the earth.

That night something set Mom off. I will imagine it was a missed appointment or a phone call to a new customer not returned. She grabbed a bowl of peas, swimming in their weak canned brine, and with her other hand took the white plastic butter dish. She glanced at Dad and bit back a word that would fall past his ears, ignored. Some bile rose in her throat, and her stomach clenched. With a flick of the wrist, she sent the stick of butter sailing to the floor. It hit so hard that a pale, loose glop flew up and stuck to the ceiling. The whole rest of the time we lived in that house, the one-inch grease spot was there on the ceiling above the phone, collecting dust as a darkening birthmark. I see now that the stain stood as a sign of love: she knew to not direct that rage at us, and instead to take it out on the perishables.

Lina, I use my own rage to imagine yours. A century after you nursed Heina, I felt the gritty loneliness of breast-feeding a three-month-old in a union hall lobby. I sat on the cigarette-scarred carpet, listening to the burbles and laughter of a political planning retreat beyond the doorway. I needed the sharp debate and challenge of the meeting, but I was also relieved to be yanked outside by my son's need. As I drove home from the meeting hours later in a snowstorm, the car skidded on an exit ramp. I whipped the wheel against the force of the rotation. My poor baby screamed in his cold infant car seat, a blue wall of sound. Lina, even as I learned mothering, as I perfected the art of scraping by, I could not pull away from the routine of making a new world. It had fed me when nothing else could.

My German timelines showed that a meltdown approached for the Buschmann family. I collected a string of dates listing massive strikes in the Ruhr mines. These would spell upheaval for the young family, church excommunication and blacklists and lost jobs and relocation.

The smells of coal and sweat and smoke poured from the packed meeting hall out into the street, mingling with the sea-crash of voices. Lina clutched her six-week-old baby with one arm tightly beneath her shawl. Heina, two and a half, grasped her free hand. With the same blue eyes and trusting round face of his father, he absorbed the crowds, enthralled.

Men in wrinkled, dirty coats offered flyers and newspapers. Lina took one and read the Polish masthead across the top of a newspaper, *Zjednoczenie Zawodowe Polskie*. She handed it back to the man, a dark-eyed Slav with cheekbones like basket handles. He muttered at her, a Polish phrase with the hard consonants. Another man said loudly in German, "Idiot—you'll get arrested for speaking Polish at meetings. They'll shut us down." The Kaiser wanted the Poles' muscles but not their mouths.

Two men behind Lina told picket stories about the brave Polish women who caught scabs' wives bringing lunch pails to their strikebreaking husbands. The women stole the lunches and smeared the women with horseshit. "Don't mess with the Poles!" one man howled. Germans driven even to starvation wouldn't do that, Lina thought.

She craned her neck over the crowds, but couldn't see Heinrich anywhere. The baby, Josef, cried out against her breast, and she looked down into his small heart-shaped face. He'd be a child closer to her heart, someone who understood her.

"Jupp, shhhh," she said, bouncing the baby. Elbows jostled her, and she had half a mind to lash out at this stupid crowd, which should part before her and show her a chair. She felt a pang of hunger for one clear political thought uninterrupted by a child's sticky hand or mewling. This was not out of hatred for the child, no, but born of frustration for the half revolution in these halls.

Lina pushed into the massive hall decked with bunting and blanketed with a layer of pipe smoke and soot from the oil lamps. There was Heinrich, hauling chairs to the front of the stage. He leaned forward to talk with a man in a black sailor's hat and then roared, his laughter carrying above the noise. Her heart filled with a burst of pride for this strong man, and then she swallowed back a tinge of bitterness. He had what he needed here in this hall, and he hadn't waited for her or even looked for her.

Meetings dragged on after rallies and pickets, and arguments followed the late-night sounds of her husband and always three or four other men tromping up the stairs. Heinrich came home with a ripped coat, crying, on the night the Kaiser called in the army to fire into crowds of striking miners. He sat up twice during the night flinching from the hooves of imagined police horses. On February 9, 1905, he opened the door holding a handkerchief to his split lip. "The unions sold us out," he said, "and when they handed out their leaflets announcing the end of the strike, we miners ripped them up, turned over the tables and scattered those cowards to the wind."

Heinrich had a feeling that worse was to come. More than two hundred thousand men yelled on the picket lines, the biggest strike in Europe's history. But the union's coffers ran dry, and it retreated in the face of escalating violence. By all accounts the miners lost, getting by with a shortened shift but no pay increase or contract. The only positive, said Heinrich, was that the Polish, the Catholic, and the socialist miners had all worked together for once and forged a tenuous coalition.

Two days after the picket lines came down, Heinrich left to report for his first day shift, and Lina leaned back in a chair, enjoying the warmth of a rare February sun falling through the window. Heina sat on the bed petting a stuffed bear, a present from a miner's wife. Baby Jupp rolled on the covers, curling the edges of his mouth into a smile.

Lina bundled up the boys, took her basket from the cupboard, and headed down to the small grocery store at the corner of Viktoriastraße, across the street from Auguste Viktoria Mineshaft 1. She passed the wives of two miners who'd been active in the strike, and they each smiled widely as if greeting family. In the store Heina inspected the candy in the huge round glass containers on the counter. Lina motioned to the storekeeper and said, "A half kilo of butter, please, a loaf of bread, and coffee." The heavy woman with sagging eyes pulled out a ledger book.

"Not on credit," said Lina. She dug into her pocket, searching for the thin envelope with the last payout from the strike fund. "I have cash."

The woman stared at her impassively. "What's your last name?"

Lina scowled. "Buschmann. But I told you, I have cash."

The woman traced her finger down a column of names, shook her head. "Can't take your money. You're on the list."

Lina put her forearms on the counter. "What list?" The woman pulled the book away. "What list?" Lina demanded loudly, knowing it was a blacklist from the strike. "What does the strike have to do with you?" she yelled. "What business is it of yours?"

An older woman sidled up to Lina. "Dear, it's the same with my daughter's husband. The mine owners . . . But if you'd like, I can buy your groceries for you—"

Lina yanked Heina's hand fiercely and stumbled out, clutching Jupp. She tried four others stores, and at the last one she walked in the door with wild eyes, already yelling. She came home empty-handed, both children crying, and opened the door to see Heinrich sitting at the table.

Heinrich reached for Heina's hand, pulling the boy up onto his lap. "There's no work for me here. The union will fight it, but it's going to take at least six months, lots of noise," he said. He raised his eyebrows in a painful show of optimism. "I'll find something, don't worry."

During the next days Heinrich left to look for work, and the long evenings filled with meetings at the union hall and meager dinners scraped together from donations. Heina tried to catch a smile from distracted Papa, whose eyes traced the floorboards. When the door slammed Heina waited, barely breathing. If Mama started to cry he stayed absolutely still until she stopped. Then when she stirred, he sat up and reached across the bed for her, watching for a smile from her drawn face.

Heina drank down his mother's unhappiness as she told him stories about her youth, about running away from home to become the maid of a colonel, about waking up early in the cold to start a fire in the huge kitchen that had been bigger than their whole apartment, with copper pots that gleamed like the sun. She said she'd decked the dinner table with silver candlesticks and piles of fruit and chocolate. She painted a fairytale world of all the things she didn't have and underscored it with bitterness as each daydream dissolved.

In the next months Heina may have imagined the family as part of a circus: they packed and moved like a sideshow. Mine owners passed the blacklists to the landlords, who evicted the family twice. They moved north to Rhade when Papa found a post at the mine there. The water came from a pump out in front, and behind the brick house ran a cold creek, Am Kalten Bach.

A few weeks later, I imagine Heinrich came home with that shine in his eyes and told Lina about a new organizing committee.

"You know I am supportive," Lina said. "I married you. *Aber jetzt ist es schluß.*" This is the end, she said, *schluß*, a tangle of consonants all soft and blurry with the meaning as firm and sharp as an axe blade.

Heinrich couldn't stand her look of fury, those spots of glowing coal in her head. He went out for a walk, hoping to discover a new view of their situation. What, exactly, was he supposed to do? The heat in the mines made your head spin. Lina had not seen the foot of a twelve-year-old apprentice hauler crushed under the wheels of a coal wagon. That crushed foot, and a thousand other sights just like it, the coughing men joking and spitting blood—how could a man take that and still call himself a man?

I imagine my own dad felt that too, the rage at stupid bosses and the choice of whether to come home and drink yourself numb or to quit: *That's it, I've had it, pack your stuff, we're leaving tonight. There's nothing for us here.*

So Heinrich Sr. did something—maybe something as simple as taking a rock and a few nails, pounding up a flyer for a miners' meeting—and then it really was *schluß*. One day in 1907 he got the summons from the court notifying him that the Catholic Church had officially excommunicated him because of his political work. We still have the fancy certificate with its ornate inked border, which looks like a first-place spelling bee prize if you can't read the words. Maybe his miner friends took him to the pub that night and toasted him. But walking home from the bar,

he knew they had to leave Rhade. And maybe the risks had become deadly. A family story contains another mysterious bead of
possible truth: that a man named Heinz Tulke saved Heinrichs's
life and that someone wanted to kill him because of politics.

Whatever the details, I know that in 1907 the Buschmann family packed up their possessions and retreated to Thüringen, the
green rolling hills of southeastern Germany where Lina was born
and had run from. Lina's brother-in-law owned a bakery where
Heinrich could work until he got on his feet. And there were jobs
there—above ground—a thriving porcelain factory and the huge
Zeiss optical works.

After the long train ride Heinrich clutched his mother's hand
and stepped onto the station platform. He was five, a thin boy
with a serious look in his wide blue-gray eyes. The train station
smelled strange, like evergreen and cut wood. What was missing? The earthy tang of coal dust. The lack of that gray note in
the air made Heina afraid, and he missed the blanket that had
always protected him. The sky flourished itself nakedly, a piercing, gaudy blue. But this, his parents said, was home.

2

Sweet Heinrich

The bell on the door clanged, and Heina looked up from the tower of matchboxes he'd built on the counter. A group of women in feathered hats and imposing bustles maneuvered into the candy store for their Saturday shopping. The words "Der Süsse Heinrich," Sweet Heinrich, looped across the storefront glass in gold paint, and the window glinted in the glare of the sun.

"Mutti!" Heina called. He didn't want to serve the women, because those fancy sorts of ladies always seemed to make a big deal about how smart he was and how quickly he could add the numbers and wrap their candy, matches, and magazines into a parcel. But the compliments seemed to contain a slightly mocking tone. Heina couldn't figure it out. He was ten, after all, and he'd already stood in Papa's place as the man of the house for three months last year when his father shipped off for army reservist training. Yet the ladies in the shop always treated him like a boy.

"Guten Tag!" said an older woman as she laid eyes on Heina.

"Are you the man of this establishment? Are you the Sweet Hein-rich?" More embarrassment.

His mother pulled aside the storeroom curtain, smoothing her apron as she put on her smile for the customers. With her black hair held up with pins, she looked quite beautiful. She seemed so much calmer here in Jena, despite the debt for the store, despite the ledger books and daily hauling of big sacks of groceries. She did cry when they visited relatives. Heina couldn't quite piece it together, but his grandparents sometimes tucked in their lips with angry silence and awkwardness at Sunday dinner. It had something to do with Papa and the Sozialdemokratische Partei Deutschlands. But Mama loved this city of culture, she said, the beautiful old university and the lovely buildings with white plaster and heavy timbers.

Mama's eyelids drooped slightly as a customer recited a long shopping list. Heina rolled a cone from a large sheet of paper, then grabbed the glass lid from the jar of cough drops and scooped a quarter kilo into the cone. He avoided the eyes of the customers but smiled at his mother as they maneuvered around each other in the space behind the counter.

When they first came to Jena, Papa worked nights in the bakery with Uncle Arno. He came home every morning with warm rolls, his mustache white with flour, then pulled closed the bedroom curtain with a snap and fell into bed. Family lore tells me that Papa Heinrich was mentioned in the newspaper for saving a baker's apprentice who fell into a huge vat of rising dough. I imagine Papa Heinrich woke up silent and moody each afternoon, staring out the window or mumbling to himself as he read the newspaper. If both Mama and Papa happened to be in the apartment, Heina held his breath, making himself invisible with a book propped in front of him as he tried to interpret the half sentences and sighs between his parents.

"Your sister's husband doesn't even like me," Heinrich muttered to Lina one morning. "I don't say a thing about the party, but while we're waiting for the dough to rise, he goads me like we're some sort of disease. *Donnerwetter*, I'm a bigger German patriot than he is—I've been in the military reserves for ten years!"

Lina slammed a bowl onto the table. "He has to mock everything," she said. "And my sister just puts her head down and waits for it to pass. But you already know this, so why complain and fight with him?"

Heinrich grumbled, and Lina turned and riveted him with her eyes. "He may tease you, Heinrich Buschmann, but that bakery is safer than any stupid assembly line. It's free bread, and all you have to do is ignore one bitter old man. Not strong enough to handle that?"

Heina, I know only a general outline of your family's life in Thüringen. I know about the jaunty name "Sweet Heinrich," a silly bit of sunlight to show me your papa's sense of humor. I know the family took on a huge debt to set up shop, one that compounded and chased them long after they'd left again for the Ruhr. My mother heard stories about the debt, and the receipts for payment remain in a family folder in Germany in Uncle Klaus's living room, a warning about creditors transmitted through generations. I don't know exactly why your family took the huge risk to open a store; maybe your parents, worn down from the struggles of organizing, decided to try a completely different way of making ends meet.

I know, too, the chest-clench of an overhead conversation about money, the unsolvable anxiety. I feel your breath stop as you listen, duck, wait for it to pass. As a nervous ten-year-old girl, I tried to piece together snippets of my parents' anger, days of money stress rolled into a heavy cloud cover. How do you tell a child that this doesn't mean we hate each other, that this doesn't mean we're doomed? It was probably no accident that as the good-girl eldest daughter in the eco-conscious seventies I decided to help. At age seven or eight, I made signs for the light switches that said, "Turn it off," following the advice of the cartoon public service commercials showing Mr. Electricity escaping and leaping with crackling abandon. I taped a sign to each light switch. Save a penny, save your soul.

Heinrich Sr. baked rolls and bread for two long years. Then one day in 1909, he might have come home laughing, booming with joy.

"I'm hired on at the porcelain factory," he said, pride swelling his chest, "and we're going to unionize the place! We've got seven union men already hired on. I'll be a clay mixer, the hardest work, so the guys will be hungry to organize."

Heina, curled in bed with a book, put his hand over his mouth to hide a smile. Papa glowed like the yellow sun. But without even looking at Mama, Heina could feel the storm approaching. He bent over his illustrated copy of The Working Man Builds the World.

"Klar, clearly, I'm for the union," said Lina. She stepped from the washboard and toward Heinrich with her wet hands raised. Her finger jabbed the air. "If you go on strike again, don't bother telling me the strike benefits will cover the debt payments from the store. What will we eat—candy?"

His parents sat, stood, paced, and talked until the wash water got cold, until Heina put his head down and Jupp started to cry. Heina woke up with his face pressed against the corner of his book, a spot of drool on the paper, and the sound of his mother dumping the wash water out onto the front step. Mama had shut the curtain that blocked off the bedroom, and a ball of orange candle flame shone through the red-and-white striped sheet. He shut his book, reached for his sleeping shirt, and tried to guess from their voices which one would win and which one of them would be unhappy.

Papa came home from the porcelain factory dusted white with clay mix instead of flour. His hacking cough returned. A section of his thumb got ripped half off in the first few weeks, smashed in a huge mixing machine. But Papa couldn't stop talking about the job. At night he'd wake them up to tell them how the organizing committee grew like rising dough.

I know almost nothing about Papa Heinrich other than the storybook tales of saved lives, death threats, and jolly laughter. I want to hear him, to see a magic electrical current pass between son and father, a twined cord of politics and familiarity that I imagine sustained Heina through all the struggles that followed. I imagine this for myself in order to be warmed by that distant sun. Like learning to make fire, Heina found his own first rush of political power and learned from his papa how a weak boy could claim the world. I imagine the moment to feel that power from the inside out.

Heinrich Sr. mussed Heina's hair and tore a sheet of butcher paper from the roll on the store counter. He rolled a cone and poured a scoop of colored hard candy.

Mama set small parcels into an old woman's basket, checking the list and adding the total. She glanced up to give Heinrich a look about the packet of sweets.

"*Was, denn?* What? I'm the Sweet Heinrich—I need to stay sweet!" Humming, he turned back to the shelves to grab a box of matches. When the women left he said, "The candy isn't for me, my dear. It's for kids of the workers, for the leafleting in support of the SPD Reichstag candidates."

Papa with his sunshine face giving candy to other children? Jealousy made a sound come from Heina's mouth: "Papa," Heina said, "I could help you."

His father turned to focus on Heina. "You could?"

Heina nodded. "Jupp can help Mama here."

Papa drummed his thick fingers on the counter. "It's work, you know, and you have to make sure people get the flyer. You have to have a loud voice and not be afraid. You have to say, over and over again, 'Vote for so-and-so.'" Papa was suddenly very serious, as if the whole world had stopped for this conversation.

Heina nodded. "I even know the candidates, and I know they're going to stand up to the capitalists and fight for a free, democratic Germany."

Mama called out, "Jupp!"

The shop door banged behind them. Papa put his hand on Heina's back. He explained they would leaflet in the town square among the stalls of the weekend grocery market piled high with shiny vegetables and sausages. Papa Heinrich reached into his pocket and unfolded the cone of bonbons, shaking them toward Heina.

"Go on," he said, "fill your pockets. They're good for your throat when you're yelling." Heina reached in and grabbed a handful of the red and yellow candies, dusted with grainy sugar. He shivered to think he'd found such happiness by accident, just by asking a question.

Heina took a stack of the leaflets and stood near a corner of the music hall with the pink marble façade. Papa disappeared around a corner. Men and women walked by, their eyes intently surveying shop windows or the traffic in the streets. Heina's stomach sank. Why had he agreed to do this? He would probably be too weak to give out even one flyer, and then he would double over with one of his coughing fits and his father would have to take him home.

A huge man rushed past and bumped into Heina's head with his elbow. Heina bunched the pile of leaflets under one arm as he reached up to rub the sore spot on his head. Frustration and anger made him open his mouth, and although he wanted to swear at that big, fat, elbow-swinging man, he screamed out, "SPD!" The grown-ups around him stopped in surprise at his outburst and then made more space for him on the sidewalk.

Further down the sidewalk, another leafleter yelled, "A vote for Germany's future—SPD!"

Heina tried this phrase twice under his breath, then yelled it into the street. The first flyer was the hardest. He stood with his arm outstretched, eyes half closed. He felt a tug on his fingers and opened his eyes to see a young woman with a long blond braid. She took the flyer and nodded politely, moving on through the crowd holding his flyer in her hand, the flyer he had given her, as if it were the most acceptable and normal thing in the world.

Heina beamed, and it became an intoxicating game. Who would take the next flyer, and could he guess by the look on their faces who might listen? A young man with coal dust on his face might grimace and shake his head, and then an older high-society lady might smile and stop to take the flyer and fold it carefully into her handbag. You never could tell.

Heina learned his techniques quickly. It worked best to hold a flyer as near as possible to a man or woman's free hand so they just had to open their fingers. A woman took a flyer, glanced at it, and tossed it in the gutter. Then a man in a black sailor's cap walked by, hands in his pockets, and stopped in front of Heina. He took a flyer and skimmed it with a half smile.

"Hey, little man, how will you be voting?" asked the man.

Heina hesitated, not knowing if this man would poke fun at him. "I'm not old enough to vote," Heina said.

The man nodded and folded the flyer. "And you're not a party member?"

Heina glanced over his shoulder, searching for his father in the crowd. Looking again at the man in front of him, Heina noticed a familiar symbol on his lapel pin, a red "S" in the middle of a wheel. That stood for Solidarity, the workers' bicycle club, which sponsored trips all around the area's green hills. His father kept a red flag from the Marl Solidarity club wrapped in tissue paper in his army trunk.

The man broke into a smile, laughing with satisfaction at Heina's suspicion. "Frisch Auf!" he said, the slogan of the bicycle club, "Look alive!" The man added, "Listen, little man, you're young for leafleting. Remember, if a cop asks you whether you're an SPD member, always say no. Young people aren't allowed to join." Then the man bellowed out above the heads of the crowd, "Heinrich—I've caught your next of kin!"

Papa Heinrich jogged over. "Causing trouble?" he said, smiling. The apples of his cheeks nearly hid his eyes.

Heina got another stack of leaflets from his father and felt more manly and adult than ever in his whole life, even when he worked in the shop or went to buy groceries for his mother. On the walk home, his father was tired but jubilant, the same way as after a long bike ride with Solidarity up to the famous castles in the hills.

"Did you notice more women than men took flyers?" Papa asked. Heina thought back over his day. Yes, it was true. "There's a reason for that, son—it has to do with the woman's economic position in the family. There's a smart man named August Bebel who writes very well on the subject. I think your mother has a pamphlet, and of course her beloved Clara Zetkin has something to say about women's mixed consciousness as well." Papa laughed to himself at this joke, which Heina did not understand.

"Tell me what else you noticed. How did different people respond to you today?"

Heina considered and spoke. Papa studied his observations slowly and carefully like coins. "Yes," Papa said, nodding and looking at a tree or a lamppost as they walked, "you're right about that. Let me explain why some of the young workers might act that way . . ." Heinrich tried to pay attention to each word, resisting a tide of happiness that threatened to blot out his vision and turn everything pearly and soft. There would be nothing finer, he decided, than to grow into a man exactly like Papa.

Heina, you have no way to know, but listen close: I played the same street corner games, over and over. My country dropped bombs on Iraq in 2003, and I stood on a corner with flyers. Cars drove past the demonstration, the drivers' faces registering shock and curiosity. A beat-up pickup truck with American flags flying from the antenna rolled to an almost-stop, and I tensed for a yell, a middle finger. This flannel-clad man gave us a two-second thumbs-up, stopping traffic as he made eye contact of the sort seldom exchanged between strangers. I felt an adrenaline street corner thrill of power, too, a shy person finding an inner circus clown, the safety of repeated phrases, the magic of that elemental exchange, the raw power of direct eye contact in a world built for avoiding face-to-face moments of indecision. I did it at nineteen and for every year thereafter: Save the old-growth forests, buy this newspaper. Here, Stranger, take a flyer. Sign my clipboard.

I know that electricity, which will wrap around your heart and tug. After the Buschmann family had spent six years in Thüringen, my timelines and books tell me they happened to return to Marl exactly when the mines once again exploded with labor unrest. Guessing about Papa Heinrich, I can only imagine that the heat and power of that engine was too hard to resist.

In March of 1912 Heinrich slammed the door behind him, breathless.

"If you got fired, so help me God, I will kill you," Lina said.

"No," he said, laying a newspaper on the table. "Look." A black banner of letters jumbled across the top of the page: "Ruhr Miners Strike!"

Papa read the articles aloud, stopping to comment and explain, maybe so the whole family could hear or maybe to savor the words. There in that kitchen, with the strike headlines bathed in the golden glow from the oil lamp, was love. Heina would have stayed in that moment forever if he could: a tiny boy, doomed to be different from his father, doomed to be lung-sick, privileged to come up out of the mines, wanting his father's rough hands and hearty, friendly laugh. Heina is the boy just outside that circle of light.

My mother tells me that Heina hunted his entire life for his papa's approval. He served the revolution in its various guises, driven to extremes of sacrifice, even after Papa was no longer around to bestow the approving nod. Little boy, I hungered for heroes too. I put my imaginary silver locket of you on my imaginary revolutionary altar, "Anti-Nazi Grandfather," an icon beside gold-dusted images of Emma Goldman, Aung San Suu Kyi from Burma, César Chávez. These half-loved, half-feared fierce deities served as inspiration and also as a hard-tipped prod to keep my body in motion. But on hateful days I'd squirm and ask whether César took a mental-health day to go shoe shopping, or if Emma would have needed to zone out behind a *Glamour* magazine. Little boy, I summon you so that you will live in my heart, keep me company, instead of floating above me in the sky or unreachable on some cold altar.

Papa left without dinner that evening to join a strike support committee. Lina came up from the cellar with a load of wash from the basement clothesline, her eyes holding a calm but far-away look. "Your father can't stand being away," she said, either finding acceptance or swallowing the inevitable. "That's his fight." Four days later the party headquarters in the Ruhr issued a general call for help. Kaiser Wilhelm II—a man so stupid he was said to never have read the German constitution—called in five thousand troops with two machine gun units to open fire on an outdoor miners' meeting in the Ruhr.

Walking down the street toward school the next morning, Heina identified the socialists in the crowds by their brooding looks and red eyes. In the socialist lending library he heard a whispered conversation, "I bet it's going to get bad again—next thing you know they'll make the SPD illegal. We've already been declared *Reichsfeinde*, public enemy number one."—"I don't know if I can take another ten years underground."

Sometime in these tumultuous months in southeast Germany, my great-papa Heinrich hung a red flag from a mountainside, or so the story goes. In 1913 the German government and the generals geared up for a European war, and Russia grew more powerful by the minute, breathing down Germany's eastern collar. The SPD, historically opposed to militarism, did an about-face and endorsed the war buildup. Local SPD radicals, supportive of the Russian socialist movement, felt betrayed by their sellout hawkish leaders.

In my heated and wild-eyed version of the story, Papa Heinrich shinnied up a flagpole with a red cloth, the scarlet color announcing, "I am still a Red—against the war and for the international working class!"

More than sixty years later, at a high school bus stop in small-town Illinois, my brother Glenn bellowed in my direction, "Bolshevik! Commie girlie!" He doesn't remember this; I know he meant nothing by it, nothing more than a cranky brother in the

cold war Midwest teasing his sister about her weird refusal to curl
her hair, her weird preference for books over beer. The smell of
warm dirt from the Illinois cornfields enveloped a group of us
kids lugging book bags, lighting cigarettes. Under my ripped blue
flannel I probably wore one of the T-shirts I'd hand painted, using
a toothpick to spell out a quote about the threat of nuclear war.
What I knew about politics was driving the country roads at night
in my Chevy Cavalier with U2 and the Dead Kennedys blasting
from the stereo. Cresting over gentle hills as corn stubble blurred
by in the dark, the heady plastic smell of a new cassette meant music and the liner notes, the semaphore of history and something-
not-right. But the fact that we were both related to a Red of some
shade? Never. I would never, ever have believed it.

And the farther you get from these struggles, the easier they
are to romanticize. Heinrich, a military reservist, had been raised
as a soldier. Could he have resisted the patriotic fervor as the
government vowed to embrace even the dirty socialists as good
Germans as long as they promised to support the war in return?

The red flag whipped and flapped in the breeze over Thüringen, and I choose to believe that rumor. Our Buschmann stories
retain those events that caused loss and trauma; I wonder if this
story stuck in the thin fabric of family lore because trouble came
Papa Heinrich's way as a result. Maybe the red flag flew after
some last straw in an escalating strike effort at the porcelain factory, and maybe Heinrich lost his job. Or maybe this flag—a thin
pennant or massive banner—held a solidarity message for the
Ruhr miners. I do know that some explosion in Jena or unbear-
able longing for home sent the Buschmanns packing in 1913.
Papa Heinrich slipped the unpaid debt note into a leather wallet,
sold the contents of the store, and maybe put that money toward
train tickets. Lina, as I imagine her, had a feather in her hat, a
harried look, and a son on each hand.

Heina's world frayed once again into tatters held together by the opposing forces of Papa Heinrich and Lina. I imagine Heina at age eleven: just old enough to have his own attachment to Jena, a crush on a blond- or dark-haired girl in school, to have faced up to a bully, to have his favorite routes for walking. As the train pulled away, he tried all possible mental tricks to avert chaos and tears. He could look at the steely joy in his father's face. He could look at his mother's pressed lips and feel shame at his weakness. He could look out the window—no, don't look out the window at the green hills, at the castle, don't look at the bridge and the town wall and the station fading away.

3

We Are All Germans Now

Any twelve-year-old boy might have wondered about the mysterious seeds that burst to launch the Great War. In June 1914 someone important named Ferdinand was killed. The world spun and burned as conflict flared along buried fuses. Less than two months later, the army called Papa Heinrich to active duty as part of the first mobilizations.

I imagine fiery arguments over the kitchen table as two socialists debated the merits of fighting the Reich's war. Maybe Papa brought in an armload of the four morning papers and laid them right over the breakfast dishes. The shouts back and forth across the apartment changed from "I can't believe you're wearing that jacket" to "Russia will invade. We know Tsar Nicholas is crazy!" and "It's always France, I tell you."

On August 1, 1914, the day before Papa boarded the train far away to the front, noise billowed from a huge parade in the streets, and the brass band and cheers made Mama and Papa shout even louder. It hadn't started out as a fight. Papa buttoned his brown army dress jacket and stood in front of the mirror in the hall. He reached for his cap and stuck out his lower lip, regarding his reflection. Then he flashed Heina a smile. Heina stood transfixed, wondering what it would be like to hold and fire Papa's rifle, to ride away toward war.

"This war will be quick, or at least that's what the generals tell us," Papa said.

Mama pushed through the kitchen door holding an empty vase and a packet of newspapers and letters. She stopped and stared at Papa, eyes pinched into rage. "What are you *doing*?"

Heina's heart fluttered. Had he done something to provoke her? But no, Papa was her target.

Papa reached to put his arms around her waist. "My love, my little Dragon, there's a parade today, and then tomorrow I'm off to be killed," he said. "You don't want to be cross with me now, do you?"

"You're joining that fool parade, play-acting the happy soldier?" She set down the vase and unfolded the newspaper, pointing to a headline and turning her hot-coal eyes on Heina. "Look, son. The Kaiser says that there are no more enemies of the state. 'We are all Germans now,' he says, even though yesterday we were damned socialists, evil communists." Her delicate, heart-shaped face hardened. "I want you to understand that when war comes, so do the promises and lies."

Papa took his rifle on his shoulder as if lifting an umbrella or a rake. "I'm not afraid to do my part, Lina," he said. He winked at Heina and shut the door behind him.

The soldiers crowded the streets, wearing puffy yellow flowers in their buttonholes. Many had ivy and greenery tied to their rifle barrels, and they smiled and waved casually as they strode in loose rows down the cobblestones, nodding to the throng of well-wishers on the sidewalks. Fabric and garlands draped the balconies of the apartments across the street and down the block. Heina stood at the window, hidden in the curtains, as the thump of the bass drum rattled the glass and the golden horns blasted only one message: On to Victory.

For years Papa had gone away to reservist training, where he camped and shot at targets and came back with funny stories. He smoked a long porcelain tobacco pipe decorated with the names of his reservist buddies, which still hangs in my uncle Klaus's living room. The bowl of the pipe is painted in tiny script with jokes about coming home drunk and illustrated with a tiny painting of a woman kicking a guy out of a doorway. Heina might have imagined Papa going to war and bringing home a thrilling batch of new stories. At night Heina might have dreamed of rifle fire the way a protected child imagines the pop-pop of war as a natural occurrence like a storm or the seasons.

I imagine Heina bathed in images of far-off war, using my own experience as a compass. The green hills of Vietnam seeped into my head through the evening news in the early 1970s. My cartoon war dream still visits me thirty years later. I watch myself in a tiny soldier's uniform, flanked by massive men in green camouflage, holding guns. The earth beneath us bucks and rolls like the ocean, and I wait to see my own face reappear from the folds of the swelling earth.

In the 1980s I collected more images. Television news flashed an icon of a downed jet on a multicolored map, and the announcer's voice said Soviet-something-or-other, threats, embassies, a crisis that seemed primed for escalation to nuclear war. I tucked my knees under my thin nightgown, decorated with a cartoon giraffe, and I waited for the bombs. This was it. This was *always* it. The morbid child's prayer, "If I should die before I wake," was a rosary of white-hot destruction. My eyes pricked with worry. I

chewed on a piece of my hair and asked Mom what would happen, knowing she had no hotline to the White House. Go to bed,
she said finally. A kid can't predict the future, so I reasoned that
if I did the work of fearing the bombs each night, I would have
to be wrong and so there would be no bombs. I wrote a letter to
President Ronald Reagan, begging him to stop the arms race.
Jellybeans, I wrote; just think about the fact that if we all die,
you'll never eat another jellybean. Weeks later I received a thick
envelope from the White House containing a glossy newsletter,
photos of Reagan smiling and posing with children, the text of
letters from kids thanking him for being such a great president.
I studied each page; my letter did not appear. It seemed that no
other kid in the United States had worries. I was alone.

Heina might have clipped a map of the western front from the
newspaper and tacked it on the wall near his bed. I imagine dark-
eyed elfish Jupp, ten years old, standing beneath the map and
asking, "Where is Papa now?" as if Heina could look into the
map like a crystal ball and see in the newsprint the small figure
of his father, with a thick imposing belly and his hat pulled down
over his eyes. Despite Mama's dour lectures, it was almost impossible not to get caught up in the excitement. The hard reality
of the map seemed to cut away the vagueness and confusion of
normal life.

They waited for six long weeks for Papa. The newspaper reported resounding victories and minor setbacks. At school the
boys massed in opposing armies every recess. When they walked
home for lunch, they did so with high marching steps. Other
than missing Papa, Heina had never been so happy. The faces of
friends and strangers seemed to glow with a noble love. His father made up a critical link in a chain of men as they crested a hill
somewhere in western Germany and headed in their grand loop

into France, where they would pinch Paris like a flea. And when the girls at school heard you were a soldier's son, their heads seemed to dip slightly and they looked up at you through dark eyelashes with such respect that you'd think for a second you had gone to the front yourself. Finally, Mama received a postcard with the date and time of Papa's incoming train.

Heina and Jupp heard the shush of a knapsack against the wood floor, the clomp-clomp of one heavy boot and then the other. A stink of camphor and smoke and mold drifted in from the hall. Papa walked into the kitchen in his slippers, but for a moment Heina thought some crazy soldier had entered the wrong house. Papa's cheeks had sunken into his face and his belly was smaller. His beard stood out in patchy bristles and his eyes were ghostly, empty, ringed with wrinkles and dark lines. "Boys!" he said, raising his arms to muss their hair with his big hands.

Jupp squirmed around to face his father. "Did you see the tanks, Papa? What about the machine guns? Was it loud and exciting? Have we won?"

Papa glanced at Mama. "It was loud," he said. "There were a lot of brave men we should be proud of." Something wasn't right. Papa's voice still boomed when he said "proud of," *stolz darauf*. But his eyes seemed to slink away rather than snap and dance.

After breakfast the next day, Papa pointed to the map in the newspaper. "We were only here, and this battle information is all wrong," he said to Mama. Another time it was a phrase in the newspaper he read: "'Almost done' with this war? No, I think not." And he laughed with a bitter, rueful sound that gave Heina the chills.

Then Papa went back to work at the mine, and Heina was actually glad to have his father out of the house in the evenings. In his classmates' dining rooms, pictures of Generals Ludendorff and Hindenburg hung on the walls, surrounded by rousing

marching tunes played on every phonograph. Heina imagined
the soldiers tromping through the dark, unable to hear the music that urged them onward.

In the spring of 1915 Heina turned thirteen and the sun drew
the flowers from the dead earth. The boys played war in the
woods near the school. Heina tramped through the gritty mud,
commanding his imaginary troops to look sharp. He wondered
secretly and with only half his heart whether his father had not
been strong enough to endure war.

Like a soldier, Heina accepted the food shortages with grim
resolve. He moved his plate closer to his chin and spooned up
thin celery and potato soup with quick motions, then reached for
a slice of K ration potato bread.

His father looked over at him. "Heina, it's okay to be upset
about this terrible food. You *have* to be upset about it," he said.
"There's such a thing as being too strong. Sometimes you have
to admit: this is not enough."

Heina scowled at his father, a very rare thing, and then washed
his face clean of it. "Ja, Papa," he said.

Jupp rapped his spoon against the table by accident and then
burst out laughing. Mama didn't even react. Was Heina imagining it, or would he himself have gotten a sharp look? Jupp stuck
out his tongue at Heina on the sly, and Heina had to bite his
knuckle not to laugh.

"Lina, the one good thing about this war is that when it's done,
the Kaiser will have to accept the SPD as legitimate. So many SPD
boys have died for him," Papa said.

Mama sighed, annoyed. "You don't know what you're talking
about," she snapped.

"Oh Lina, my little Dragon, tell me why."

Mama rattled off a list of dates, the Kaiser's past betrayals of
the SPD and the socialists. "We're too trusting, Heinrich."

Mama and Papa loved to argue and yell about politics, but the drama grated on Heina's nerves. If he ever got married, he vowed, he would never have every day and every night filled with nothing but politics and the SPD—from breakfast through laundry to the last kiss good night. Heina looked down into his pale yellow soup, which had dissolved into clear broth with a thin layer of potato at the bottom.

The best way to handle meals, Heina decided, was to eat fast and leave the table. He stayed busy the whole day, like Papa the steam engine, reading the SPD paper, walking, doing schoolwork, or working on the scrap-collecting drives at the school. He was training, he told himself, and this would make him stronger. He found an iron wheel hub in the ditch behind the apartment, and every day he lifted it with each arm until his muscles shook. One day his mother found him as she was doing laundry and said, "Heina, don't be a fool! Think about the energy you're wasting. There goes dinner!"

During the June break from school, Marl city leaders asked the children who weren't working on family farms to sort metal for the war drive. After a day of sorting in the school gymnasium, Heina's hands were dirty and cut, and his clothes smelled like grease, tin cans, and old screws. As he walked down Viktoriastraße, he could only think about washing his face and going to bed.

Up ahead a roar of voices echoed against the brick buildings, rousing Heina from his sleepwalk. Miners spilled out of the Auguste Viktoria Shaft 1 onto the street. A streetcar was stuck in the crowd, and its bell clanged and clanged again. Buggies and trucks stopped amid the surge of the rally, and a speaker on a platform motioned for the workers to move toward the mine entrance.

Was Papa working at A-V? Heina moved toward the platform,

enveloped in the roar and the bustle of bodies. A few men recognized him and patted his back. The chant "Money for food"
rippled through the crowd, passed from one mouth to the next.
Miners jostled, spreading the wet smell of coal dust and dirt.
This was what Papa meant. The correct response to bad soup,
Heina realized, was to yell about it, not just to toughen yourself
up to accept it.

It looked like chaos, the men's mouths chewing the air in anger, but it was impossible to miss the undertone of jubilation,
the sheer joy of exertion on one's own behalf. Every detail had
been composed with forethought, agreed upon. How loud, what
area, what to say, whom to target . . . Papa had a hand in this
creation, this mechanism of coordinated humans. Heina felt a
curiosity to watch Papa work, to see the inner workings of this
science of change, to understand how these plans were made.

Heina, I wonder if you felt what I did, an almost spiritual sense
of peace and possibility when first watching a demonstration being planned. At my small private college in Minnesota, I found
myself in a rust-orange seat in the student lounge for my first
meeting of the campus Public Interest Research Group, started
years before by Ralph Nader. An organizer flipped sheets on a
big pad of paper and asked us what we wanted to accomplish
on campus. She listened to us and made a list with a big black
marker. Then we worked through our options as she showed us
how to take these broad goals and break them down into manageable parts and campaigns. I fell in love in that instant with
her long black hair, her Chinese-Irish round and freckled face, in
love with her addictive courage and competence and daring. She
was a Pippi Longstocking with a clipboard. We drew a calendar;
we made a strategy chart; we were off.

Strangely enough, it's still impossible for me to disconnect the alcohol-solvent smell of a permanent marker from the hope of liberation. I was shy, but I had always loved story problems in math classes. And these charts were nothing more than story problems, games of the imagination where you charted possibilities, focused your resources, and then leapt out into an unsuspecting world. Before we knew it, we were collecting petitions to save Minnesota forests, and I had organized a panel discussion. People came for discussion, ideas snapping in the air, letters written, further plans made. The nuclear family had been a poor approximation of this drug of purposeful closeness, and I am still baffled by anyone who fails to be intoxicated, who steers clear of the temptation to alter external reality.

I will always try to reach back and share this drug with my younger self. Forever after, when I yell at a demonstration, a small part of me is trying to reach a girl I imagine is a block away, wondering what all the noise and picket signs are about. I know she's sitting in her mom's '83 Cutlass with the windows down, waiting for the stoplight to change, waiting to turn eighteen so the mystery of her life will start. She's picking glitter fingernail polish off her gnawed-down nails, she's got a squinting and sad look to her eyes because she doesn't know how to get out of this boxed-in life, because everything is so scary and the world might end any day now. Sandra, Monique, Kiara, Betsy, if you come to our party, you can make some noise, and sometimes people actually listen.

The crowd dispersed. A demonstration always made Heina feel choked up and warm, but the feeling faded as he walked alone toward home. A man with a strange shape passed him. The man's upper body tilted as he walked head down with an overcoat around his shoulders. One empty sleeve had been pinned up in a fold against itself: he was a war hero. The man's footsteps

receded, and Heina's heart raced. His hands crept together, fingers twining around each other. How would you find work with
one hand? How would the man live? Had he seen his hand after
he'd lost it during the battle? Heina's head swam with the fire of
the demonstration translated into a rough and wild fear for his
father, who was headed back to the front.

Days later, Mama spread a thin layer of bacon grease on a slice
of bread and covered it with another slice. Heina smelled the
grease, most of the family's weekly ration. It was a special gift,
because Papa was due to board a train in his soldier's uniform.

Papa warmed his hands at the stove. "It's miserable out there,"
he said quietly. "Not two weeks after Christmas and back again.
Fighting over some chunk of France I don't even want."

Heina sat on the hall bench, tying his shoes as he called to mind
every recent memory of Papa as if trying to cement the images in
a scrapbook. They spent Christmas at a meeting at the SPD hall
with red candles and songs, where they exchanged small presents.
But then a fight had broken out, with chairs shoved back roughly.
A man raised his voice to curse General Ludendorff, who had
been quoted in the papers about Germany's need for "breeding
grounds" in the East. "How dare you support that racist?" the man
bawled to his opponent, who retorted, "Are you so weak that you
don't want Germany to win?" And then fists flew.

Now, Heina heard a muffle of whispered phrases through
the open kitchen door, last-minute household decisions about
money and the future. Mama whispered something about "soldier's pension" and "Don't worry, we'll be fine." The rations
kept shrinking, and most families needed extra money to buy
groceries on the black market.

Heina leaned forward, propping his hands on his knees and
lost for a moment in studying the strange terrain of his knobbly
knuckles and flat fingernails. These were strong, young man's

fingers. Working hands. Heina rose and leaned into the kitchen, and the words pushed themselves out of his mouth.

"Papa," he said, "I'll go into the mines. I know boys who haul coal and tend the horses. I'll see Herr Evenrude about a position." Heina waited to feel Mama's hand on his wrist, to hear a restrained "Ja."

But Papa let loose a steam-engine roar: "Your lungs are like paper lanterns! You would be dead in two years."

Heina closed his eyes, and to his horror tears fell down his cheeks. Instinctively he folded his arms around his torso to cover the scar that hid a collapsed section of lung. No kind murmur came from Mama's lips to soften Papa's roar. They were disgusted with him.

Papa pushed back his chair and grabbed his son by the shoulders, led him out of the kitchen onto the back stoop. "Son, you have a *brain*. You're intelligent. Look, you've had more schooling than all of your forefathers combined."

Heina opened his eyes. He stared out at the snowed-over garden marked with stakes, the grate where they grilled sausages in the summer, the gnarled apple tree hanging above the neighbor's wall like a witch's hand. He sniffed. This babyish crying could never be erased now. Papa held onto Heina's shoulder and explained that office work might be safer. That was noble, too, for the union movement, because the miners were losing leverage. Besides, he said in a low string of words, the pay wouldn't be enough as a hauler to help Mama with even basic expenses.

As Papa grabbed his pack and handshakes were traded all around, Heina turned his face down to avoid Papa's eyes, ashamed at his outburst and the tears. Then Heina headed to school with his near-empty book bag, shuffling through the slush on the cobblestones. His spindly body had failed him by refusing to copy his father's barrel chest and huge biceps. He hated mirrors in the locker rooms at the Workingman's Youth Club, hated to look at that uneven, pale chest with the misshapen dent on one side where the doctors had taken out part of a rib to get at his lung.

That evening Heina went to bed before supper to avoid Mama's piercing, judging eyes. She was sure to hate him now. She revered Papa's strength, and she always laughed to watch Jupp sprint effortlessly after a soccer ball with a wide, elastic smile. And Papa and Jupp could melt Mama, wink at her and make her laugh, but Heina could only duck and get out of the way.

Heina curled in bed under the thick goose-down comforter and imagined his future fading away. He would never stand on stage at a miners' strike with his fist held high, never raise the lantern in some cavernous tunnel, never greet fellow union members at dirty meeting places smelling of smoke and coal and filled with laughter. He cried as if he were giving up his whole childhood, the most comforting sights and sounds and smells, the mine.

Heina woke up with a clogged throat and hacking cough. Acrid sweet and sour odors wafted in from the kitchen, the old wives' cure for a cough, hot milk and honey with a thick slice of onion. Kids would fake health to avoid that drink of warring bitter and mild, a noxious brew, like Mama versus Heina. Mama pushed open the bedroom door and handed him the glass. He gagged it down.

"It's terrible, isn't it?" she said, and reached to smooth the hair on his forehead. He tried not to tense under her touch. She was being so nice and he wanted to burrow and hide. It was horrible, first crying in front of Papa, then getting sick like a child. He drained the glass, and his stomach pitched.

Mama reached into her apron pocket and drew out a folded piece of paper. "This is for a week from Monday, Heina." She touched the nape of his neck lightly with her fingertips, then turned and left, closing the door behind her.

Heina opened the paper. It was a letter from Jan Pyra's Handelsschule, a secretarial technical school in Recklinghausen, and it read, "Thank you, Heinrich Buschmann Jr., for enrolling in a nine-month course of study."

He pressed his lips together and fought back tears. Mama always said, "Heina, your house is built too near the water," the gentle rebuke for the strange sight of a son whose eyes misted at the slightest provocation—just like Papa. Where had Mama gotten the money to pay for school? Mama and Papa must have decided as they walked to the train station. They had put their intelligent heads together to organize his future. He would work in an office with slanted desks, lead pencils, and windows streaming sunlight, and he would have *ein Beruf*, a trade. The word came from the verb *rufen*, to call, and connoted a calling, with the honor and specialized skills that the noble word carried.

Heina, so much of your life lies beyond my imagining, but I know the mixed pride and shame of the pencil pushers. The kids at my huge farm-town public school in New Lenox, Illinois, were expected to cut their shaggy '80s hair and get to work in landscaping firms, or sell auto parts, drive delivery trucks, work as receptionists or nurses, or join the army. To glory in books, to be shipped here and there for tests and classes, was a privilege; to go out of state for college marked me as "think-you're-so-smart" and "nerd," a gift beyond anything my family had known.

It went to my head, of course, and then I was set straight. Working in Dad's office one summer, endlessly stapling and collating radiation safety test kits and mailings, sitting next to a shelf of survey meters, I said to Dad, "I don't think I'm cut out for manual labor."

He, son-of-a-butcher, every-possible-jobber before he opened
his business, combined a gentle turn of the lips with a hard and
even look in his sharp, dark eyes. "There's nothing wrong with
manual labor," he said. "It's just as good as any other kind of
work." This necessary string of words flipped and rolled for
years in the tumbler of my brain.

But lines are drawn and cuts are made. When you try, you feel
a permanent pulling at the messy scar tissue: you can't go back.
The half jest, half jab at the local bar went, "You think you're so
smart, college girl." *I feel smart here*, I wanted to say, *but at college I feel like a hayseed imbecile.* They see the studying and thinking
behind your eyes, they'll hate you for it down at the bar, so you
learn how to turn it off, hide it. Still, the two worlds will never
come together. That would be one version of the revolution, I
guess, when the bitterness is gone, when the terrain of calluses
on a palm wouldn't map a story of denial and blunted potential.

On his first day at Pyra, Heina left before daylight and walked
the six kilometers to school in a light rain. He climbed the front
steps of a large stone building and followed a metal arrow to a
door at the end of the hall, where "Pyra Schule" was painted in
black script on the door glass.

Heina opened the door to a row of high desks. At each desk
a copier or clerk trainee hunched over a slanted surface without the benefit of a chair. On the far wall a floor-to-ceiling open
cabinet overflowed with office implements. Students milled in to
grab paper, ink, rags, and to set up their desks.

Heina approached a chubby blond boy. "I'm new. What do I
do?" he asked.

"Back there," said the boy, motioning with his head to another door. Heina walked down the aisle between a row of desks.
Serious young men nodded at him politely as he passed. "Tag,"

they said, and "Guten Tag," in a range of accents, a high German hard *g* at the end of *Tag*, the way they were taught in school, and the soft *g* that sounded like *ch*, the way folks here in the Ruhr talked.

Heina was thrown midlesson into a course on dictation. Herr Pyra stood at the front of the classroom in a jacket and vest, reeling off complex phrases and subclauses that marked the high art of German bureaucratese. Heina sharpened a quill with his penknife, but it kept clogging and blurbing out huge lumps of solidified ink, and his paper pad soaked through with black splotches.

At 11:30 Herr Pyra abruptly checked his watch and walked out of the classroom. Heina leaned his elbow against his desk and looked with dismay at the mess in front of him. To his left and right boys wiped their quills with rags and tightened the lids on their ink canisters.

Too tired for politeness, Heina called out, "What now?"

A thin boy, already equipped with glasses, turned around and smiled. "It's time to run to the common room. Half hour for *Mittagspause*, and you can even buy some coffee at the canteen. Look, man, you've got this huge ink splotch on your lip."

Heina followed the boys to the basement, rubbing at his blue lip with his shirt cuff. The boys pushed at each other, joked and yelped, bragged about being on the list for a job here or across town, moaned about Pyra. "Oh, I'm going to complain to the Stenographers' Union," one boy said, and the others laughed. When they sat down with their coffee and bread, Heina couldn't stop himself from asking, "Where's the union office?"

"It started in Bochum four years ago," someone shouted down the table. "But it's small, hardly does anything because we're not really organized yet." Heina bit his bread to keep from smiling. Papa would be thrilled: a union!

The boys seemed to sort themselves into two groups, the ones whose fathers had been bureaucrats and the ones whose fathers mined coal, farmed, and worked with shovels and hammers. Despite a jovial familiarity among all the boys, Heina sensed the differences, from the color and elasticity of the skin, which showed how much vegetables and meat you'd gotten as a child, to collars smudged with sweat and grease or freshly pressed, which indicated whether the mother had help with laundry and money for soap.

The first true shock came on the last Monday in January, a week after Heina started. Herr Pyra suddenly stopped in mid-dictation. He walked halfway down the far aisle near the windows, and the boys straightened their backs, pushing off against the desks to stand arrow straight. Heina's leg muscles still twitched after standing for hours on end, and he'd copied the secret habit of leaning with his hips against the top desk drawer to take the pressure off his aching feet.

Some were too slow. Pyra stopped near an overweight boy with a curl of greasy hair on his forehead. Pyra's cane whistled through the air and struck the boy's back with a whack that resounded through the classroom. The boy emptied his lungs with an *oof* and leaned over his desk; it had got him in the kidneys.

At lunch break, a few of them leaned over to touch their toes, groaning to ease their cramped backs. The boy who'd been whipped was silent and red-faced. Heading down the staircase to the common room, Heina fell in step with a tall, thin boy named Otto.

"How can Pyra get away with that?" Heina asked.

"Because he knows we'll get it worse when we're on the job," said Otto. Heina scowled, half opened his mouth as if to speak. Otto sighed. "Look, this isn't as bad as mines, but we're going to be *Lehrlinge*—apprentices—for at least a few years when we get jobs. And the Lehrlinge are absolutely fair game. If you have a cruel boss, you'll get whipped. Mind what I say, I know it's true because my older brother was a shopkeeper's apprentice, and he came home with black and blue marks across his knuckles."

In the lunchroom the boys first ate in silence and gradually began to kid the boy who'd been whipped. He looked for a moment like he might cry, then he punched one of them in the arm and started to laugh. In between joking and eating, several of them chimed in to add their horror stories about jobs. Timo said, "It's worth it, and better than losing a hand in some bloody mine explosion." Joachim said, "If you can't take this, you're not a man." Another said, "No, I'm not taking that. It's wrong, and boy, I'll deck Pyra when he comes my way with that whip."

"Anyway, that's why I'm a member of the Arbeiterjugend," Otto said. He passed a card around, with his signature and the logo "AJ": Worker Youth. "It's like a union for young people, started in 1904 by a guy in Berlin. Some locksmith's apprentice hanged himself because he'd been beaten and tormented so badly, and that got people riled up."

The boys nodded and made noises of approval and shock in their throats, but only Heina hung back on the stairs with Otto when the others shuffled toward afternoon classes.

"Do they work with the SPD?" Heina asked. "How do I sign up?"

Otto gave a half smile. "Oh, the good old SPD," he said. "The unions and the SPD have been trying to shut us down since '06."

Heina studied the stone floor, queasy. Had he misheard? The SPD would actively fight against youth organizing? Otto glanced at the ornate clock on the wall. "Don't want to get a whack on the ear, Buschmann. Let's go." The boy's crooked smile, the ironic and friendly curl of his lip, and the way he moved his arm like a wave in the direction of the classroom caught Heina's breath in his chest. This was a real young man, someone with confidence, and his freckles and dark blond hair and dirty collar seemed to glow with vitality and intelligence.

It's a little like falling in love with hope itself. My very first surge of political desire centered on a head of lovely purple hair. At sixteen, in the post-punk wasteland of 1987, I wanted so badly to dye my hair blue, which I imagined would set me free in some vague but definite way. Mom said no, vowed she'd throw me out of the house, so I didn't do it. But then I saw that beautiful purple head.

I'd tagged along with my boyfriend's family for an expedition to an art fair in Chicago's Hyde Park. We threaded our way through rows of white tents, past smudges of oil paint on canvas, through crowds of stylish people flashing bare arms and silver jewelry. Turning a corner, I saw the purple-haired woman. I walked toward her booth, and she handed me a pamphlet about animal rights and a postcard about monkeys and cruel lab experiments. It seemed like a reasonable thing to oppose. If Ms. Purple Hair hated it, I did too. I printed my name on the group's mailing list.

My entry into politics started with that signature, prompted by a beautiful dye job, and bulk mail laid my path to the American Left. The animal rights group sent me mass-printed photos of puppies in cages, and they asked me for money. I sent checks. I was rich anyway with all that money from waitressing at Pizza Hut. They sent me notices for protests on Michigan Avenue, where they would dump red paint on ladies wearing fur coats, but I never went.

The group sold my name as part of a list to various political magazines, and I began to get bulk mail from them all. I joined Greenpeace and read its magazine. Alarmed at the state of the dangerous world, I made a hand-drawn flyer about dioxin, a cancer-causing chemical in paper products. I left the flyers in front of the toilet paper and paper towels at the local grocery store where my high school friends stole cases of whipped cream to suck out the nitrous for a high. I didn't tell anyone about this weirdly nerdy act of deviance. I was a worrier, a hole-in-the-ozone, greenhouse-effect, AIDS-babies, 3:00 a.m.-wide-awake-staring-at-the-ceiling ball of anxiety. I worried about the nuclear waste my father's company worked with, knew much more than the average high schooler about the lack of a permanent storage facility for it, was aware of the short-and long-term dangers of radiation poisoning. Greenpeace was my escape valve and a window to sanity: at least there were other worriers like me, living far away in big cities.

At around the same time, Dad took on a contract to oversee radiation safety for a transport company that shipped barrels of nuclear waste to temporary storage sites. And he'd apparently noticed my subscription to *Greenpeace* magazine.

He stormed into the kitchen one day after work, looking massive and efficient in his white button-down shirt with the cuffs rolled up.

He dropped his briefcase and pinned me with his eyes. "You didn't call Greenpeace about the job in Massachusetts, did you?"

I froze. We stood on opposite sides of the kitchen counter. I wanted to slink down below his line of sight. I knew the company worked with a big "de-con" job on the East Coast. But why would I report on my father? He hadn't even done anything wrong. I probably stammered, opened my mouth in shock. I might have said "No" with as much ridicule and vowel stretching as I could muster, to communicate the fact that the accusation itself was offensive, the teenager's only defense.

"Greenpeace trucks have been following our guys near the job site," he snapped, an office-sharp version of himself.

I shrank and shook my head. I got a strange guilty feeling that he *did* hold me responsible. I couldn't deny that I gave money to the people who were, apparently, stalking his employer's radiation trucks. I was smart, but I was a smart seventeen-year-old Pizza Hut waitress, not savvy enough to coordinate a coastal surveillance of my father. Later, as I mulled this over, I had to admit it was impressive that he noticed anything about me. I took it as a kind of a backhanded compliment, like an acknowledgment that I might be smart and powerful enough to do something that devious or confrontational.

Otto pulled Heina aside every few days to share updates about the youth worker group's activities and pass him the group's newspaper with its bold red and black masthead. Heina put the folded paper under his copybook. During pauses in the lessons, he ran his ink-stained finger down the newsprint, scanning the "Letters to the Editor" page for fiery invectives from kids his age, precocious leaders demanding that the SPD step up to the plate and say no to the war.

Heina came home one evening and slung his leather satchel on the kitchen chair. He'd passed a practice test in dictation, part of what he needed to get his certificate.

"Mama, *gibt's Essen?*" he asked. "Any food?"

Mama turned around with a knife in her hands and sadness or fury in her reddened eyes. "Nichts," she said. "Nothing. Damn turnips for dinner. I'm sorry, there are no potatoes anywhere, not even on the black market."

She was crying over turnips? Heina loosened his collar and kicked off his shoes, searching for his house slippers on the mat near the door. Jupp ran into the room, gangly and huge, and collided like a battering ram against Heina's side. They wrestled, giggling, and Heina felt a wave of tension from Mama's direction. "Jupp," he whispered. "Es reicht jetzt." That's enough.

Jupp looked up at Heina with dark, playful eyes. "You're afraid because you know I could beat you up already, Herr Clerk."

Heina shoved him away and sat down at the corner kitchen bench. A postcard leaned against the saltshaker on the table. "Is it from Papa?" he called out.

His mother paused, then said, "I know you can read." Heina widened his eyes to her back in sarcastic shock at her foul mood. He held the card with his fingertips, studying the dirty smudges and the light swirls of ink made by Papa's thick hands. He squinted to read in the dim light.

"My dear family: Everything is splendid here, and we are winning decisively. Verdun is such a picture I cannot describe—I will be home soon. So many men are already returning to their places of origin."

This was the strident and meaningless language that would pass the troop mailroom censor. But his father had underlined random words three or four times and thrown in two or three exclamation points after each sentence, almost as if he were being devilishly sarcastic. Heina reread the last phrase, "returning to their places of origin." Ashes to ashes, dust to dust. "Things aren't going well at this Verdun battle—is that what you get from this, Mama?"

On May 2, one month after Heina turned fourteen, Otto ran into the classroom and slapped a folded newspaper on Heina's desk. "They've arrested Karl Liebknecht!"

Papa had often invoked Liebknecht's name, and the newspaper photo showed a careful, small man with spectacles speaking at platforms above teeming crowds, urging the SPD to dissociate itself from the war. It was hard to dislike a radical whose name literally meant "beloved servant." Heina scanned the article, catching only the basics: ten thousand workers in Berlin had rallied for an early morning May Day celebration, and Liebknecht had shouted from the platform, "Down with the war! Down with the government!"

A few weeks later Liebknecht still sat in jail. Otto came up to Heina's desk before class, clicking his tongue and shaking his head. "Did you hear what your SPD's gone and done?"

"What now?" Heina asked, rolling his eyes. Some other backtrack or show of spinelessness, he imaged. But it was worse.

"They've launched a purge," Otto said, all kidding gone and his eyes hard with anger. "They kicked out the independent leaders from the party."

Heina had worked earnestly at stoking his cynicism, but the news hit like a blow to the sternum. His body offered up fond visceral memories: the smell of the damp and musty SPD hall with its red banners and rows of books, where Heina had been toasted on his birthday, where the Little Red Workers' Groups had recited poems and staged plays. Heina felt a flash of wordless bewilderment, like a child betrayed by a parent in a fit of rage. He struggled to find the thread of rational thought. This should be no surprise. He was an adult. Yet the insanity wounded him all the same.

And why wasn't Papa here to make sense of the SPD, of its splits and the internal fury? What good would it do to kick people out—like a man, wild with anger, slapping his wife when he wanted to smack his boss? The image that came to Heina's mind was Mama, standing over the cooking turnips, fierce with rage and exhaustion, turning with a knife in her hand, unpredictable and irrational in her fear.

Lina, Jupp, Heina, and Heinrich Buschmann.

Hedwig and Friedchen Klejdzinski.

Above: Jupp and Heina Buschmann.

Left: Klaus, Friedchen, and Gerhild Buschmann (my mother). This was probably taken in 1947, which would make Friedchen about forty-three; she looks much older.

Facing page top: Possibly an SAJ camping trip; Friedchen is smiling and seated in the middle behind the couple at front center; Heina is standing in the last row, far right.

Right: The photo my mother calls the "wedding photo" because we don't have a wedding picture of Heina and Friedchen. This was probably taken on an SAJ camping trip or gathering, with friends gathered around goofing off.

Heina Buschmann near retirement, around 1963.

4

Make It New

Three hundred socialists sat in the dark, some holding hands, some giggling and whispering to each other. The stage lights bloomed to reveal Karl Schmidt. He wore a sandwich board painted in sloppy script: "Welcome to the SPD 1916 Christmas play. Our apologies: no paper, ink, or money were available for printing programs." The crowd roared, and a miner sitting across from Heina pounded the table with his fist and wiped away tears of laughter.

SPD local history from the winter of 1916 reveals bleak humor and bitter jokes about the lack of food. But I have to imagine the living of it. Heina might have watched the off-key children's chorus on stage as the kids fidgeted and meandered through holiday and revolutionary standbys. Heina tried to catch his father's eye, but Papa stared down at his fingernails, hands splayed flat on the tabletop as if the smooth wood might buck like a wild horse and run away. Since Papa had returned from the front in October, he'd worn a numb and distanced face.

Papa had returned right away to the mines. I imagine that within a few days, he coughed constantly and spat blood into a handkerchief. He wouldn't say whether he'd breathed in poison gas at Verdun, and he didn't complain. I know that in these months the miners' union appointed him to run the miners' cooperative grocery, but I don't know whether he was truly sick and shell-shocked, or whether he bounced back from military service like a vibrant circus clown. Meanwhile, Heina graduated from Pyra in September and placed his name on a long list for open secretarial positions. Father and son would both be clerks.

Lina caught Heina looking at Papa, and a scowl flitted across her face. She tapped Jupp on the shoulder and turned her wrist, motioning for a look at his watch. Already restless. She was beside herself with nervous energy, and the more withdrawn Papa became the more she turned irritable and worried. Jupp gave her a sympathetic smile, rolling his eyes as the children strained for a high note. She smiled back and lowered her eyes, as if embarrassed that her impatience had extended even to a group of six-year-olds. She put her hand up to her neck, running her fingers along the simple silver necklace she wore, and something about the gesture made Heina's heart ache. It was childlike and lost, as if she were searching for something to hold onto now that Papa had retreated and taken away his laughter and his booming joy.

The children filed offstage to heavy applause. The curtain parted again, and a local SPD leader appeared wearing an apron and a frazzled, abused blond wig. He waved a wooden spoon at a stove that had been fashioned from a table and a piece of cardboard.

"Hmmm," said the cook in falsetto. "What shall I cook for dinner?" He rummaged in his pot and brought up slips of paper. "Look, ration cards!" He paused as he studied them, licking his lips. "I think I'll bake a cake. I don't have any eggs, but that's no matter. Just add two eggs' worth of ration cards, and beat well." The audience laughed at the familiar joke, which had been printed in the papers and told on the street with many variations. It was better to laugh about the lack of food and the surplus of ration cards than to complain about eating breaded turnip cutlets for dinner or potato-peel cake for dessert.

After the show men and women stood in groups, smoking and talking, and the children ran through the hall in packs, dodging the legs of their parents. Heina stood by Papa, who grunted when the local miners' union leader, Guido Heiland, approached. In place of a greeting, Guido said, "Heinrich! Na, it's got to end soon, don't you think?"

Papa ruffled his mustache with his lips and said, "I think we're doing our part here, pulling thirty thousand last month to the antiwar demo. We need to get the war finished before Heina gets a call-up card." Papa clasped Heina fiercely on the shoulder. All males seventeen to sixty had been ordered to the front. In two and a half years Heina would be fair game. He silently thanked his parents for not meeting and marrying a year sooner.

Heina's personnel file reveals that he got a job with the Recklinghausen County administration in mid-February 1917. When he opened the official letter about the post, I imagine he felt chosen, rescued, and manly—a provider. Maybe his mother even patted him on the neck. Maybe she made a deal with a neighbor to obtain an egg, which she recklessly used to make the most greasy and succulent potato pancakes Heina had ever tasted. It was, after all, a huge break for the family: a government salary. The money itself wasn't much, actually shockingly little, as the second letter with the numbers revealed, but it was reliable. The mines might catch fire or collapse but no one could live without bureaucrats.

Each morning Heina rode his bicycle six kilometers down the gentle sloping curve from home, past the old school, near the Gänsebrink Park where the farmers led their geese, and through the farmlands. The first few days on the job Heina attempted to piece together a daily schedule amid the clatter of adding machines and the swift footsteps and murmurs of the other clerks. He leafed through file pouches filled with forms, each peppered with mysterious abbreviations. He realized he would have to endure receiving insufficient instructions, blundering through a task, and then waiting to be yelled at or worse.

He stood at his desk while his dictation copy was being proofread. To forget the ache in his legs, he stared out the window at the traffic on the street below. His eyes drifted eastward toward the river. Far away from these file folders and blotters, thousands of kilometers away, Moscow blazed. The newspapers relayed stories of Lenin and Kerensky, radical and moderate, shouting past midnight, yelling in meeting halls and rallying their supporters as they fought about the establishment of the soviets. Outside the meeting halls, amid the spires and onion-topped churches of a Russian autumn, bullets flew as the tsar's forces took aim at the revolutionaries.

Those Russian questions continued to rage in the minds of socialists everywhere, but Heina might have laughed to imagine a granddaughter listening to those same arguments one century later across the Atlantic Ocean in a bar in Boston. Hungry for radical politics after college, I accidentally fell in love with a tough-guy socialist and signed on with a strident organization whose meetings were peppered with phrases like "the Fourth International" and "the means of production will be seized by the working class."

I ate a few baskets of free bar popcorn, spongy and stale with the taste of cigarette smoke. Voices raised on an esoteric question: whether the peasants in the Soviet Union before the revolution were truly reactionary or whether they were members of a rural working class. There was a correct answer, of course (peasants are reactionary), and Lenin couldn't be argued with. When the members of the socialist group opened their mouths I fell silent, even though my affection for the fields, for my paternal grandfather who had scraped by as a butcher and farmer, made me question Lenin's universal relevance. I would get past it, I vowed, leave my softness and doubt in the dust on the way to the postbourgeois Red heaven. With enough faking and caffeine, I could push through the filmy wisps and Mardi Gras bead curtains of my personality. If I clenched my teeth and focused, I could make myself think in bullet points.

Most of what I'd known of communists or socialists up until that point came from *Rocky IV* and a few days in high school history class when we learned about Stalin's mass murders and Khrushchev taking off his shoe to pound on a podium and threaten nuclear annihilation. Heina, I approached the first bare edges of your world, dulled and simplified like an image that has been copied over and over for a century, rendering it almost unreadable. Maybe I was drawn to this smoky bar because of a version of you I only sensed.

I joined the group and stood on street corners, selling their newspaper for fifty cents, not knowing I was looking for you, thrilled to be around a real live grown-up group of anticapitalists who did normal things like buy cat food and toilet paper while at the same time decrying capitalism, criticizing the Soviet Union and U.S. imperialism.

Heina stood at his desk and braced his weight on his arms, trying to approximate a push-up. He was almost fifteen, after all, and needed to be a strong man whether or not he was a clerk. Schneeweiß, a supervisor, happened to shuffle by and saw Heina fooling and rocking on his arms. Long-legged Schneeweiß approached Heina's desk and asked with a hint of sarcasm, "Nothing to do?"

Heina began to say, "Stretching," but the sounds faded on his lips. Schneeweiß reached for a letter drying on Heina's blotter. Heina grabbed for it fruitlessly, like a child, and immediately regretted his loss of control. Schneeweiß held the long letter at the top and ripped it down the middle.

"Start again. You need the practice," he said and walked away.

Heina shifted his weight to his heels and looked out the window, fuming and mortified, avoiding the glances of the six other clerks, who would shake their heads in sympathy after Schneeweiß was well out of sight. Heina's ears burned. Oh, to scream! Oh, for a pickaxe, for the loud jostling and swearing of the black-faced miners instead of these young men with clean collars and ears, instead of Schneeweiß with his wire-rimmed glasses and hair combed razor straight across his forehead.

To add to Heina's rage, Schneeweiß was an SPD member, an elected local leader. I have invented Schneeweiß, but there were many like him, SPD leaders who did not act their politics but instead sat back and mouthed their whispers about the need for national discipline, the need to support the war. With sad sacks like that in charge, it was no wonder the SPD was tearing itself apart from the inside. Liebknecht and Rosa Luxemburg stood on their soapboxes and proclaimed an end to all this limp-noodle politics. Then they acted, formed their own party, the Independent Social Democrats, the USPD. They took a hundred thousand SPD members with them. That, Heina thought, would show people like Schneeweiß, would make somebody in Berlin sit up and take notice.

Papa seemed sickened by the interparty warfare, and his old friends came by to sit around the kitchen table and smoke and curse. "How can we have strength without unity?" they thundered, reminding Heina of the old hall in Jena decked in red, of the organizers at the porcelain plant with the rough hands and breathless speeches. These men had laid their lives on the line for the SPD, had split heads—their own and others'—for the party. "This generation is different," Papa said. "They want to fight with each other." Another man took a pull on his pipe and released white smoke from lips shrouded in a gray beard. "Oh, Heinrich, nostalgia. Marx would be laughing at you . . . Tell me, you don't remember the splits in the party conference of '07?"

A thrill of excitement rose up Heina's spine as he imagined a newer, more radical party. Couldn't these men smell delicious change, a new era coming with the heather-scented spring air, with the radical winds from the East? Maybe that was what they meant by "discipline": bite down, move steadily ahead, don't get too excited by all these crazy dreams.

Heina, how do you rein in that jazzed-up, whacked-out joy? Or is it better to ride that electric charge into the sunset of explosions and possibility . . . You can call it groupthink, or the power of people who realize they all want the same thing.

Way back in college, before my brush with the socialists and just after I'd discovered activism, the Gulf War turned normal days into television vigils. I boarded a bus to my first antiwar rally. We stood on a multileveled plaza in downtown Minneapolis as sound and snow washed over us. Speakers yelled through a microphone and cheap, crackling amplifier, and I strained to hear the words through the pops and squeals of feedback. I stamped my feet in the slush and wondered when we would march. Papier-mâché puppets bobbed: caricatures of the president, a war-hungry dragon, a top-hatted oil baron, cartoonish faces softening as wet snow pelted down. Daylight faded, and the crowd morphed into a slow-moving amoeba, gathering itself up the street and stretching thin. I clapped in time to a chant and looked at the closed and darkened windows of apartments we passed.

Along the route, as we shuffled under the blue-gray sky, I saw flames. We passed a corner parking lot, and fire roared out of a Dumpster. Black-clad kids, with the anarchy symbol of a huge encircled A inked in red or white on the back of their black sweatshirts and jackets, whooped and ran, the flat soles of Converse sneakers smacking the icy pavement. A small group pushed over metal newspaper boxes and papers spilling onto the street. Others slapped stickers with the logo "Lie$" onto the boxes. Most of the kids wore bandannas across their faces, tied at the back of their heads like bank robbers, so police and witnesses wouldn't recognize them. The orange splashes of light looked beautiful in the blue night. I imagined then that this was like the French Revolution—to the barricades!

That march was a political carnival ride, a slow-moving boat in a loud echoing hall, "It's a Radical World After All." I was a child there, in the patches of color, puppets, faces, and flyers, not understanding the messages. My shoes were soaked, and the smell of burning trash engulfed us as we jogged past the Dumpster and scattered. But the togetherness around that large campfire couldn't keep the sadness at bay. I couldn't quite imagine myself in those black sneakers, couldn't firebomb a Dumpster and then say to my fellow punks, "Oh shit, I have to go study for my botany final." But the Gulf War and faraway raining bombs taught me to want a consuming, avenging fire.

The roar of a demonstration surged in Heina's blood, in the echoes he must have heard even while in the womb. Yet I imagine the noise never failed to quicken his pulse. Stumbling down the stairs of the county building, Heina hit the bottom of the stone steps to a burst of May sun. The iron clock on the city building read 5:00 p.m. but the light was as bright as midday. Instead of hopping on his bicycle and taking a left toward home, he turned right. Walking toward the angular town square at the lowest point in Recklinghausen, Heina stopped to glance at the newspapers on the corner stand. The sun drew color into the faces of people passing. The muffled crash of rhythmic chanting, then a pause and the single thread of a speaker's voice, then the response of the crowd, echoed from behind the town square monument. From a block away, Heina saw the placards of a demonstration against the war.

Stepping onto the curb toward the rally, Heina saw signs with the logo of the USPD, the new Independent Social Democratic Party. Heina's smile froze on his face. What would Papa think if he knew Heina had stumbled here? The speaker on the platform lambasted the SPD for failing to stand up to the Kaiser, for voting to fund the war machine.

Heina inched closer, the heat of the sun pressing the back of his head. Young women with baskets hanging from their arms wove in and out of the small crowd, handing out flowers and pamphlets. Amid the German girls with their tiny wan faces and blond hair, Heina noticed a dark-haired woman, her strong nose and chin giving her a look of seriousness and confidence. Heina put out his hand for a flyer, then pretended to read the words. The woman's dark hair, tied in braids, turned the sunlight to a molten glow. Had he seen her at one of the huge SPD youth group May Day camps? Her shoulders turned away from him as she sought a path through the crowd.

"Are you a USPD member?" he asked, his voice too loud and hoarse. He cleared his throat. She turned and met his eyes with a clear look. Heina forgot for a moment what he'd asked and stuck his hand out mutely. Her fingers brushed his.

"They gave me a sandwich to help with the pamphlets," she said. "But I'm thinking about joining. Do you have a question about the program?"

"What will your parents say?" he asked. When the words came out of his mouth, he realized how childish the question sounded. A real man wouldn't care about parental approval.

"My parents? They don't care much about politics, but I do."

He opened his mouth, mind blank. She gave him a curious look, a half smile, and passed on through the crowd. Heina watched her go, then composed his face in an expression he hoped was serious, critical, intelligent, and revolutionary. He folded the flyer carefully and placed it in his pocket. He knew politics in this small town. He knew if he went to another USPD event he'd see her again.

A week later Jupp hunted for the battered soccer ball amid the tangle of rakes and buckets in the garden shed. "Heina," he said, "come on, take a shot!" Jupp rolled the ball across the lawn toward Heina, who kicked it back. Jupp dove for the ball, hair flying. Heina couldn't concentrate on the thump-thump of a soccer volley in the walled cage of the backyard. The SPD had shut down most of its youth activities at the hall, and the boys' lives had become so narrow.

The side gate squeaked, and Herr Strauss, a short man with a felt hat, stepped into the yard. "Having fun, boys?" he called.

Heina shrugged. "It's okay," he said. "But even with the war, the SPD should open the youth league back up so kids have something to do."

Strauss squinted at Heina from behind his glasses, then turned and called up the back steps into the kitchen, "Heinrich!"

"Nice job," whispered Jupp sarcastically. He elbowed Heina, still panting from running.

Papa appeared at the top of the kitchen stairs in a knitted vest and house slippers.

"I found our youth commission leader in your backyard," Strauss said. Heina reddened and put the ball on the ground, tapped it toward Jupp. "No, enough of that for now," said Strauss. "Come on inside—the local committee will be here soon. We need to put your ideas on the agenda."

Heina wiped his forehead, scooted a chair into the crowded kitchen, and tried to avoid the eyes of the SPD committee members, feeling like a dirty kid called in from a backyard game. At the end of the meeting, Heina leaned forward and added in a too-soft voice a few sentences about the need for youth activities.

The members shook hands and most filed out, leaving only Strauss and Paul Rhode, one of the area leaders, a man with a restless energy and a stern look. Strauss leaned back in his chair. "Heina, you're an organizer. There are many party members who feel in their hearts what's right, but they don't *do*," Strauss said. He smoothed his neatly trimmed beard and continued. "Those people will corner you at a bar, tell you their beliefs for hours, and that makes them feel good. But that talk doesn't change the world." What exactly was Strauss getting at? It felt like a round-about challenge.

Rhode drained his coffee cup and set it on the table. "You could be a leader like your father. But do you know what that means? It means you must always be thinking. It means you never come to a meeting without a proposal or a suggestion."

This, like so many others, is an imagined moment. Whether it happened over dinner, in a single meeting, or over the course of a week or a year, my grandfather Heina somehow grew from a child to a political adult, and his shoulders were judged strong enough to help support the burden of making a new world.

Maybe Heina panicked at scheduling a youth meeting. Maybe he was distracted with worry that no one would attend. But with that sick feeling in the pit of his stomach came the knowledge that this was what *really* mattered, more than his work at the county administration or any other concern. The knowledge arrived with the drugs of esteem and respect. Men at the meetings now called him "Buschmann" and slapped him on the back, comparing him favorably to his father. Those seconds of rough familiarity made up for so much. The respect seemed to heal the divot of missing bone in his rib cage and broaden his narrow, tight chest. It stretched his thin clerk's hands into miner's paws. When men and women worried together, when anyone around the world said, "Comrades," he was now included. His mother even treated him better, gave him an extra spoonful of food or a roll at dinner, as if he would need the fuel.

What I know is that an organizer gives up a certain kind of freedom before he or she even realizes it's gone. If you are taking your life task seriously, there is always the work of assessment to be done, the work of analysis (even while you are gardening, driving, or having sex) to figure exactly how you can help your group develop. To-do lists scroll before your eyes at the most inopportune moments.

You can always find time to constructively criticize your own leadership and the work of your organization, to think about the long road ahead, the challenge of developing skills within your ranks. You earnestly believe your actions matter, and with that step of faith you are doing things that other people do not do, and your actions begin to create an impact. In this life there is also a way, if you are devoted or too devoted, to lose your breath through a tightness of the chest when you realize you have no idea how or where revolution can be brought about. The world becomes a wilderness of possibility and danger on a grand scale.

You begin to build your identity and personality on that lack of freedom, and you willingly trade freedom for control or the illusion of it. If you are anxious about the approaching bombs or the hunger in your neighborhood, you can finally *do* something about it. This is a theology of second chances, but in place of a wise and benevolent god you have only your fellow humans with their limitless capacity to work or to betray, to win or to fear.

In his second meeting, I imagine Heina raising a proposal in such a wavering and soft voice that a seventy-year-old miner sat forward in his chair and yelled, "What?"

Heina cleared his throat and repeated, "I propose a forum coorganized by the SPD and the independent socialists." He gripped the wooden chair seat and braced himself for raucous discussion.

"Good idea, Buschmann," Rhode grunted. A few others nodded. "All those opposed?" Silence. Rhode scribbled a note on the agenda. "Buschmann, get something together and deliver a plan next week. But I don't want this to serve as a funnel to dump all of our youth members into the Independent Party!"

Heina caught the look Papa flashed in his direction, a quick agreement with Rhode that said, *Don't be tempted, Son, don't be stupid. New and radical movements are thrilling, but the heat of that flame will burn up all we've worked for.*

Heina, I first imagined you as the stalwart SPD member, an unintelligible icon who always kept party discipline, a firm-jawed man of iron. I had envied you, Heina, because I believed you basked in a political acceptance from your revolutionary parents. I believed you felt at home in the universe in a way I could not imagine.

But three years into my research, Mom let a bit of my inheritance tumble out of her mouth. Disconnected sentences and fragments of fact from her childhood hid like unstrung beads in the pockets of her mind. "I know my dad left the SPD at some point," she said. I probed for details and she shrugged, disappointed that she did not understand the memory.

I held this shred of information alongside chronologies and histories, trying to join the ragged edges. The socialist parties had split seven or eight times, and each jumping-off point held its own significance, messages I will never receive about Heina's choices and politics. And then there's the question of the reliability of my mother's child memory. It could very well have been Heina's papa who left, or someone else entirely. But I decide to see this clue as meaningful. I imagine it was here, in Heina's youth, that the combined excitement of the Russian Revolution and heady teenage years sparked movement and fire. Heina, I listen close to this imaginary message: if we really want to change things, we are always running up against sharp edges and barbed wire, sometimes even held out by the people we love. And sometimes we hurt them in return.

Joint efforts at this time were common between the youth in the SPD and the independents, and art, plays, and recreation were central to the youth movement. It's easy to place Heina at this intersection, though I have no way of knowing. I fabricate a modest proposal: a short hike and visit to a photo exhibit, "The Industrial Pride of the Ruhr," followed by a youth-led antiwar rally.

At the miners' union hall, a young man with a weathered face led a group of young people through the photo exhibit. Pointing to a large photo of a foundry glowing with smoke and molten metal, he said, "This steel mill is useful to the working class, so we might see it as beautiful. We need steel, and there's no reason to love this steel plant any less than we love the forest."

Heina surveyed the crowd of about forty kids, some of them SPD youth members, some USPD youth. A good showing of middle-class kids from various nature clubs had also turned out, wearing their characteristic "reform" clothes that drove the adults crazy, loose tunics and short pants for the men, and blousy unrestraining shifts for the women. Research showed me that such exhibits opened in those years throughout the Ruhr, urging nature-loving teens to open their hearts to workers as well as trees, to appreciate the social realities of the working class.

Heina surreptitiously glanced at the women, hoping the dark-haired girl from the Recklinghausen demo would appear. He didn't see her. To distract himself, he considered the first photo: a man with a smudged face resting his hands on the handle of a wheeled cart piled with steel bars and twisted metal. In the background, the darkness of the mill building was lit by the cracked and riddled shine of orange-hot steel in a blast furnace.

The man had a bemused look in his eyes, a question: What is so picturesque here, Mr. Photographer? But the scene, particularly the man's strong hands, captivated Heina and reminded him of his own father's massive palms and fingers. This photo was flanked by two landscape shots, one of a rolling horizon dotted with smoke stacks and the other of a factory nestled in a valley. Heina had to admit it was difficult to feel the gut-stirring reaction of beauty for a common factory, but old ways of thinking had to be challenged.

After the photo exhibit, the group followed a path through a small forest preserve. Heina breathed more deeply as they moved into the cool pines.

A young man, Willi, fell in step next to Heina. "Like the exhibit?" Heina asked.

"I don't know," Willi said, eyes scanning the gravel path as if he were searching for words. "I understand the factories are important, but shouldn't the land be everyone's first priority? It's the one thing all Germans share." Willi took a pamphlet from the back pocket of his wool hiking knickers. Heina reached for the palm-sized booklet and read the cover, a tract by a well-known right-wing environmentalist who had won over a large portion of the middle-class youth movement during these years.

The group wandered down the road toward the rally site, and Willi pointed to the smokestacks on the horizon. "This place used to be just farmlands and forests, but now it's all mines and steel mills. You go for a short walk and come home coated in coal dust. I know the Poles don't mind living in filth, but I think Germans want to protect our country."

Heina inhaled and held his breath, swallowing a desire to blast this young man with a barrage of words. "That fellow who wrote your pamphlet . . . he's quite an anti-Semite, you know," Heina said. "All that business about our 'roots deep in the German soil.'"

"You can't discredit this guy just because he's a little prejudiced. He's from another generation," Willi said. "His ideas are food for thought at least."

Heina raised his hand, bargaining for time to formulate a response, but a flurry of activity at the far north of the open plaza distracted him. Organizers moved through the crowd, handing out cardboard signs. A USPD member clambered onto the small stage and launched a chant against the war. Otto from the Pyra Institute then began to speak in a clear and rousing voice about the need for a united youth movement against the war. He finished by calling out, "And from the SPD, we have . . ." A USPD

member motioned to Heina and said, "Come on, man, you organized this thing. Get up here and say something."

The world turned momentarily black in front of Heina's eyes,
and he pushed his way through the crowd, cursing himself. How,
after all the planning meetings, had it slipped his mind that he
would also have to speak? He hoped that when he opened his
mouth, something vaguely comprehensible would come out.

5

The Promise of Power

I see Heina as a boy-man caught in a swirling torrent. War's burdens pushed many Germans to raise their voices and their weapons against the government. Putting myself in Heina's shoes, I hear voices from above, the confusing tumult of men and women making plans as a deafening backdrop to the daily challenge of finding food for three meals.

Heina clutched a small sack of potatoes. Men and women passing on the street corner prodded him with their shoulders and elbows. Where was Papa? He'd been here just a moment ago, haggling over the price of potatoes at a black-market stand. These hard-bargain potatoes looked like shriveled dead people's toes, but they were potatoes, after all. For four weeks that April it's quite possible the Buschmann family had eaten nothing but turnips, as the "Turnip Winter" of 1916–17 forced the inventiveness of fried turnip cutlets. There—from the direction of the tobacco shop came Papa's embarrassing Buschmann laugh-howl. Papa stood on the steps next to Guido

Heiland, the charismatic miner who'd come to Marl in 1912 to
organize the SPD.

"Hamburg and Bremen have formed Workers' and Soldiers'
Councils!" Heiland yelled, cupping his hands against his mouth
to broadcast the news. "Comrades, join us tonight at the hall,
8:00. We must plan, or the revolution will start without us!"

The shouts of response and assent rose up like a wave. Heina
strained on tiptoe to see. He leaned forward and his paper sack
ripped. Potatoes tumbled onto the cobblestones, and he squatted down to scoop them into his jacket pockets. One rolled off
into the gutter. He angled through the crowd and crept toward
the tobacco shop, locating Papa in the crowd.

"When the revolution gets here, we'll finally get the miners'
issues settled—and we'll win!" boomed Papa.

Heina squeezed next to Papa and lifted the flap of Papa's jacket
pocket, thinking to deposit the rest of the potatoes without in-
terrupting Papa's conversations. Quick as a shot Papa's strong
hand snapped down and caught Heina's wrist in a vice grip.

"Heina!" he hissed. "You don't sneak up on a war veteran like
that. I thought you were a pickpocket or a cop."

Heina held out a potato. "I've got to put these somewhere,
Papa. That sack busted."

As the shouting rang on around him, Papa looked quickly
to the left and right and nudged a blond man with a handlebar
mustache. "Comrade Franks," he said, "let my son use your
handkerchief." Franks flourished his wrinkled red hankie. Papa
tied the potatoes in a bundle.

"Go give these to your mother. Tell her . . ." Papa stopped and
considered. "Tell her it looks like revolution is about to break.
Ask her to come to the hall with some supper."

Three days later, November 9, 1918, the German Revolution
exploded. Papa announced over dinner that the Kaiser, embat-

tled in Berlin and unable to control the strikes and protests in every corner of the country, had abdicated.

"Who's in power, then?" Jupp asked. He leaned over his soup, his curly hair falling in front of his eyes. There was no school, no work. Everyone was on holiday.

"We are," said Papa, "so finish your food, because this is history. We'll see the end of war before the week is through." Papa leaned back and laughed, his eyes bright as stars. "The munitions workers in Kiel decided they've had enough. Boom, a strike!" He smacked the table hard, and the plates rang like bells. "The soldiers coming back from the front are sick of war, hungry and armed: good people to have on our side."

Would Papa and Mama never get done with their soup? Finish up and let's go! Heina had wanted to leave the house last night, but Papa said it was too dangerous after dark. Instead Heina had stood at the open window, listening to the street noises of yelling and chanting, the cracking of a fire, rifle shots of warning, and late at night a crowd running down the street singing a revolutionary song in laughing voices.

In one lifetime Heina saw three German governments crumble into dust. In 1990 the Berlin Wall disintegrated piece by piece, and two cocoons ripped open as living creatures mingled and touched each other's faces after what seemed an eternal separation. Each subway train in Berlin stopped at every station, a prosaic sea change. No more would western trains zoom past a bleak fluorescent blur of communism, no more would eastern trains halt in midtrack and reverse. I rode the Berlin trains that fall as a student, grateful to live this history.

Even the most jaded Berlin cynic in a black turtleneck stood at the spontaneous gatherings and mumbled in time to the chants: "Unser Deutschland," our Germany. To an outsider, this might have seemed a frightening refrain of German nationalism, but at the time it sounded only a long-buried hope from Heina's era that Germany might forge a path determined by direct democracy. At that moment in the fall of 1990 all questions could be asked. Some wondered if the fall of the wall meant West Germany could also remake itself, if the conservative government led by Chancellor Kohl would crumble in the face of the people's desire to form a completely new country out of east and west.

Returning one night from an evening at a German pub, we rode an old East German train that rose on elevated tracks from an underground station. Flames leapt from the street below. A house on fire or a chemical explosion? The old East German subway car had no safety controls on its doors, so my classmate Lewis heaved on the brass handle to force open the door as we sped above the fire.

"Look!" he screamed against the wind, the light of the flames reflecting in his glasses. "It's the Autonomen. Holy shit!" The Autonomen, or the Autonomous, was a long-standing and loosely organized band of anarchists in Berlin. To take direct action against the housing shortage in West Berlin, the anarchists had transformed vacant buildings into vast squatter communities, often refurbishing walls, pirating electricity, and performing wild and fanciful decorating schemes. They would soon spread eastward, reclaiming the empty spaces of the other Berlin.

"The street at Kreuzberger Platz is dug up . . . They're dropping huge pieces of pavement on the cop cars!" Lewis yelled. "Get up! You've got to see this!"

I grabbed a brass pole near the door as the wind blew my hair over my eyes. Fire exploded below at a barricade near a police car. The street was furrowed like a plowed field. Orange fire streaked down from a balcony against the blue night. Lewis braced himself against the open doors, filling the car with cold and the light of fire. As we rolled away I had to repeat to myself what I had seen to make sure I had not imagined it. In three months I would see the flaming Dumpsters of the antiwar protests in Minneapolis. On both nights I stood stunned at these acts that were simply not allowed and therefore technically invisible, unseeable. I realized how much momentum and anger it would take for someone like me to propel myself beyond the realm of normal expectations.

Standing at that window, Heina felt his old personality dissolve. His lungs expanded, and even the flesh that helped him breathe seemed to be infused with freedom. People like Papa had seized the country for themselves, which meant no one was Kaiser and yet everyone was Kaiser. The SPD's plans on paper would sketch themselves on the earth: the unions would run the factories and mines, and no one would ever stomp on Heina's toes or scream in his face at work again. Maybe bosses at work would be elected, there would be potatoes to eat, and workers would get vacation time for hiking. Maybe it meant an end forever to that taken-hostage feeling of knowing the bigwigs and industrialists could wage war for as long as they wanted. It meant that the warm feeling in his Worker Youth meetings would spread out and flow through the streets.

The Buschmann family walked toward the old town center, and Mama Lina pulled at the boys' collars to keep them near. Miners and factory workers stood at street corners with their arms crossed, some cradling rifles. They looked like rambunctious children as they beamed with smiles and nodded at everyone who passed. Heina saw an unaccustomed splash of red from the newsstand. Overnight, the *Daily Spectator* had become the *Red Flag*, and the headline read, "German Republic Declared!"

They stood for hours, the whole day, shoulder to shoulder in the town square behind the church. The crowd listened to speeches beneath the red banner, and Heina tucked his hands in his armpits to keep warm in the early evening chill. Men and women ran around the edges of the crowd to pull each other into urgent conversations in the city hall, now occupied by the Workers' and Soldiers' Council of Marl. Sandwiches and rolls were handed through the crowd as the sun glared behind the city building. Party leaders rushed into a meeting. An hour later a line of men and women strode out onto the stage, some with determined gazes and others unable to hold back broad smiles.

A woman called out, "Comrades! I present to you the newly appointed Workers' and Soldiers' Council of Marl-Hüls!" Heina scanned the faces and recognized many from SPD functions and from meetings around his parents' kitchen table. Impressive—about half the group came from the new Independent Social Democratic Party. Heina applauded with the crowd until his palms were sore, but a small feeling of disappointment curled in his chest.

Trying to make a joke of it, he leaned over to his mother, who was scowling intently. "Mama," Heina said. "I'd have voted for Papa, wouldn't you?"

"Papa has a position," she said. "He's one of the new local administrators. He helped the committee get organized." I'd come across this fact—that Heinrich had been a key administrator in the revolutionary government—in a slim paperback volume on the history of Marl, and I might have missed its significance entirely had I not known what upheaval gripped Germany in these months. I imagine that Lina started her analyzing and murmuring, explaining the factions represented by each person on the committee. Heina nodded and pretended to follow Mama's detailed analysis, but squatted down to reach quickly for a pebble near his shoe. He tucked it into his pocket, thinking that someday he would show his children this stone and tell them about the moment it stood for.

Papa pushed through the crowd to reach them. "Heina—listen, we need a favor from you."

"*Schatz*, sweetheart, it's getting late," Mama said to Papa. "There's a curfew, and Heina's not yet seventeen."

Papa ruffled his moustache with his lip, his gaze firm. "This is man's work. Don't worry, I'll have a soldier bring him home in an hour."

"Man's work," his mother scoffed. "If you'd read August Bebel at all, you'd know it's 'Comrade' now."

Heina clutched the stone in his pocket and tried to assemble his face into a serious, manly look. With a nudge on the shoulder Papa propelled Heina through the crowd on the city hall steps. The city shield above the doorway had been draped in red cloth, and a man with a rifle yelled for people to get back. Maybe the council wanted him to have a role in a decision-making session, maybe even vote as one of the youth leaders! Then someday soon he'd be up on that stage, and Mama would have to nod and give a grudging, quiet smile.

Instead of turning toward the meeting room, Papa led the way toward another door. "Son," he said, "I need you to take one of the bicycles in the courtyard there and go to Meier's Print Shop across town—by the old church and the bridge, *ja*? There will be a bundle of posters. Say you're from the Marl Council. Bring them back here. Okay?"

Heina pushed open the door and wheeled a bicycle toward the road. Papa reappeared with a slip of paper. "In case any of the patrols stops you," he said. "It's got Guido's signature." Papa stood for a second, looking around the courtyard. "You'll remember this day, won't you?" he asked, his eyes misting and shining bright blue in the half-light. Heina's throat tightened.

Love and admiration for his father, for the confusion and excitement, took away his breath. He nodded.

Heina rode from the printers with the flat package of posters balanced against the handlebars, almost hoping a patrol of men with red armbands would stop him so he could show them the paper to prove his official business. He stopped to adjust the load and peeled back the wrapping to look inside the package. "All Citizens of Marl," the text began in large letters. Below the headline ran a list of crimes now punishable by death or imprisonment during this period of upheaval: looting, carrying a gun without permission, and hoarding groceries.

Within weeks the surge of energy in the Workers' and Soldiers' Councils across Germany gave way in some cities to furious infighting as socialist activists laid out their goals for the new republic and saw just how far each would dare move toward revolution. I have no idea where Papa Heinrich stood in these battles. Because he was a miner, I will guess that he continued to take the miners' position, usually more left-wing than that held by many SPD functionaries. I can only imagine the long hours of trying to establish a working Soviet-modeled committee and the heartbreak in watching it deadlock. And I have to imagine him bringing that heartbreak home and transforming it into a silent ache that hung over the family.

"Go and ask your father if he wants a sandwich," Mama said to Jupp, who rolled his eyes with dread.

"Why do I have to be the one to do it?" Jupp pulled himself off the kitchen bench, sighing, then hurried back in. "Papa's coming," he whispered.

Papa leaned into the kitchen, bracing himself against the doorframe. Over the last month he had lost weight and collected new wrinkles under his eyes, exhausted with running back and forth between the miners' co-op, union meetings, and the Workers' Council.

"We asked the council today to formally support the miners' strike," he said. Then in a roar, "They said NO!" His eyes reddened with sadness and rage.

Triumphant red flags still hung from the lampposts, but each day's newspaper brought bad news. The Congress of Workers' and Soldiers' Councils, elected in Berlin, had seated 2 women out of 496 delegates. Mama shook her head grimly, tracing her finger down the newspaper column of names. "Rosa Luxemburg isn't on this list. I'm no Bolshevik, but only an idiot would say she isn't one of the smartest people in the country, man or woman."

Were these the birth pangs of the new republic or the premature death throes? During the last two weeks of 1918 the country seemed poised to plunge into chaos. Two days before Christmas naval officers in Berlin went on strike because they hadn't been paid in weeks. Noske, the new SPD head of police, called in the Kaiser's conservative troops to brutally crush the strike. The SPD press avoided the story, and the far-left papers hurled condemnation and news of a massacre. Moderates flinched in fear as far-left militias began arming against further attacks, and street fighting exploded in Berlin.

Christmas passed with barely a celebration. Three days later the independents, including Rosa Luxemburg, pulled out of the new socialist government to establish the German Communist Party. Local independent socialist groups debated in worried and muted tones whether to move left and declare themselves communists.

Papa sucked on his pipe, leaning over the newspaper-strewn kitchen table. "You can't set this kind of thing—a new country!—in motion and then decide you've had enough. *Nicht wahr?* Is it not true?" He looked up to get confirmation from Lina, who carefully poured bacon grease from the frying pan into the grease canister.

She sighed in annoyance. "Papa, *es reicht schon*. Enough already." He'd been expressing his shock at the communists for two days straight, expecting someone in the house to give him a decent and rational explanation for the split.

Heina didn't know what to think. Depending on which party newspaper you read, each perspective sounded so logical. He began to look forward to the distraction of mindless work, the copying and the ink on his fingers, the rattling of the windows in the drafty Recklinghausen administration building. The Congress in Berlin had decided to keep the old administrative structures in place for now, so Heina still had a job. The banner hanging above the Recklinghausen City Hall still proclaimed the victory of the Workers' Council. Heina wanted to take down the piece of embroidered silk, either to save it as a memento or to shield it, like a hopeful, wide-eyed child, from the reality of the unreliable world.

We rounded a corner on one of Leipzig's cobblestone streets, absorbing the last night in East Germany before the official 1990 German Reunion celebration. Our student group passed a church where a cluster of lit candles sputtered on the curved stone threshold of a doorway. I had seen a similar memorial in Prague: a massive ring of colored candles in a city square, an anonymous memorial to the students in the crushed Prague Spring revolution of 1968–69. The candles in Prague had been set and lit for years, accumulating a multicolored geology of wax rivulets like a foot-tall Bundt cake. The white candles in Leipzig looked naked and new, hard-edged and tall. We stopped to ask what it meant.

"That's for the dead revolution," an older woman said in English, her eyes searching our American faces to gauge whether we might understand. "The people who started the democracy movement didn't want capitalism, but now it's what we'll get. No one wants to celebrate tonight."

In Leipzig's medieval town square a sparse crowd huddled in a light rain. A mostly drunk rock band mouthed a slurred welcome into the microphones and played cover tunes, including "Back in the USSR," like a Disney version of the soundtrack of freedom. The noise echoed against the old pocked and crumbling stone.

My friends and I sported the scruffy hippie look, but we stood out in the crowd in our American-style windbreakers and jeans, every zipper pull and pants pocket screaming a logo. We shouted to each other over the noise of the band, rolled our eyes, debating whether to leave and where to find a bar.

A young guy with bad skin leaned toward us and asked in a shout if we were Americans. One of our group smiled and instinctively lied. "Canadian," he said.

The kid must not have believed him. Pale hands flew toward us, and a few shoves sent one of our group stumbling. We ran, ducked, and shielded our heads as chunks of terra cotta—either broken flower pots or roof tiles—rained around us and smashed on the slick cobblestones. I remember sprinting through the dark down a side street as orange-red shards ricocheted.

They chased us, screaming, "Ausländer raus!"—the skinhead battle cry, Foreigners out. In Germany my complexion was taken to be Turkish and had earned me growled threats and the occasional refusal of service at the rougher sort of bar, but this skirmish attacked our money, our Americanness. We dashed into the train station, arms windmilling, soles slapping concrete as we scanned the lit boards of clacking letters for any train headed west.

Then the roof seemed to cave in: a blast of sound exploded,

shaking the ancient glass windows in their casings—like dooms-day. Simultaneously the soot-blackened trains all sounded their horns in the shell of the station, a deafening salute to the last midnight in the former East Germany. The sound waves receded, leaving a thick, clogged silence.

An engine huffed. We found a train and slammed our bodies into seats, panting. Get me out of this dark, sooty country, get me out of the past, I wanted to yell, urging the train to move. I did not know how to navigate a world without the oasis of 7-Elevens and credit cards to save me from whatever midnight trouble might find me. I still don't know what those kids might have done to us because I don't know who they were. Maybe skinheads. Or maybe they just wanted us out of their country so they could have it, briefly, for themselves.

Heina might have told me then that revolutions of every stripe, like people, live and breathe. Like any other living thing, they hold the capacity to mutate, to turn mangy and mean, to take side alleys and lose their way. And I imagine I would have cut my eyes at him, the way a real nineteen-year-old granddaughter might get sarcastic and impatient and then regret it. Heina, I wouldn't have bothered to look for you if I had wanted to watch a marionette show ending with a lesson for children, the homily that making revolution is inherently dangerous and flawed. He would open his mouth, looking for an entry point to reply, frustrated to tell me what I had misunderstood. We both know power is grasped and overthrown, grasped and overthrown. What I want to know is how to live through the pounding of that surf.

Tell me, Opa, which scenario frightened you more in your teenage years: a bloody revolution from the Left, or an orderly and respectable progression of tyranny from the Right? Which of those poor old puppets, worn but still eminently serviceable, cast the more ominous shadow?

In early January 1919 I know only that Heina must have paid close attention to this puppet show as revolutionary charges parried with reaction. A huge street battle raged in Berlin, and the SPD police arrested Rosa Luxemburg and Karl Liebknecht. The communists occupied a newspaper building in protest. In Heina's neighborhood and throughout the county, the right wing reorganized. As Heina walked home from work one evening he may have passed two unfamiliar men with rifles. He nodded in greeting, and they glared back.

"Get on home, son," a man said.

"Why, Comrade?" Heina asked. "What's going on?"

The man abruptly lunged and swung his rifle butt at Heina's thigh. Heina turned and sprinted, the man yelling behind him, "Don't you give me that 'Comrade' shit, you Red!"

Panting, Heina opened the apartment door and ran inside, slamming it behind him. Mama rushed out from the kitchen, forehead knotted at the racket. "Who are those men?" Heina asked.

Papa stood in the kitchen doorway, coughing and wheezing. "You've met the right-wing militia, the Freikorps. They're patrolling the miners' neighborhoods to keep us in line. Our so-called Revolutionary Council is doing everything it can to appease those thugs."

The next morning before work Heina became mired in a thick crowd gathered around the newspaper stand. The news flew from mouth to ear: Luxemburg and Liebknecht had been shot in Berlin "while attempting to escape."

"How could a person attempt to bust out of the most highly guarded cell in the Berlin jail?" asked a woman clutching a crumpled paper.

The SPD paper offered no clues. Heina opened the independent paper and read, "The prisoners' bodies were found, mutilated, in a drainage ditch."

"The SPD has blood on its hands!" said a boy.

"No, it was the right-wing idiots on the police payroll. Hire the last administration's lackeys, and look what you get," a gruff voice replied.

Heina must have closed his eyes to imagine in that hollow moment the last seconds of Rosa Luxemburg, just a woman named Rosa, who cowered as a man in uniform struck her. Or maybe she was stoic to the end, having prepared herself for this. Who was the man who took the air from the lungs of Germany's Lenin? Did he choke back a retch as the blood of a woman pooled on the stone? Or maybe he felt fully and feverishly alive, a flutter of personal triumph as if he with his own weapon had saved the Fatherland.

With a revolution crumbing and the knife-edge of extremism glinting, a young man of sixteen must have felt the responsibility to act. If my guess is correct and Heina chose this time to rebel against the SPD, there must have been a moment of decision, a first step. Maybe a flyer on the cluttered message board near the door caught his eye: "Young People, the Government, and the War: A lecture and discussion at the Miners' Hall . . ." The meeting was Saturday—tonight—sponsored by the Independent Social Democratic youth group.

That evening Heina made a sandwich for dinner and waved to his mother on his way out. She didn't look up from her newspaper as he passed. Outside the night wind peppered his skin with tiny ice crystals, but he inhaled deeply as he walked. It was good to get his legs moving, to work out some of this energy. Was he nervous that he might see that dark-haired girl from the rally a few months ago? Or maybe he feared the desire and anger in his own heart. Heina had somehow forgotten to mention to Papa that he was headed to this meeting.

Rows of chairs lined the hall's rough wood floor, and the space bustled with warmth and light. Heina shook hands with kids he knew from the SPD youth group and other former SPD activists who'd joined the independents or the Ruhr's first communist groups. They sprawled on the floor and straddled chairs, talking loudly. Heina ran his hand through his hair and laughed over some cynical joke about the SPD government. This scenario, or something like it, was likely, as young people moved left of their parents and toward both the socialists and the communists.

"So, my father—he just can't imagine anything besides the SPD," a guy named Fritz complained. "It's like he's married to it!"

"I think it's our duty to make up our own minds," a girl added.

The conversation turned serious and loud as the young people nodded and confessed their feelings of disillusionment and betrayal. Heina took off his jacket. As he listened to a friend's point about the local SPD, he felt the gentle brush of goose bumps, the realization that this hall was home. Honesty lived here, and so did hope, in the eyes of these young people willing to come out on a Saturday night to talk politics.

The speaker climbed toward the podium, but the din in the hall refused to abate. Squinting through tiny glasses, the speaker began his lecture. Conversations faded reluctantly, and the kids around Heina began to nod in agreement with the speaker, who first laid out what they already knew about the SPD and then analyzed the reasons why the country needed an independent push from the Left.

The question-and-answer session after the lecture threatened to disintegrate. Kids from the new communist youth group stood and invited everyone to join their organization, and someone from the SPD group protested, saying they needed to devise a German and not a Soviet solution. Altogether there were five organizations in attendance vying for membership, with tensions among them barely controlled. The speaker pounded on the podium with a gavel twice, three times, the wood sounding as if it would split.

As the lecture dissolved into clumps of conversation, Heina pulled on his jacket and realized he'd forgotten to eat his sandwich. He unwrapped it and was about to take a bite when he saw the dark-haired girl walking toward him, holding the arm of another young woman. Heina stuffed his sandwich in his pocket.

"Comrade, hello there!" he called out.

She smiled and blushed. "Good evening, Comrade," she said. They introduced all around, and Heina learned the dark-haired girl was named Elfriede Klejdzinski, but everyone called her Friedchen. I have no idea where my grandparents met—it might well have been earlier in the SPD youth group—but part of me loves the romance of Heina's youthful rebellion twined with infatuation. So I'll leave this moment be.

"What did you think of the lecture?" she asked. The bold raucousness of the meeting seemed to charge the air in the emptying hall, and it made Heina reckless.

"There's lots to discuss, nicht? I could walk you home so we can talk about it. If you wouldn't mind." Friedchen's friend grinned and pushed her on the elbow toward Heina.

Near the hall exit, two long tables were scattered with membership forms. A group of kids leaned on their elbows and scratched their names in the blanks, joining the independents. His heart filled with the evening, Heina looked at Friedchen with a daring smile, grabbed a membership card, and printed his name.

Heina, I know that delicious sense of falling in love with the hope of a new family. I dove into the storm surge, though I didn't realize as I approached the surf of radicalism that the first place I'd land was the hospital.

The upheavals for me were not as massive as a German revolution, but maybe the seismic echoes of the Berlin Wall crashing down had started it all. By the time I returned from studying in Germany in late 1990, plans for the first Gulf War had been launched. Back in the United States I threw myself into campus antiwar organizations, working every night to help plan rallies, to edit an antiwar poetry collection, to raise money for a bus trip to Washington DC. The snow and the springtime of 1991 presented a never-ending palindrome of a year that still makes my shoulders knit with remembered worry and overwhelming sadness. Something had to be done. How did one change the course of one's own country?

I spent the next summer in a crowded attic apartment near campus, talking politics and itching with the sadness of a broken dream. Drawing strategy charts and planning timelines for logical campus campaigns had not stopped a war or made a dent on the evening news. Unlike the students who raged on campus in the sixties, our groups with their careful media strategies had remained strangely invisible. We drew thousands to rallies, but then we seemed not to exist. And that stoked my hunger to be heard at any cost.

During the day I traveled the back roads of southeastern Minnesota to interview farmers as part of an internship in environmentally sustainable farming with the Minnesota Department of Agriculture. At night I had sex with my long-haired boyfriend from New York. I subsisted on dense vegan homemade bread, cereal with apple juice instead of milk, and too much coffee. I was hungry and jittery all the time.

One quiet afternoon that summer my boyfriend and I lugged our bags of dirty clothes into the basement laundry room of a campus dorm. Maybe we joked and tickled each other. I remember that I laughed as I pulled laundry from a dryer. I stood up quickly to put quarters in the machine. I saw spots and sat down, thinking I'd had a simple rush of blood to my head. Somehow I ended up in the hallway outside the laundry room. I must have walked in a swerving line to clear my head. I slid down the wall and found myself pressed to the cool cement floor, eyes closed, unable to catch my breath.

My mind shrank to a small point inside a body that felt as massive and empty as space. The muscles of my chest and throat clenched in a choke, so I gave in and sipped air in thimblefuls. The voices of my boyfriend and someone else shouted to call 911. Those sounds announced an irrelevant crisis, almost funny because it spooled out on the other side of the world. I couldn't seem to open my heavy eyes. Admit it: I didn't want to. The deep black pool beneath my closed eyelids invited me to stay and rest. I remember cold on my skin as a bit of spit trickled down my chin. I imagine that shallow breathing and a lack of oxygen had worked together to shut down my whirring brain.

Depression and exhaustion, those vague words, draw a crayon circle around the symptoms that triggered this moment. The words with their state-of-being ion endings present an illusory comfort, describe a problem without providing an answer. On that basement floor I had no experience with depression or admitting I might be "sad," so those forces grabbed me bodily to demand my attention.

In the box of the ambulance with its metallic echo of clambering and chopped words, a knuckling of hard plastic dug into my sternum. The EMTs rubbed this sensitive area as a pain stimulus to shock me awake. It seemed to take too much energy to respond. Maybe they wondered as they yelled my name if I was an overdose case. My boyfriend might have told them herbal tea was the strongest thing I'd consumed that afternoon. In the ER they cut my black Earth First T-shirt down the middle to get to my chest, maybe for CPR. I fought to maintain my safe, dark bubble.

Then a nurse in the ER said softly: "Sonya." I opened my eyes to the sweet kindness in her voice.

I know I spent a few days and nights in the hospital. After the electrodes and monitors and tests, the doctors declared me free of heart problems and epilepsy. They sent me home. That night and the next day I blacked out again and again. My roommates, nineteen and twenty and as mystified as I was, watched helplessly and then had to cart me back to the hospital, where more tests produced no more answers. I quit my job because I was afraid to drive. Mom drove up from Chicago to take me to the Mayo Clinic an hour away, where a short-tempered emergency room resident examined me and dryly commented that this might be "in my head" without providing suggestions for what to do next. I tell myself this was fifteen years ago, that such a strange mind-body split would not happen today, that a woman who could not breathe would at least be handed a pamphlet on panic attacks.

As we drove away from the clinic I repeated two fantasy solutions. Either I had to get in my car, drive somewhere far out west like Wyoming, and get a waitressing job. Or I had to shoot myself. "In My Head" was a seemingly insoluble problem. I didn't know a thing about panic or therapy. Mom next took me to a neurologist in Chicago who did tests and declared me biologically healthy. Mom demanded I see a counselor, which I adamantly refused. I imagined the counselor would tell me to stop being dramatic and to shape up.

That fall I drove back to Minnesota and registered for classes, thinking I would show this humiliating "In My Head" thing who was boss. Before my first class started, I sat on the floor near a bank of payphones in the student center, counting the black blotches fogging my vision and trying to decide whom of my tapped-out friends to call for yet another crisis. I couldn't bother anyone, I was too much of a bother already. My pocket calendar contained a long list of political meetings that made my windpipe fold like origami. Was my to-do list the problem or the solution? Maybe the concrete, real world could reclaim the territory invaded by this problem In My Head.

Crying and scattered, I waited for the blotches to disappear. In these weeks I wrote in my journals only sporadically, so I am not sure what led me to the bold and blind decision to quit school and move alone to Minneapolis. I must have talked this plan over with friends, laid out the steps, but looking back, I am amazed that my escape from My Head was to move sixty miles away where I knew no one and had no job. I assume it was the closest I could imagine then to my Wyoming fantasy.

After I'd made my plans I walked to the college treasurer's office in the first floor of an ornate red brick building off the campus quad.

"I need to see the tuition check from my mom. She needs the check number," I said to the receptionist. She directed me to a bookkeeper, who located the check with surprising speed and handed it over with a smile and a slightly baffled look.

I took the check with my mother's careful slanting signature and turned away. I pushed open the heavy wooden doors, bursting into the crisp blue of a Minnesota fall morning, and I ripped the check into tiny pieces.

Those tuition checks had delivered me from small-town Illinois into a kind of Disneyland of trust, a place where young adults had free rein, could learn the skills and boldness necessary to seize their parents' checks. Sending me to that fancy hothouse of academia and activism equipped me with the skills I needed to leave it. But I was also a young woman aware of consequences and the bottom line, needing to rescue a check before it cleared, not a girl able to pack her car and leave school with hair flying and a foot pounding the gas pedal. If I quit school, I would take care of the details first.

Heina, this moment would probably have broken your heart in the same way it broke my mom's. She'd been lured to immigrate to the United States by a seedy relative's promise of a college education that never materialized. Instead she earned her GED after three kids were born. To thank her for her dream denied, I handed back my ticket to college so I could go hunt down my sanity in Minneapolis. And to top it off, I wanted her to understand, to be happy for me.

Your papa may have felt that betrayal, too, if it's true that you left the safety and respectability of the SPD he'd given his life to build. At the time, Heina, I imagine that the lure of finding your own life was irresistible. And I understand that necessity.

Jupp rolled over in bed to turn toward Heina. "Where were you?" Jupp asked.

Heina unbuttoned his shirt, smiling in the dark. "At a meeting. And then I walked a girl home."

Jupp leaned up on one arm. "What girl?"

"Friedchen Klejdzinski," Heina said, practicing the sounds on his tongue. "She's very intelligent."

"I'm sure she's pretty, too," Jupp said. "Not bad, old man." Girls in giggling bunches already followed Jupp home from school and offered to do his chores during summer work camp.

Heina folded his shirt over a chair. "Have you heard about the independent youth group?" Heina asked. "This lecture I attended . . . They have a sharp analysis of the government and the war."

Jupp's head jerked back slightly, the outlines of his curls bobbing in the dark. "The independents, huh? Heina, you know they're Bolsheviks."

Heina climbed into bed and pushed Jupp over to make some room. "They're not Bolsheviks, for God's sake. I mean, some of them are very left, but you don't have to be a Bolshevik to be a little critical of the SPD."

"Dad's going to kill you," Jupp whispered.

"About what, the girl or the meeting?"

"Don't be dumb," Jupp said. "Papa knows the truth about the SPD better than you do. You can't just go and leave whenever you feel like it."

"Well, Dad doesn't need to know, all right? I'm a man, I bring in a salary, and I can afford to have my own opinions. I'll probably talk to him about it anyway," Heina said. Jupp's resistance gave him a thrill of emphatic delight. He *was* a man, after all.

The next day at dinner as they cut rolls and spread war-ration margarine, Jupp announced, "Heina has a girlfriend, and she's Polish."

Heina glared at Jupp, and Jupp smiled back. Mama set down her fork with a click, her eyebrows arched in a controlled gesture of expectation. Papa leaned back and coughed into his fist, hiding a smile.

"So! Where did you meet her?" Papa asked.

"At a meeting," Jupp sang. Heina kicked him desperately under the table.

Papa scowled. "I thought the SPD youth meetings were on Monday nights. Was it the folk-singing group?"

Heina opened his mouth to speak. "The independents," he said, watching as Papa's sharp eyes narrowed. Papa heard the depth of Heina's half-second pause and sensed that attendance at this meeting meant more than another panel coorganized with the SPD. Heina couldn't lie to him, even when he carefully gave only a portion of the truth.

Papa chewed a piece of bread, the bristles of his mustache fanning. Maybe the older man felt a metallic pang of pride, sharp and small as a tack, for this quiet son who kept his own counsel and made his decisions, consequences be damned. But there would be consequences. Maybe Papa's heart muscles tightened to see Heina as a barometer for the health of the SPD and for Germany's youth. His eyes closed, shutting off their approval and light. He turned away.

I can't remember the words I used to tell Mom I'd left school, and I don't know whether I was careful or blunt. I used politics and metaphors of struggle and resistance to avoid thinking about how much I'd hurt her. Yeah, I was having panic attacks, but the cool thing was there were all these awesome anarchists and political activists in the Twin Cities. It was going to be so amazing! I can't remember telling her, and the absence of that memory lets me know that I didn't listen to her response, whatever it was.

A few days after the honeymoon rush of a fresh decision, I stood at a payphone in St. Paul outside the agricultural sciences library at the University of Minnesota. I had returned a few monographs after I slapped together the overdue final report for my internship. My possessions pushed like silly children's noses and faces against every window of my Chevy Cavalier. I dialed the code to Mom's calling card and probably played with the metal phone cord, then smacked the weighted metal trapdoor of the change return that covered the curved recess where quarters sometimes hid.

"Mom, I was wondering if I could borrow a few hundred dollars for a security deposit on an apartment. I'll pay you back, I promise," I said. I bargained, told her I'd had a change of heart. I'd go to therapy in exchange for a break from school.

"No," Mom said, tight and hard. She worried that if I left school, I would never go back. That fear derailed everything she had hoped for her daughter. "I don't think I can talk about this right now." She hung up.

I opened my car door and sat down in what was now my living room. Cassette tapes littered the front seat, and stickers from bands and political groups plastered the dashboard. I breathed deeply, scanning my body for the prickles of a panic attack. Strangely, I was okay. Tonight I would drive an hour back down to campus to crash with friends, and tomorrow I'd drop off some stuff at my new rented room. Rent money would eventually materialize when my new landlord let me clean her house and wash her storm windows.

A week later I tried again with Mom, wanting to tell her about the politics in Minneapolis, the anarchist kids, my room (with a window!), my job at a coffee shop. *Look, Mom,* I wanted to say, running to her with a treasure like a snail shell, a pretty rock in my open palm: *I built another life!*

Silence on the crackling phone line. I could practically hear her swallow, see her biting her lip, her pained eyes darting as she stood alone in the kitchen in Illinois. "You're turning your back on everything I stand for," she said, more weepy than irate, and so there was hope. "I feel like you're rejecting my life and all the choices I've made."

I choked on her sadness, but a breath of exhilaration opened my windpipe. Mom had unintentionally pointed out the back-door to adulthood. I'd never considered judging her. I hadn't thought it was possible.

I stood in the living room of my landlord's house, looking through a window I'd cleaned out into the Minneapolis night. A mixture of chaos and wiry strength churned in me. Didn't she understand this was the opposite of judgment? I had to shave my head and get a tattoo and be wild to see that I was separate from her. That's not judgment, that's acceptance.

And I made these choices carefully, none so irrevocable as to deny me permanent access to the good-girl track. Once I started I wanted more, each buzz of freedom pointing toward the world and away from the problems In My Head. I discovered which bakeries to visit at closing time for free bread. I sold my books. I tried to live for three days on kale and bagels I bought on sale at the community food co-op. In an end to that particular experiment, I threw up in traffic all over my Chevy's steering wheel and dashboard. Apparently a body can take only so much roughage.

In political meetings with the blue-haired and tattooed from the Revolutionary Anarchist Bowling League who wanted a different revolution than top-down Red Russia, who baked cakes to celebrate the anarchist Haymarket Martyrs of Chicago, I felt free. And look, Ma, no panic attack this week. Did I lie in bed at night and cry? Sure, I was mood swinging my way back and forth between therapy, coffee shop, and political rally, but for age twenty, I see little remarkable in that. We were all running from Red Russia and its aftermath, like planets and space matter scattering outward after the Big Bang of 1917.

Did Papa Heinrich feel an inner revolution as he slowly developed disgust for the SPD? I may never know. I know that coal veins ran in Papa Heinrich's flesh. I know his family tree branched downward, underground, instead of toward the sun. In February of 1919 miners' strikes loomed, and the miners needed to eat, but the reigning socialists in Berlin said the country needed coal. The SPD sent the army toward the Ruhr, weapons drawn, ready to smash the strike. So Papa Heinrich had to choose a side.

I imagine Heina listening from the sitting room. Guido Hei-

land sat at the kitchen table with Mama and Papa, sighing about
the Workers' Council and the approaching Reich troops.

"We have to seize the mines so the army doesn't occupy them,"
Papa said. "Flood them, maybe? But we still have their weapons
to face."

"The answer is obvious: a general strike," Heiland said bitterly. "I proposed it in council, but not one man had the courage to support the idea. I stood up and said, 'I used to think the
Bolsheviks were the biggest enemy, but now I think it's a shame
we're not all Bolsheviks.'"

I know from Heiland's quotes in a book on Marl history that
the Buschmanns' close friend did call for exactly such a radical
solution, to no avail. A few men stood to support him, but all
agreed the time was too short, the odds against them.

The oven in the dining room had gone cold, but Heina didn't
get up and stir the wood inside. He didn't want his parents and
Heiland to know he was eavesdropping. He cupped his hands
around his mouth and blew into them. It was scary to think that
Guido Heiland, a strong-willed man with a decisive squint, did
not know what would come next. How could the fire of the previous summer have disappeared? The German Revolution! Boldness in the crush of the town square felt second nature when victory was already assured. But when the weather turned cold and
uncertain, people ducked their heads, willing to fade into their
own quiet spaces. Heina's revulsion at these people who refused
to stand up with Papa and Guido faded as quickly as it had arisen.
It was so easy to turn your disappointment into a sharp weapon
and to lash out at your neighbor. It was much more difficult to
analyze a situation, to turn a trap to your own advantage.

Multiple accounts tell the tale of the Reich army approaching
from the north and the west and smashing into nearby Dorsten.
The independent socialists, the miners, and the communists

grabbed their guns—old hunting rifles, pistols from the Great War, and pickaxes—and gathered in town centers and churchyards, waiting. Men with SPD pins on their lapels stood in those crowds, too, but the party leaders were nowhere to be seen, and the party newspapers remained mute.

Maybe one of Papa's friends pounded at the door, breathless, calling into the kitchen, "The Reich troops are marching!" Heina pulled back the curtains as the thrumming rain of boot-clad feet echoed from the street. A few blocks over, on the main road between Recklinghausen and Marl, a contingent of armed police from Berlin stormed down the cobblestone with their weapons, stomping in time toward Marl center. Their goal was to unseat the Workers' and Soldiers' Council, which Berlin had declared to be violent, too left wing, and the knife-edge of a Soviet threat to the country. Heina's hands were slicked with sweat. Last night Papa's friends had stopped by to pass on rumors of boys Heina's age dying in the Dorsten street fights. And now it was too late to do anything but listen to the troops march into their town.

The next day people in Marl did what they knew how to do. The mines and the schools shut down. Local accounts tell of a thousand people marching to city hall in Recklinghausen with a red flag to lead them, as if the color red itself would remind the SPD leaders in the hall and the SPD members in Berlin of their principles. Then on February 17, 1919, blood was spilled.

Maybe Heina snuck out of the apartment, needing to get away from his parents' suffocating political arguments. His mother could do nothing but snipe at his father's optimism and cluck her tongue critically, and his father could only shake his head and rub his big hands restlessly along his thighs or comb through each newspaper for small shreds of hope.

The cold air seemed amazingly still, and it took Heina a few seconds to notice the source of the silence: no groaning of the mine shaft pulleys or roaring of a demonstration. Quiet patrols of armed miners shuffled back and forth in front of the mine shaft gate.

At a corner near a deserted pub Heina saw a poster with the jagged German iron eagle. The bird's thin beak hung open as it screeched a slogan: "Comrade! Help Me! Defend me against Bolshevism, the Polish Threat, and Hunger! Join the Freikorps!" Heina grabbed the poster's curled edge and ripped it across the middle. The Freikorps promised to protect the power of the mine owners, the factory owners, and everyone else who had it good under the Kaiser. Heina chuckled at the scrap of paper in his hand, a long strip emblazoned with the phrase "the Polish Threat." It was disgusting and hilarious to think of Friedchen's family as a threat matched by starvation.

As he walked back up the stairs to their apartment, the door slammed open and Papa jumped down the stairs, grabbing Heina by the collar.

"God in Heaven!" Papa growled, his face red. "Where have you been?"

"I'm sorry," Heina gasped. "Just around the block. What . . .?"

Papa let go of Heina's jacket. "Federal troops and the Freikorps are shooting communists in the Recklinghausen town square. They've thrown a hundred Sparts in jail, and they're going to kill them all." Papa's ice-blue eyes were bullets. He explained that if the Spartacists, a communist group, were being assassinated, everyone with Red tendencies was in danger. "Go out only with a gun. And if you've still got that independent youth card, burn or bury it."

Heina numbly followed Papa upstairs. Had Papa lost his mind? Public assassinations in Recklinghausen? Under the Kaiser's rule, Reds got at worst a few years' jail time.

Heina sat on the sofa crammed against the dining room wall.

The ticking of the mantel clock seemed to surge forward and race like a bomb's timer. That clock was built in Poland, given to Papa by a friend from the regiment. Every object and painting hanging on the walls, every book on the shelves, told a story. And each object held a message about the possibility of revolution, about a vast network of people across Germany willing to fight for freedom. Everything in this home expressed this confidence, but outside the world had been turned upside down.

Heina imagined that someday after the war he'd tell his children about this terrible repression. He wondered if the children of the future would be able to picture civil war in Germany and an armed invasion of the Ruhr. He pulled the independent socialist card from his wallet and studied the bright red logo. How could he rip it up? His name appeared on a membership roster anyway, and that list was more likely than this card to fall into the wrong hands. Heina walked into his room and squatted in front of a bookshelf. He slipped the card randomly between the pages of a volume on Jena SPD history, then shoved the book under the bottom of the stack. The card may never have existed, the story is my fiction, but I don't want to see Heina destroy this imagined token of youthful rebellion.

Socialists in the Ruhr gathered in the spring of 1919 to debate, flinging stern German phrases and volleys of harsh consonants. Two weeks passed. Cities in the Ruhr collapsed before the troops. The SPD police chief rounded up and executed twelve hundred protestors in Berlin. Bavaria—the land of cream puffs and lovely coffee, known today for composers and men in lederhosen—raised a red flag and declared itself a Soviet republic. The Freikorps were sent in with little discipline and no clear orders, and one thousand died in Munich.

On June 28, with Germany facing internal combustion, the Treaty of Versailles was signed to end the Great War. Germany, habituated to battle, flexed its muscles and prepared to beat itself to a pulp. The Buschmann family must have continued to scrape by while spending endless hours in meetings to plan resistance.

Nine months later, in March 1920, Heina was waiting to turn eighteen, and a right-wing general named Kapp tried to take over the government. History seems to fragment here, to spin into shards of stories that come together in a scattered mosaic. All the history books explain that "the workers" stopped Kapp's putsch with a general strike that swept the country. Few accounts describe the fragmentation within those workers' ranks or tell who had the courage to call for this strike.

Ruhr workers then watched troops approach in another wave toward their rivers and cities. The Red Army gathered in self-defense and fired its weapons, believing this to be another surge of the right-wing coup. Facing a deadlock in fighting and a blockaded string of cities, the Red Army sent telegrams off to Berlin. "Help us," the Red Army bleated, and the response clarified the issue: No, those troops are ours. You are being attacked by your SPD government.

After I told Mom that Heinrich Sr. held office in the revolutionary government, she went back to her piles of photos and unearthed a military-style group portrait: three rows of scruffily clad men and one woman. The group included Heina, Jupp, and Papa Heinrich.

Mom said she'd always assumed the photo was taken during one of the wars. The men wear big-buttoned, double-breasted jackets that seem to be cut from a similar pattern and black military-style caps with an insignia. Some of the men wear belts with an attached loop that stretches over a shoulder. Heina and Jupp, faces thin and smooth, stand in the back row, far left. Their jackets are new and pale, and Heina glances slightly to the left of the camera with a serious and earnest expression.

The photo is mysterious for reasons of ideology. If it was taken in the '20s, when Heina was in his late teens, this group might have been a local contingent of the Red Army willing to die to keep the "red" in the SPD.

But the photo might show a second or third militia, the moderate Reichsbanner Schwarz-Rot-Gold, or Black-Red-Gold, or the later and more radical Iron Front, both formed to defend the republic from the Nazis. I already know from other sources that Heina joined the Black-Red-Gold. But is this photo from the '20s, from the radical independent/socialist/communist Red Army? The truth is, I want Heina to be pulled to the far left, because this dancing with and running from the Red tide has been a current in my own life. I want to know how far these men wandered or were pushed.

Mom studied Heina's smooth face in the photo and declared the image to be of Heina in his teens, not nearing thirty. I took the photo to a camera shop for a professional enlargement. I compared our mystery photo to another, dated photo from 1922, and Heina's face looked similar. Then I reconsidered. We round-faced Buschmanns don't show our age, which makes the guesswork difficult.

I went over the enlargement with a magnifying glass and saw one man wearing a sash that looked tricolored in its shades of gray, which might denote the Black-Red-Gold. Still, my great-grandfather's moustache is gray-toned here, not the snow-white it would be in the years leading up to World War II.

I might imagine Heina's serious thrill in donning a uniform, even as he wrestled with the socialist youth groups' stance against the growing militarism that gripped the country from left to right. I could picture Heina guarding a storehouse of groceries or holding a weapon at watch duty. But I don't write these scenes. Something in me resists.

We Reds love our militant images. My friends have proudly hung posters of Nicaraguan Sandinista women freedom fighters carrying babies and rifles, or socialist realist montages of muscled youth marching forward to defend the revolution. I romanticize this strength, too, and it's not for nothing that we call a hard-line radical a militant. Maybe it's so attractive because grabbing a rifle is one sure way to get a line or two in the history books, so it's the only image we have of ourselves. And there is also the universal seduction of the gun, the sense that when a weapon is drawn, the drone of daily life breaks open, giving way to a clear and narrow purpose.

But I won't imagine teenage Heina holding a weapon or squinting with fear, wondering what it would be like to be killed by an advancing army. Maybe this is selfish; it's true I love this young stranger who will make me possible. I tell myself the scene can go unwritten because his life will be filled with such moments, which freeze and seem so proud but have such poison and betrayal at their heart.

All the farmers' horses in Marl were requisitioned as a last-ditch attempt to help the Red Army flee from the advancing SPD government troops, according to local history. I lead Heina and Jupp away from the front lines, imagine them going door-to-door to ask for horses. Three doors might have been slammed in their faces, but at the fourth house they might have received the reins of a small mare and a thin plow horse, which they led to the Marl square.

The right-wing authorities, backed by the Freikorps, seized power and sentenced the independent socialist leaders to death. Four young miners, all under age twenty-one, were executed in the town square of Recklinghausen, where I had walked obliviously many times in childhood to eat gummi bears or admire the Easter-egg German cobblestones. Otto Ernst from Bockholt, Georg Engelmann and Emil Suhr from Langenbochum, and Ernst Brockhaus from Linden died this way: the first young man was required to dig his own grave while singing a patriotic song, and he then was shot while kneeling in front of the grave. The next young man took the shovel, was told to fill dirt in on top of his friend's body, and then was ordered to dig another grave for himself. Then the third went down singing and probably sobbing, then the fourth. Public outrage ignited days later when pedestrians saw hands and feet protruding from the hastily filled graves.

Heina must have known those boys named Otto, Georg, Emil, and Ernst, and he must have been haunted by the thought of them, shot on the ground where he'd attended his first USPD demonstration, on the same bit of earth he'd crossed after work. Maybe in his nightmares he found himself as one of those boys, singing while shoveling. I imagine he had known Emil as an acquaintance at youth meetings, seen him laughing and tucking his hands inside the sleeves of his shirts, which were always too large. Or maybe it was because Heina was almost exactly their age. Somehow they'd gotten caught for signing an independent card at one point, or agreeing in the heat of the moment to do some sabotage or sentry duty, making a choice that in context seemed small and logical, as boys do.

Papa continued, unshaken. He ate his breakfast, resolute in every movement of chewing bread and snapping straight the newspaper's pages. He brushed the crumbs from his shirt and headed off to the miners' co-op or a union meeting. Heina fought to hide a deep sadness that scared him. In the weeks after those particular murders, he had to force himself to walk up the hill toward the county offices or to help with peeling potatoes when he wanted only to collapse on his bed.

What was wrong with him? If he were a true revolutionary,

this would only have ignited his radical passions and made him stronger. He had to work doubly hard to hide his softness from Papa, who was a real man, a real miner, a real political socialist. And those boys, those shallow graves—they stood for the full measure that politics could demand. If Heina was weak inside, he needed to push himself twice as hard to compensate. If Socialism herself came forward, clad in red robes, and asked you to lay down your life in any of three thousand ways, the answer had to be yes, without hesitation.

Meanwhile, a new balance of power in Berlin formed around a wobbly coalition that included some of the old Kaiser's conservatives. Hindenburg, the leader of the German military, announced that the Great War had been lost because Jews and Marxists had stabbed Germany in the back. A *Dolchstoß* is a stab in the back with a dagger. When I was young I heard the phrase "They stabbed us in the back!" so many times in my relatives' brief and angry comments on German history, never understanding who had done the stabbing. It turns out that for every perspective on German history, there's a backstabber. Some Germans—and many others—love their own outrage at being a victim, which seems to free them to hate, to plot revenge.

And these were Heina's teenage years, when he could still giggle at Jupp, horse around like a boy, look up from the newspaper with innocent light in his eyes. So I have to imagine moments of necessary freedom in the midst of the madness.

I imagine an afternoon: Heina stepped off the path and leaned up a slope covered with scattered birch and pine trees. He reached for a straight, stout stick and handed it to Friedchen. She smiled back at him, shy but amused at his gallantry. She knew about his weaknesses, the fear of the future, and she listened to his giddy hope about politics, about groups he wanted to organize here in Marl, this project and that meeting.

Hardly breaking stride, she raised the stick and gave it a thump on the ground to test it for rot or dryness. A hard shudder met her hand, and the stick held. She nodded at Heina and wiped a trickle of sweat from her temple.

The silence in the woods helped them pretend the chaos in the cities was manageable. Since the revolution and the putsch, the last two years had seen a splintering and explosion of socialist organizations. Most of the independent socialists had gone over to the communists. Heina agonized about the choice, listened to other independent kids as they tried to convince him to join the communist youth group, but it was a step too far. The communist group seemed a bit loud and out of touch, proclaiming with a visible hollowness that the revolution was around the corner, when the revolution had been shot in the back of the neck. Heina had listened to and watched Papa, mulling over whether he should rejoin the SPD and fight for that old, beaten party to make it something new.

Heina's endless buzz of thoughts and questions scattered as Erndt yelled forward to the small group of hikers, "Let's stop here for a bit, all right?" Erndt motioned to a clearing up-hill, and they shrugged off their packs and tossed them on the ground.

"Have any of you decided to go to Bielefeld for the youth fest in August?" asked Karsten, flopping onto the grass. Since the first youth celebration in Weimar last year, he had raved about the demonstrations and the huge crowds. "You all have to see this Erich Ollenhauer fellow speak. He lost an arm in the war, and he wants young people to organize. He's so clear and smart."

Karsten ran his hand along his girlfriend Anna's thigh, and she rolled away from him, her short hair and loose dress fanning out in whirls as she laughed. The health craze had spread from the middle-class youths to the socialists. The women in all the youth groups had started sewing loose smock dresses, comfortable as nightshirts, and wearing them without corsets. It was important to breathe, as important as life itself. The young people had to unite, anyway, and together they would figure out how to do things differently, to somehow not end up as murderers, cynics, and the walking dead.

Erndt sprawled on the tall grass, matting it down, chin tilted up so his face caught the full warmth of the sun. "Beer, I'd love a beer," he sang. "Friedchen, did you bring any? Check in your knapsack for a stray beer."

Heina reddened and looked down. Erndt tried to include Friedchen in every joke, even if she didn't say much, anxious about impressing these fast-talking politicos. Her eyes laughed and her mouth stayed prim, slightly upturned. "No, Erndt, nothing here," she said.

Erndt had listened in private to the developing tale of Heina's woe, his parents' refusal to sanction his planned marriage to Friedchen. Heina's mother had picked out a shop owner's daughter instead, a bland girl she insisted on inviting over for dinners and coffee. How could Mama hate a miner's daughter? Friedchen's father had followed the wave of Polish immigrants into Germany's industrial area. Was it a Polish thing or just the fact that Friedchen's family was poor? It was too much for his mother, the supposed revolutionary who'd married a poor man herself.

With all the guts his parents had passed onto him, Heina quietly said to Mama, "Fine, then. It's not your choice, and I'll marry her anyway." He battled and swallowed his guilt, slicing it with a razor point of clarity. No drama, no yelling, just shivering and saying what had to be said.

Friedchen loved Heina's intelligence, his political involvement, and his open-mindedness, but she also feared this determination, this sharp will. She studied the broad slope of Heina's forehead as he leaned in to respond to a comment from Erndt about the Versailles Treaty payments and the industrialists. Friedchen didn't hear Heina's words. She only saw this river of politics in front of her, and she felt as though she had to keep Heina near her against its current. She felt a flash of foreboding, as if the political demands on him would only increase as he gave more time and energy.

War-surplus canteens were passed around. Friedchen shivered as her lips touched the cold metal. Men now dead had sipped from these necks, most likely. She wouldn't say things like that aloud to this group, but Heina would understand. He seemed to sense the chill that passed through Friedchen, and he leaned into her side, looking up at her and squinting in the sun. There was a rustle of a canvas knapsack, and Karsten leapt to his feet with the newest of toys from his uncle: a portable camera with a complex tripod.

"Don't move," he cried, then took five minutes unpacking the pieces and setting up the camera as the young people posed. "Look, I'm about to capture young love. We'll send it straight to Goethe's grave to keep up the old man's spirits."

Friedchen glanced down at Heina and he leaned back on his elbow, touching her side with his shoulder. She threaded her arm around him, grasping his collar, already wanting this photo, a chance to see her man of motion temporarily at rest.

Mom stood at the kitchen counter sorting through a stack of family photographs. I sat in a chair near the counter, maybe tucking a strand of long hair behind my ear. Or maybe I'd already shaved my head. I don't remember when in college I studied my grandparents' photos for the first time with political eyes.

Mom handed me a photo of a young couple in a clearing,

surrounded by friends in goofy poses, blades of grass in their mouths, a German hippie pantomime. I recognized the young man with the high forehead and serious eyes: a smooth-faced version of Heina. He leaned against my grandmother, Friedchen, who wore a simple smock dress and looked apprehensively upward and past the camera. Her arm wrapped around the top of Heina's shoulders, fingers curled at his collar, as if she didn't want to lose hold of him. With her free hand she loosely grasped fern fronds in her lap.

I had seen old-fashioned German photos like these many times before in family albums, with rows of clowning young people holding guitars and flags, striking casual poses, wide smiles, guys and girls with their arms around each other. All Germans love their daily constitutional walks in the woods, so I'd never really paid much attention to these weird photographs.

I'm not sure why Mom unearthed the photos that day. Maybe the sight of a tattooed anarchist daughter at the airport gate had driven her to find an explanation somewhere in our battered and hacksawed family tree. More likely she was trying to connect and reclaim me in those months when I brought my anarchism into my parents' house, as I sat on my mom's bed and talked for hours about Goldman and Kropotkin and she patiently mulled over my words. During one of these visits home my dad had carried The Anarchist Cookbook up to my bedroom as a peace offering. He had used his interest in conspiracies and living "off the grid" to find me a copy of the 1970s bomb-making relic. I scowled doubtfully, maybe even lectured him about how I wasn't into making bombs. I probably said, "Jesus, Dad. That will get you on a CIA watch list, and it was probably written by the CIA anyway." As far as I remember, I did not accept the gift and never had the book in my possession. But I wish I had it now as a fond souvenir of that strange and sweet moment.

So at the time, filled with my own ideas, I didn't see politics in these family photos. I saw dead Germans with nothing to tell me, a bureaucrat and his long-suffering bride. I might have asked why they posed so weirdly.

"That's what they did for fun," Mom said. "They were kind of like hippies."

"Hippies?" I asked, doubting that she knew anything about politics besides what I told her.

In my 1990s hippiedom I had lived in a vegan co-op at school and taken a never-ending bus trip back and forth from Minnesota to Washington DC for protests. My first political boyfriend was a smashingly beautiful young man with great polar fleece jackets. We made out in the campus arboretum, held hands at antiwar protests. Then we both moved leftward along the continuum from soy milk to shaved heads.

"You know, nature lovers," Mom said. "On Sundays when the other kids went to church, my dad always took us for long walks instead. He always told us, 'My God is in the forest.'"

Weirdly enough, the radical currents in the U.S. student movement in the mid-1990s had turned to study German radicalism and the Greens, and I had recently joined a Youth Green Party study group at school. The bit about skipping church for hikes and a forest God caught my attention.

"Lots of camping, free love, and flowers in their hair," Mom said. "And everybody was having babies out of wedlock. That's how Aunt Inge happened."

I widened my eyes. My German aunt Inge, stern, imposing and proper—a love child. If there was an imagined moment that stirred my connection to Heina and Friedchen, way back before the history fell in as mortar around the heavy stones of affection, this was it. My grandparents found God in the trees and hooked up in the woods. They were cool kids with problems.

6

A Lash of the Whip

Heina built one of the first socialist youth centers in his region. Today the plot of land in the woods near a school bears no marker or trace of his name. Perhaps that's because it wasn't Heina alone who erected the building and filled the structure with purpose. The movement provided the passion, the volunteers, and the effort, and Heina's silent way of deferring to his organization may explain perfectly why he felt comfortable being lost to history.

I think I understand Heina's desire for four walls and a roof, a place where young people could gather for meetings. They'd never again have to shout their agenda items in a noisy pub or beg the local conservative SPD leaders for a lousy meeting room. The SPD leaders granted the socialist youth group such favors but kept a mental tally, referring to it during every conflict, like an itemized bill where the total cost was lifelong obedience.

The headline in the socialist youth newspaper read, "Young people as a true political force? If so, we need our own institutions." In the newspaper pages I read at the local youth movement archive, young activists described their successes at building youth homes. The German socialist movement had built itself as a social force by building walls and rooms. The youth groups then dared to suggest that the protective or suffocating umbrella of the SPD didn't provide necessary shelter or room to grow.

Heina and his group wrote letters to the county offices in Recklinghausen. They asked for financial assistance or a plot of land on which to build a youth home. I know those details because my uncle Klaus went downstairs to the cellar one morning to look through a stack of photos and papers for more information about Heina.

He came upstairs slightly red-faced and triumphant. "Na!" he said, laying a musty file folder on the dining room table.

Inside we found letters and documents providing a layer-by-layer geologic account of Heina's political life, everything from a membership card in a socialist first-aid society to newspaper articles with inscrutable notes in the margins to illegible to-do lists to newspaper clippings of obituaries of dead comrades. It seemed like the contents of a scrapbook that Heina never had time to complete. Half of the file contained the complete correspondence of the youth home's construction, filled with the terse and careful loops of 1920s German officialese. In the front pocket of the folder were two copies of the youth home's plans. An architectural diagram on blue paper showed how the various beams were to be bolted together to secure the roof and walls. The other, a rough hand-drawn schematic of the floor plan, named each area: "great room," "reading room," "sitting room," and "building manager's apartment." Heina, maybe to remind himself of this first difficult act, had saved the complete record of his victory, marking out the territory he had liberated.

I imagine Heina furrowing his brow at the end of a youth group meeting. They'd drafted the letter to strongly request support from the county. How would this sit with the county directors, who were also his employers? I see Heina's comrades pulling on their jackets and chatting about the details of the next demonstration against Germany's military buildup. Friedchen fanned her hand over the drying ink on the meeting minutes and brushed loose hair off her face. They had a plan for the coming week, and a letter to post. This was what also made Papa's eyes shine: feeling all these people working together on a shared project was some glimmer of heaven on earth.

After Heina's private worry that they'd asked for too much, he was shocked by their success. The young socialists negotiated the free lease of a parcel of land next to a school, at the edge of a park called Gänsebrink, the Goose Brook, where peasant women brought their geese to water. The area was a four-block walk from Heina's home. Letters went to county financial officers requesting a low-interest loan. The rest of the deal proceeded with a long string of tiny favors cobbled together. The SAJ couldn't afford to build from scratch, so a small log cabin was dismantled in Serbia and shipped to Germany as part of a complex reparations arrangement after the war. A local lumber cooperative and builders' union arranged the transport and paid for shipping. The disassembled log cabin was delivered by truck in July 1924, along with the plans, six rolls of roof paper, nails, bolts, window glass and hinges, and one bucket of asphalt mix.

I know, Heina, how a simple room can be the anchor for a new world. During my Gulf War political immersion, I mapped the cross streets of Minneapolis. My guiding stars were the radical bookstores, the lesbian-owned pancake house, the independent coffee shops, the anarchist community centers, the punk rock newspaper, the college campus locations for Anti-Racist Action meetings, and the organic food co-ops. If I could find a way to bind myself to a routine in this alternate universe, I could stabilize and then paste together a new life.

After leaving school I got a job at the Well, a coffee shop in a rambling white Victorian house on a main drag in Uptown, a hipster/rocker neighborhood of Minneapolis. When I arrived for my first day of work, my new boss—a sweet ex-addict chain-smoking epileptic who didn't like to take his medication—looked at me through his thick glasses and said, "Who are you?"

By the end of my first day I learned that all of the staff members except for me and two other employees were in recovery from one addiction or another, drawn together from the well-known string of drug rehab clinics surrounding Minneapolis. Recovering addicts lined up for triple mocha caffeine buzzes and told stories about snorting coke off the hoods of pickup trucks. The owner ushered movie star visitors—in Minneapolis for rehab—back toward the kitchen and had them sign the wall above the ice cream cooler with a permanent marker.

At the Well, I never really knew when my shift would end, because the dishwasher who was supposed to arrive for the evening shift had had only a few months of sobriety after years of heroin. Time was not his strong suit, and management considered this an understandable excuse. The cook smoked while mixing baked goods, and he made organic muffins with chunks of peach, fat purple blueberries, and sometimes cigarette ash. He disappeared to his basement apartment to have grand mal seizures while the staff drank coffee and made very bad cappuccinos. At the Well I felt safe, because all the fucked-up was right out in the open.

One crisp day that fall four gorgeous young people took a table in my section. They had the Minneapolis '90s punk rock look: rough, choppy haircuts; black Converse high-top sneakers; and dirty, tight jeans. I had met them at an anarchist conference that summer, where I had picked up the Youth Green 'zines they made with the logo of a muscular, raised fist clutching a sunflower. I wrote their order on my blue pad, then quietly introduced myself and recited the friend-of-a-friend pedigree necessary in anarchist circles for an immediate bond. Laura, with her shaved head and eyes the color of sandblasted blue-green beach glass, pulled out her pen and wrote her phone number on a napkin. "You should come to one of our meetings," she said. My heart fluttered; I felt like I'd been asked to the prom.

At my first meeting of the anarchist collective, I sat with arms clasped around bent knees. I was in awe and love with the women in the group, their stories about whipping off their shirts and shouting at demonstrations, their shaved heads and homemade 'zines and devilish good looks. We held study groups to learn about radical democracy and nonhierarchical methods of organization, and I sat on the floor in someone's cool grungy apartment, holding a photocopied article containing a sea of words about radical democracy by some French theorist guy. I tried so hard and utterly failed to follow the conversation. A few weeks later I was officially inducted into the collective with a mock ritual that included being crowned with a battered football helmet and touched on both shoulders with a Wiffle bat.

AWOL (our name was an acronym with meanings that shifted depending on our mood: A World of Love, Anarchists Without Lutefisk) got together on a few Saturday afternoons to write a street-theater skit for an upcoming rally. The demo had been organized to protest a plan to store nuclear waste in aboveground casks across from a Native American reservation on the floodplains of the Mississippi. I made a prop for the skit with an empty plastic container that had once held Twizzlers licorice, a gift from my mom for my first month at college. I added a flashlight, green tissue paper, and lots of duct tape. The container had seen a strange lifecycle: purchased at Sam's Warehouse by my parents, paid for with money earned by nuclear waste disposal, contents eaten by a hippie-turned-anarchist, and then morphed into a prop in a protest against nuclear waste. I told the street theater team that I couldn't go to the protest because I had to work. I'm sure I could have gotten out of my shift at the Well. I think I was glad to have an excuse, because calling my mom for bail money was more than I could handle.

In the folder of Heina's political life, I found proof of his rebellious streak, a letter from the youth group to its elders and SPD party leaders. It began: "The Worker-Youth meeting gathered on June 29, 1923, hereby protests against the dictatorial vote of the supervisory committee . . ."

Dictatorial—a fine word, full of outrage against the local SPD party machine, which wanted to control the fiery youth group led by Heina. The handwritten draft of a letter, signed with his name, showed clearly that Heina manned the left wing in the socialist youth organization. The early 1920s pitted the youth in a frothing national battle against the SPD, which crept rightward in its desire to purchase a bit of security on what seemed like a sinking ship.

Sitting at Uncle Klaus's dining room table with yellowed documents scattered around me, I dragged my finger slowly across a copy of a socialist youth group agenda. I struggled with the old-fashioned script, which seemed almost like a different alphabet. I leaned over to ask Aunt Christa the meaning of a word I couldn't make out.

Aunt Christa's voice caught in her throat. "Look here," she said, pointing to the bottom of a set of handwritten meeting minutes on the table. The careful signature written there: "Friedchen Klejdzinski, youth group treasurer."

A swirl of ink, something as simple as a signature, changed how my family saw its own story. Our women have sighed over many cups of coffee, "Poor Friedchen, poor Friedchen," pitying her for suffering through her husband Heina's fanatical devotion to politics, his raving, insatiable mistress. In the rush to avenge Friedchen we'd narrowed her story to hide one fact: she was an activist. I didn't know the exact degree of her involvement, but it was clear that becoming an elected socialist youth group officer required a certain level of commitment. We called Uncle Klaus in to tell him the news, and he pushed out his lips and raised his eyebrows. On the phone with Mom that evening I told her what we'd found. She paused, and I could almost hear the rush of her thoughts as she tried to imagine these scenes in order to better know her mother. "I want a copy of that document, that signature," she said, as if hungry for tangible proof.

What I know is that Heina, a smooth-faced and optimistic twenty-two-year-old, organized a construction project and squeezed major donations from local governments during the aftermath of Germany's 1923 economic crash. I imagine that Friedchen, this mysterious woman with her own small or large hunger for politics, found it effortless to fall in love with Heina, a quiet young man with a knack for building permanent structures from scraps.

Heina pulled a canvas tarp over the rolls of roof paper, then leaned to pick through a box of hardware. Earlier today, after the grand unveiling of the wagon loaded with supplies, his father and eight other miners had rummaged through the piles and called out what was missing. Franz Rupprecht said, "These window frames are nearly rotten."

The men struggled with the heavy support beams most of the morning under the August sun. Finally, toward evening, a house-shaped frame stood above the earth. Heina hoped the process of revealing this miraculous building would ensnare the men, and they would work into the evening. But as the light faded the men tossed down their tools and asked who was buying the beer.

Now the sun angled orange through the trees, and Heina realized the tools and parts in his hands were half invisible in the blue shadows. He sat on his heels. Remember this, he told himself: the sight of a real building frame standing hollow in dark lines against the forest; a truckload of timber and iron hinges, after almost a year of begging and worrying.

"That can't be Heina Buschmann, actually standing still," said a voice behind him. Heina turned. Friedchen stood on the path with her bicycle, her hair in braids. He walked toward her and covered her hands with his on the handlebars, then leaned in to kiss her on the cheek.

"You're coated with Serbian log cabin mud," she said, studying his half-wild, exhausted face, his blue eyes looking bleached by the sun. She'd never seen him look this boyish and relieved—not at the youth fest last month in Nuremberg in the midst of a joyous march of thousands under red banners, not after a knockdown battle at an SPD meeting last week.

He pushed his hands through his hair, then motioned toward the pile of materials. "We'll need more money," he said, laughing ruefully. "Rotten window frames, missing pieces . . ."

"I brought you a sandwich," she said. "Don't you have to work tomorrow? You'll be dead on your feet, and your mother is going to make you hose down in the backyard before coming in."

"I think I forgot to eat today. This is the best-looking liverwurst in the world." He wrapped his arms around her waist and buried his sweat-streaked face in her neck, lifting her off the ground. Biting into the sandwich, wiping crumbs away with the back of one hand, he motioned into the empty space to show her the meeting room, the library.

"What did your father say about the shipping bill?" Friedchen asked.

Heina sighed. "We'll have to take up a collection. I fronted it from my savings. We're going to have to do a fund-raiser, maybe a concert or something."

She closed her eyes, willed her heart to stop thrumming. He didn't have money to be writing checks for these huge projects. He saw the worry tighten the muscles in her jaw. "Friedchen, don't worry. We'll figure it out. It's a temporary loan. I'm good for it—I've got a government job. The group will pay me back."

I drew up the flyer for the Midwest Eco-Anarchist Network (MEAN!) conference and photocopied it on red paper. The registration fee was either five dollars or whatever you wanted to pay. AWOL provided an extensive list of anarchist contacts—info shops, collectives, record labels, and anarchist 'zines—and we added the stamps. Y'all come, let's organize for some disorder.

I'd returned to school after my Minneapolis adventure to paste my college degree back together. Vanloads of black-clad, pierced, tattooed anarchists arrived and stumbled into the student center, dragging sleeping bags and cases of beer. I think it was a good conference, but I didn't absorb much of it. I spent the weekend running from meeting room to meeting room with a roll of silver duct tape and a handful of permanent markers, making signs and delivering agendas. I remember a huge pot of lentils that someone had cooked in our vegan cooperative house. I hauled the dented pot into the living room, scraping burned stuff off the bottom with a wooden spoon, wondering whether this crap was edible.

The anarchist boys with spiky hair and the anarchist girls with pink dreadlocks and fishnet stockings sprawled across the living room. My housemates shot me cranky looks as if to say, "Sonya, I'm all for the revolution and whatever, but I've got a geology midterm tomorrow." I was supposed to be an organizer and a thinker and a radical, but I missed my own darn conference to be the errand girl. Either I didn't know how to ask someone else to take care of the lentils, or I figured that if I didn't make a few sacrifices, nobody else would.

Heina, I have fantasies of your revolutionary life. Every kid wanting change here in the United States hears stories about the sixties, and we all want to crawl into those snapshots, be enfolded in a sense of belonging and community as soft and formless as a patchouli-scented cloud. But in your time the splits and infighting boiled with passions as sharp as the ice pick that pierced Trotsky's skull, riling factions to anger and betrayal.

When I started looking for you, I envied your wide selection of elders, your pantheon of graybeard supporters. But it wasn't that way, was it? I have been so sad, too, sitting in a New York apartment, being interviewed for potential membership in a social-change organization, hearing the barbs of condescension as an older male organizer mocked me with, "Listen, little girl." I have stood up and fled the droning lecture of an elder at a study institute in Vermont after he told us to stop smiling because politics was serious business. I expected too much from these movement parents, and then in a fit of rebellion I decided there were no parents, that I would explode all the categories and fuck my way to the revolution. We tried to be elders to each other, but we responded with a shortage of mercy and perspective.

We kissed plenty, but always in political parentheses. We confessed our political burnout to each other but never our need for safety. In my search for stasis in this Red Sea, I have quit, retired, withdrawn, come back a million times. I have uncomfortably found myself serving as elder to kids looking for answers, knowing I will let them down, watching as we fail to produce a conceptual technology for holding disagreement in balance with unity, as we fail to contain our missionary zeal. I thought for a while that an anarchist sleeping with a socialist produced that lovely tension of agreement/disagreement, that the bed that held us meant something for the movement. For moments at a time we laughed, and no one tried to lobby or advocate for a position or perspective, and I felt held. The history books tell me about the infighting in Weimar Germany. I add the broken heart I know to imagine that pain and doubt.

Peter, a communist youth member, might have pitched his voice above the squeal of the streetcars barreling up Viktoriastraße to call out, "New issue of the *Proletarian Worker!*" He held a stack of newspaper aloft, turning back and forth to show the front page. Heina stepped off the streetcar and pushed slowly toward Peter. The young men shook hands warmly.

"I saw the pictures of the new youth home in the paper. It looks great," said Peter, handing out a copy of the paper to a passerby and pocketing the coins.

Heina dug in his own pocket for the five pfennig to buy a communist paper. "It's good so far, but I'll tell you, it's nothing but trouble with the party," said Heina. "They can't stand it that we have a little more independence."

"Believe me, you'd be just as pissed to sit in our meetings." Peter shook his head, then nodded toward the paper he handed to Heina. "Be warned. Someone in the Central Office must have had a bad case of indigestion."

Heina laughed. "Let's figure out when we can meet to talk about united actions against the German National Youth Association. Did you hear they clobbered two Jewish kids near the synagogue on the other side of town?"

Peter sighed. "Those idiots. I'm surprised they can even tie their shoes, much less lift their truncheons."

Heina walked away and opened the paper. A huge headline beneath the fold screamed, "SPD Sells Out the Working Class!" He skimmed the article, his good mood sinking. Nothing surprising here, criticism of SPD leadership for supporting the postwar military buildup and for the SPD's growing welfare system, which the writer said "siphoned off proletarian discontent."

A horse-drawn wagon rumbled past, and one of the horses shat onto the cobblestones. A woman stepped from the curb and scooped the horseshit onto a newspaper. She'd carry those "road apples" right home to her garden to make the dirt produce a bit more. That was life, Heina wanted to yell. The Workers' Welfare Group was not radical, but it was impossible to organize corpses.

Heina crumpled the paper and stuffed it into a trash container, not out of rage but distraction. That ranting article would launch Papa into a heated tirade against the Bolsheviks. Still, you couldn't take it all so seriously. He and Peter were friends. A lot of the young people from both parties didn't get so hung up on the acronyms. The older SPD and communist comrades added to the bile of frustration and hatred as they traded salvos in print.

Turning the corner toward home, Heina brushed against the rough stucco wall of the bakery. The smell of ripe yeast pouring from the bakery's open window turned his stomach. What if he was being fooled, if good old Peter called him "Bourgeois Buschmann" behind his back? What if Peter's assignment was to keep up a good relationship with Heina just to fool the socialist youth into being docile? No—not possible. Heina had to admit that he'd done it too, sitting in the twilight outside the youth home just last week, sighing in a casual joke with Paul Plottki about Peter, who Heina said would be a perfect guy if he weren't a damn commie.

That night after work, Heina grabbed Friedchen's hand as they waited in line near the SPD hall. He rubbed the tips of his smooth fingers against the side of her palm, roughened from doing laundry. At twenty-four he was old enough to get married and start a family. Would she want to? So many activists said marriage was old-fashioned and repressive.

Friedchen stood on tiptoe to see above the crowd. "What's happening up there?" she asked, craning her neck.

Jupp jogged toward them, panting. "Somebody's shoving Paul Plottki around," he said, gasping for air.

In front of the building a circle widened in the crowd as a scuffle spilled into the street. A young man pushed at Paul's chest, knocking him down, then took off down an alley. One of the older SPD members raced away in pursuit. Paul got up and rubbed his tailbone, clutching a mess of wrinkled "Working Youth" papers.

"Those damned German Nationalists!" Heina yelled. "How did that start?"

Paul tried to catch his breath. "Not them. The communists."

Heina squatted to retrieve a stack of newspapers and smoothed them against his thigh. "Shit," he said under his breath, straightening the papers to avoid looking at Paul. Heina knew Paul's strong jaw was set with rage, the same look that had flashed in his direction at so many youth meetings. Paul and he took opposite positions weekly, battling over whether it was treason to argue with SPD leadership or to work with the communists.

"I don't know what happened, this guy appeared out of nowhere and clocked me in the chest—" said Paul.

An older woman near the door called out, "Is that what you're going to do, lie about it? I saw you start into it with that communist kid, who was only giving out flyers . . ."

The man who'd chased after the communist youth member reappeared, winded and empty-handed. "They were both screaming at each other," he said. "I don't know who started it. But throwing punches, that's crossing a line!"

Paul brushed his hands against his thighs. "I'm telling you, that guy came here looking for a fight."

"You can't get into it with them, Paul," Heina said. How stupid! He wanted to yell but couldn't bring himself to do it.

Someone in line said, "The communists are nothing but thugs! Did you see what they just did to Paul Plottki?"

Lenin's balding profile, set off in gray, graces a red flag. His trim bit of beard and moustache circles a mouth set in a determined line, and his eyes squint to focus on a point well beyond the horizon. A red star blazes beneath him. You see this face and feel a wash of strong emotion. That much is assured. But which one? Only eight years past the Russian Revolution, Lenin's image glowed like a hot poker, a physical touch to the flesh. One had to decide. The SPD declared the communists a threat and any ally of a communist to be tainted with that dangerous heat.

Socialist youth group history reveals the story of a young man named Comrade Rosendahl, a socialist youth member from the Ruhr area of Germany where Heina lived. Rosendahl took a train trip to the USSR to see Soviet Russia for himself and make up his own mind. When he returned to the coal-laden air of home, the socialist youth leaders gathered, and one agenda point called for a decision: whether to purge Rosendahl from the party as a result of that trip. The majority voted in favor of the first purge. And so there must have been a moment in 1925 when a comrade leaned over at a bar or a meeting and whispered to Heina, "They're expelling Rosendahl."

I long to see Heina's face in that moment. Did he grimace and look down at a scratch in the table's wood surface, which reminded

him of the widening and shameful scar in their movement? Or, at
the age of twenty-four, did he prize party discipline, knowing that
without it his organization would dissolve in the face of the Nazis?
Heina might have bitten the inside of his lips, looked his compan-
ion in the eyes, and said, "Rosendahl asked for it."

My imagination wanders up against a hard blank spot, not because I can't map out the possibilities but because every direction
feels one-dimensional. I hope Heina felt a tipping queasiness in
his stomach when he heard the news. I hope he was smarter than
I was at his age, that he didn't treat his politics as a hard-edged
religion complete with heretics.

My heart wants Heina to be a rebel against absolutism of all
varieties. Historical accounts with nearly a century of hindsight
will reveal the SPD's spineless and confused collapse as Hitler
marches to power, with the communists spending their vital
force tearing into the SPD. I want Heina to move against this
acidic current. I cheer him on, knowing it will be futile in the
end. I cling to my evidence, my pieces of paper, to assure myself
that Heina fought the conservative local SPD party leaders again
and again from 1923 to 1929. One family rumor tells me he left
the SPD; another story tells me he was weak, a nobody. He could
have been a sellout, an office boy, a man who gave his energy, vitality, and even his family to the SPD because the party demanded
it. Using my own life as a pattern, I can only guess that he walked
a complicated path.

The mysterious military group portrait Mom unearthed might
find its home here in the story. If not the earlier Red Army, those
military poses could have belonged to the Reichsbanner, a growing group of left-wing and centrist activists who organized
against the far-right military Freikorps, the Nazi allies. I know
Heina joined the Reichsbanner at some point before the group
was banned.

Maybe Heina stood in the back row, waiting for the group portrait to be taken, distracted and wondering what role the Reichsbanner militia would play in the SPD '26 elections. He wasn't
even an active member of this organization, but his father had
roped him and Jupp into the photo, hoping to get them more
involved. The photographer fiddled with a lever on his camera
and looked through the lens. The wide-shouldered men would
never fit into the photo's frame.

"Rutschen Sie zusammen!" Scoot yourselves together! The
men in the front row jostled their chairs and muttered. The
two rows behind them, standing on the risers used by the SPD
chorus, shuffled their feet and stood at angles. Jupp shifted his
weight from one foot to the other and stole a glance at Heina.

"Look at Papa," Jupp said out of the side of his mouth. "Doesn't
he look like he's running as Bismarck's replacement?" Papa sat
in the far right seat on the first row, his broad frame held erect.
His arms, the biceps on which he balanced knife points as a party
trick, bowed out stiffly from his hefty frame.

"He wants to be *someone*'s replacement," Heina said.

That spring Papa and Mama had become a roaring, huffing
two-headed political machine. Together, they organized a local
Hüls ticket to run as opposition candidates for the city council. Seeing Mama stump for votes with single-minded intensity
had made Heina truly afraid of her and also truly convinced that
women were equal to men. It was her idea, actually, that the two
of them run together on the ticket. She'd refused to cook anything more elaborate than sandwiches in a month, and she instead covered the kitchen table with campaign flyers and lists of
possible voters.

"Jetzt . . . los!" cried the photographer, and with the flash-
powder's explosion, the faces and forms were fixed: thirty men
and one woman, the local formation of the Reichsbanner Black-

Red-Gold. Whether their mission was to defend the republic from the extreme left or extreme right was, however, a sore spot within the group, and Heina didn't know whether they'd actually be militantly in support of anything. In their makeshift uniforms, they stood with an official red flag and the tricolors of the republic. Painted theater sets of a woodland scene and a room served as backdrops, making the militia members look like children performing a play with cast-off materials.

After the photo a group of men surrounded Heina's father to ask about the city council campaign, and the men near Heina and Jupp asked about the youth group. Heina nodded and gave the expected response: "Everything's great, going just fine." Thankfully, none of the party heads were here to narrow their eyes and question his integrity—or Papa's—for causing trouble in the party.

"Are you going to join the Reichsbanner?" Jupp asked Heina.

Heina shrugged. "I don't know. They seem sort of right wing. All this talk about reclaiming the idea of the 'Nation' and 'Patriotism' sounds like a bad idea."

Jupp's face lit up. "But doesn't it make sense? I mean, I'm not a Nazi, but I'm a German patriot, too!"

A man named August Stötzel shouted, "Men!" and waited for the chatter to die down. Stötzel, a small man with a wiry frame and intense eyes, was a family friend who had grown up with Papa and now worked the Shamrock mine. "We have a mission. We are to serve as poll guards at the upcoming elections, and I need you to be armed. We can't let what happened in Bremen last year happen here."

Several shouts went up in support. "The Sturm-Abteilung will be running scared!" someone yelled. Last year the SA—street thugs who supported the growing National Socialist Party—terrorized local elections and bullied people for votes. SA members

handed out flyers calling for an end to the "Red Terror," then
backed up their threats by driving several communist leaders out
of town under armed guard.

"I'm not such a big fan of the 'Red Terror' myself," said a
booming voice from behind Heina. "I still think we did the
right thing last year in supporting Hindenburg." Heina rolled
his eyes. No one had called the communists a "terror" until the
Nazis started doing it, and now it was accepted vocabulary. The
SPD had become incredibly tense about the growing voter block
of communists, and the party edged rightward because it feared
appearing left wing.

Stötzel, never one to duck an argument, came over to the man
who'd made the "Red Terror" comment and stood toe to toe with
him. "Comrade, have you checked your politics lately? The communists are fighting against the capitalist coalition in power in
Berlin, just like we are. And we have more to be ashamed of than
they do. Our party leadership is in bed with the capitalists." The
man blustered an inaudible reply, and several arguments ignited
across the crowd. Stötzel was listed in a local Ruhr political
history as one who later switched from the SPD to the communists.

Jupp leaned over to Heina and said with a smile, "I guess
there's going to be a brawl or two at the polls."

"And then there will be a brawl or two at the socialist youth
conference when the leadership finds out how many of us are
getting more militant," Heina said. He rubbed his temples with
his fingertips.

"I'll clock anyone who tries to stop the voting, I don't care
who," said Jupp. "Well, I've got to go find something for Mitzi to
eat." Mitzi, Jupp's German Shepherd puppy, was tied up outside
the hall. After Jupp was cornered last month and harassed by a
gang of SA, he'd gotten a sharp-toothed dog from a farmer's lit-

ter and had started taking her wherever he went. Heina took off
his hat and watched Jupp leave. Jupp would be so much braver in
a street fight than he, so much more eager to toss down his silly
Reichsbanner hat and throw a punch.

Within weeks, though, Heina worried about more than political
tensions. Maybe he could blame it on being distracted or too optimistic, but he wasn't sure how they had allowed it to happen. He
was a modern man and understood how babies were made, and
he had learned the latest health theories along with politics in an
SAJ lecture. But that one night on a camping trip, with the smell of
wet canvas in their war-surplus tent mingling with the crackle of a
campfire under pines, had apparently changed their lives.

Around the fire murmured voices and laughter joined with the
sounds of Jupp's puppy yipping in its sleep, dreaming of chasing
rabbits. Gustav leaned back against a log and argued good-na-
turedly with Rudi about the SAJ. Heina and Friedchen had each
packed a tent, but nobody batted an eye when they set one up and
left the other in its case. It was a political choice, like anything
else: they didn't have to live by the same rules as their parents'
generation, didn't have to step blindly into marriage while still
being as ignorant as children about their own bodies.

Gustav smiled as Heina and Friedchen strolled, hands clasped,
toward the tent. Jupp called out, "Just be up for the big morning
hike tomorrow, Brother."

I know that sweet hope, too, when I've been doubly pledged to
the movement because it delivered a fierce and lovely fighter
from the sea of dull and conventional partners. With the man
I'll call Larry, my socialist fiancé, I believed that every kiss, every
beer in a dark Irish bar in south Boston, gave me a view of the
revolution as reflected through a pint glass. We inhabited a secret world bound up in our private jokes and attraction but also

roped together with the taboo desire to change the world. In the
end that dream of dangerous unity made it harder to leave him. I
saw our apartment as liberated territory that had to be defended
rather than criticized.

And yet, for Heina and Friedchen, the ground really had been
liberated in those days. The SAJ group, about twenty of them,
had hiked into the Haard nature preserve that evening to prepare
for the annual May Day festival, which would last all day and into
the next night. They would wake the next morning with plenty
of work to do, herding the Hawk youth groups with their blue
shirts and red scarves into play groups, coordinating athletic
displays and choirs, gathering wood for the fire, cooking, and
planning last-minute events. Free from their jobs and worries at
home, all they had to think about was the world they wanted to
create instead of the world they had been handed. That release
made the stars glow, made the tiny red bells of the heather on the
hillsides smell twice as sweet.

That night in the tent Friedchen curled next to Heina under
the blankets. With Heina's rolled-up jacket as a pillow, they lay
on their backs and looked up at the canvas weave, discussing
politics in a shorthand they'd both grown comfortable with,
murmuring concern about Jupp, who'd gotten involved in planning and organizing for the Reichsbanner and was mired in the
political muck of that group.

"He's got such an easy confidence. That's the mark of a real
leader, I think. He's not a worrier like me," said Heina in a whisper, looking into the glint of Friedchen's eyes.

She gave him a concerned half smile. "Well, he's free from
worry because you do all his worrying for him."

That small and astute comment overwhelmed him, and blood
rushed to his face. No one else, no woman or man, could know

him so well. For two years he'd tried in oblique and general terms to gauge her reaction to the topic of marriage, but he still wasn't entirely sure what she would say. His eyes filled with tears and he looked up at the tent peak, which blurred in front of him.

"Do you . . . Would you consider, you know, doing all those old-fashioned things like marrying me and having a few kids?"

Crickets rasped outside. Heina let out a rush of hoarse whispers, apologized for pushing the issue. Then he turned his head. Luminous, she bit her lip and smiled in the dark.

In the charged air that night and the thought of a future together, their luck felt assured, embroidered like the raised golden logo on a red flag. And I imagine that for the rest of his life, the smell of a damp canvas tent or the thought of a May Day celebration would hit Heina in the chest, make him blush slightly as he tried to regain his composure.

I lay the reconstructed chronology of Heina's political activism alongside the birth dates of his children and other domestic events. A familiar choking sensation of too much happening at once creeps into my throat. I count backward nine months from the birth of Heina's eldest daughter. By day Heina's strident articles on the impending Ruhr youth festival appeared in the local socialist youth publication. These must have been written in the evenings after work as he fought back a nauseating tension and worry about his pregnant girlfriend. Or maybe politics served nicely as an escape, as the family says. I have done the same. I've thrown my energy and time into a huge organizing effort to dilute a sense of personal chaos so I could look back later and claim a greater reason for those days and that pain. It is oddly comforting to imagine Heina battling the flurrying anxiety, the crush of appointments and impossible responsibilities.

Three months later the roar of the Dortmund-bound trained filled the station. Heina shouted, his voice cracking, "Youth fest kids—this is your train!" He put his fingertips to his lips and let out a piercing whistle that reverberated through the station. Fifty kids grabbed knapsacks and bedrolls, pushing toward the train's open doors.

The national 1928 SAJ youth fest opened today, right here in the Ruhr, in Dortmund. The planning of the huge event had overwhelmed local organizers, and Heina had made weekly trips to Dortmund in the months leading up to the fest. I imagine Heina needed the exhaustion in order to sleep at night. Today he felt only half present in this train station, and whenever he closed his eyes his thoughts turned to Friedchen.

Turmoil had torn at their relationship in the weeks since that May Day night. He'd even been convinced she didn't love him. He asked her, stupidly, whether she was sure she was actually pregnant. She squinted her eyes at him in a fury and ran away crying. Some days his eyes filled with tears at work as he made lists of the overwhelming practical details: a home, money, a wedding ceremony, telling their parents. Other days, comforted by the fresh air and the beat of his footsteps, his heart filled with hope. He had a good job, and he and Friedchen had known they would have children together in any case. Nothing about this was negative if he looked at it objectively.

She'd been moody and sick, telling him first that a May Day baby was incredibly good luck, and the next day that she'd visited a homeopath her cousin had recommended to get a tea sure to provoke a miscarriage. Heina had to pinch the bridge of his nose to stop a gush of tears. He didn't realize such things were even possible. Several discussions led to the same truth: they had to tell their parents. Friedchen's Catholic parents might be furious at her out-of-wedlock baby. Mama wanted him to marry "up," a bitterly hilarious hypocrisy.

Now the SAJ kids pushed into the train, claiming cabins and

earning scowls from commuters and weekend travelers. Heina sat down and closed his eyes.

"Heina! So what do you make of the SPD now?" asked a guy named Fritz. Heina sighed and watched the cabin snap back into a blurred focus. The Berlin SPD leadership had thrown its support behind Germany's rearmament, waiting for another war.

"Ridiculous," Heina said, with an irritation that surged well beyond his feelings about the party. He rubbed his hands together and looked out the window. "Anyway, I've got to go see if the Hawks group made it into the last car." He got up and left the narrow cabin, stepping over the packs and bedrolls littering the floor.

Fritz called after him, "I hope Ollenhauer is finally going to stand up and say something critical. Otherwise this big festival is just a bunch of pretty red flags and empty slogans. If we're not militant, we're going to lose all of our members to the communists and Nazis."

Heina's head swam. He yanked down a window in the train corridor and breathed in the coal dust and wet of the rainy August morning. He leaned his head against the window frame. Should he have stayed home? He ached with confusion. What would Papa do in his shoes? That was simple. There'd be no sympathy for wanting to stay home with a pregnant girlfriend. The old man would look across the wide distance between them, thinking, "This is how my soft, office-boy son fills his time."

But Papa's words, in reality, weren't always so predictable or clear. Two nights ago Heina had a flash of resolution. Papa had fought side by side with Poles in the mines, had been a coal miner himself. Papa could not harbor prejudice against Friedchen and her family.

Heina crept into the living room, catching his father reading the Bible by candlelight. "Papa," he said softly.

Heinrich looked up and pulled off his glasses, tipping his chin in Heina's direction. "Hmm?"

"You like Friedchen, don't you?"

Papa smiled warmly. "A very good girl," he said. "I do like her." Papa liked all the Klejdzinskis, knew Friedchen's sister Hedwig as an employee at the co-op and her father as a union member.

"Do you think—what do you think Mama would say, if . . ."

Papa glanced down at the page. "I'm not your mother," he said. "But you know she would like you to take that Hammond girl on a few more dates. That's what she tells me."

Bah! Papa, freedom fighter, making a silly social argument about an arranged marriage proposition. "Mama's a good organizer, that's true, but she can't organize my whole life!" said Heina. And damn it, he'd snapped at Papa when he had planned to discuss this logically and get real advice.

Papa seemed unwilling to intercede. "You have a fight on your hands, Son. And you know your mother. I can't tell you what she'll do." Papa used the argument about women's equal rights to avoid trying to change Mama's mind.

"Do you hear how horrible that is?" Heina whispered. "Is it because Friedchen happens to be half Polish? Or is it because her papa doesn't own a grocery store like Herr Hammond?"

Papa's eyes rigidly scanned the text in front of him, and the flush in his cheeks and the flare in his nostrils meant he was fighting to control a surge of feeling—was it rage or sadness?

Twenty-four years old and unmarried, Friedchen carries the baby that will become my aunt Inge. Friedchen's father is an invalid who lost his health to the mines. Germany stands on shaky economic ground even now, less than a year away from the U.S. stock market crash in 1929 that will set off Germany's powder keg. But Friedchen can't see that coming.

Or maybe she could feel those tremors. Maybe the careful, withholding eyes I see in photographs show a sense of foreboding I can't decode. I know almost nothing about her. My mother, Friedchen's sixth child, has only a few brief memories of her, because Friedchen will die a few years after the war. In many ways this moment before her first child's birth may be her last breath of free air in the time before the Nazis and war and all the loss that is to come. She has a baby inside her, along with that dreamy hopefulness of pregnancy, the sense that her love with Heina is so strong that it now has a physical manifestation.

Can she know what waits around the corner? She might not be surprised at the extent to which Germans can hate. She's seen the articles and posters describing Poles and Jews as vermin. When she walks with her father on the way to the market and he makes a comment to himself in Polish, a German may look at him with iced-over eyes. *Immigrant. Parasite.* At least the Poles have a homeland they can dream about. She feels badly for the Jewish girls in the neighborhood who are even a step below the Poles on the pecking order of teasing, the poor Jews who get blamed for things that have nothing to do with them.

Friedchen peels potatoes for her mother, a German woman named Henriette who is out in the garden feeding the chickens. Friedchen stands at the sink at first, and then when she starts to get light-headed, she takes a bowl with the potato peelings and her knife and sits in a kitchen chair, near the small window that is open to let in the cool breeze. *Frische Luft.* Germans have a strong belief in the curative powers of drafts. If you are sick leave the window open at night and the cold will sweep the germs away. This isn't always productive in a coal town where the dust in the air will turn your clothes and skin to gray.

She turns the knife, expert at grasping a whole potato in her strong hands and whisking off the peel in one complete piece, turning it around and around to let the brown spiral fall into the bowl like the curl of a fancy girl's hairdo. Then you look in the bowl, and the spiral's shape will tell you your future. If a pregnant woman is doing the peeling, there are signs for girls and signs for boys. Friedchen wants to ask her mother what the signs look like, because she'd like to know, but then she'd have to tell her mother she's pregnant, would have to break her mama's heart. As it turns out, Friedchen's sister Hedwig will also get pregnant before marriage, confirming the stereotype of those dirty, loose girls in the poor neighborhoods. But that's not how it is at all. Freidchen loves Heina, Heina who is the best man possible, Heina who is away this weekend at the Dortmund youth fest. She wanted to go with him but felt too sick and weak to fight those pulsing crowds.

Heina showed her the newspaper articles he wrote about the fest, the careful calibration of train schedules, his advice for group organizers to buy transit passes in bulk. "Youth comrades," he wrote in the SAJ member newsletter I found in the archives from that July, "it's relevant to proclaim with the fullest force: every last one should go from your villages to the Dortmund fest. Red youth under the red flag on the red earth!" Intelligent and forceful, even in print. His days had been a blur this past month as he firmed up arrangements for the massive speaking chorus performance of Red Earth, a new play for the festival.

Friedchen stops her potato in midcurl and looks through the open door into the backyard. Something sticks in her throat, a half worry or maybe just nausea. Heina has assured her they will get married, that everything will be fine. He has a good job when so many are unemployed. He will take care of her. But he's so busy. Some weekends he moans and says, "I don't want to go to this meeting, I just want to stay home with you, my dove. I don't like to see you sick." But he always goes to his meeting anyway because he is disciplined. And if everyone were disciplined, he'd say, we'd already have revolution instead of the mess we've got now.

Friedchen's mother comes into the kitchen, triumphantly holding an egg in each hand. "Endlich!" she says, Finally! A few eggs. Friedchen smiles and looks down at the bowl, thinking about her own little egg, her baby. She will wait to tell her parents until Heina has the wedding plans finalized, until after he breaks the news to his mother. Then she'll tell her own mother. But of course her own mother already knows, notices the absence of even a trace of blood on Friedchen's side of the bed shared with Hedwig, notices the slight thickening under her chin and at her middle. Her mother is no fool.

As I write this at age thirty-two, I'm six months pregnant with my first child. I've been learning the schedule of my body, slowing and feeling the ripples and kicks of another human inside me. The first three months I was terrified, unable to see myself as a mother, unwilling to give up my former sense of self, the solid, absentminded comfort I had in my body. I pushed myself to get in the car and drive to political meetings with my stacks of agendas and flyers. If I stopped working so hard it would be a sign that motherhood would take me over, swallow me up, and leave only an empty shell. So I had to fight to retain all of my pre-baby activities, despite the morning sickness and exhaustion. I imagine this compartmentalization worked for Heina, too. A week after the youth fest he immersed himself immediately in planning protests against his own party leadership, which had voted to fund the building of tanks despite a membership veto.

As my baby became a definite presence at two and three months, my focus began to disintegrate and unhinge. I started doing what I had feared. I put off political work, started saying no to events and meetings. Most alarmingly, this seemed to occur without a shred of guilt. I was slowly becoming a different person, collecting baby supplies from thrift stores and garage sales, not out of a dogged sense of sandbagging against an incoming storm but out of a sense of excitement, the nervous expectation of meeting someone new who I would already love more fiercely than I could imagine.

Friedchen knows this. What I don't know is whether Heina does. My mother has tried to peer back into her childhood to understand her father. She can't cut through the haze of German restraint or Heina's shyness to really understand whether he was taken with his children, whether he loved them in the heart-stopping way that I already love my son. Is it fair to judge Heina, to guess that there were moments during that Dortmund weekend in August when he completely forgot about his growing baby and his future wife, when he was so swept up in the waves of planning and organizing that his own future seemed insignificant or selfish to consider?

I will have to admit to moments this August when, even with a baby in my belly, I sharpened my attention at a weekend political retreat and became in mind at least utterly unpregnant. Captivated by a discussion about the current antiwar movement, I forgot for hours at a time that someone else swam inside me. Does that mean I love this baby less? But on the other hand, can you claim to love someone—love as the verb and not the abstract concept, that plastic trophy promised in lieu of a real relationship—if your behavior can be seen as selfish, distant, withholding?

Lina pushed the loose strands of hair from her face and leaned back from her perch on the garden bench. For Papa Heinrich's twenty-fifth anniversary in the SPD, October 21, 1928, they opened the garden to a glowing evening celebration. After a ceremony down at the SPD hall, it seemed like half the neighborhood stood in their garden, drinking beer and laughing, telling stories about the four men feted tonight who'd spent their young lives in the party. My uncle Klaus discovered in his cellar a large commemorative photo mounted on cardboard of Heinrich Müntjes, Heinrich Mintart, and Heinrich and Franz Rupprecht posed to mark this occasion. In the photo the men eye the camera with bemusement, and their rough hands and wrists look strange and boyish in too-short suit jackets.

"Boys!" Lina called. "We're going to have a toast! Heina, bring that bottle of champagne from the kitchen." She sat in the center of rows of tables grouped together in the warm fall evening, amid the expanse of green they'd planted with fruit trees that spring. The family's first house had been finished last year, built by family and friends so that they'd never get evicted from another apartment because of politics.

Heina stood on the back steps, unsmilingly studying his mother. His head throbbed. He'd spent four or five hours of this beautiful evening in a state of rage and now felt wrung out and light-headed. He had half a mind to run down the stairs, grab Mama by the shoulders, and shake her, yell and demand that she admit to this happy crowd what she'd done.

Heina had told Mama that afternoon that Friedchen was coming to the party. Mama muttered a curse in her son's face. "Let her come into this garden with a pregnant belly and disgrace this whole family? Never."

Papa told Mama four months ago about the pregnancy, but she'd never acknowledged it to Heina's face. Instead Heina caught her looking at him as if waiting for an apology. On this celebration day Heina hoped Papa's wishes would trump Mama's, but Papa stepped aside as Mama stormed into the bedroom and slammed the door. Papa shrugged, the tips of his handlebar mustache dipping as he fumbled for words. "She's a little Dragon. I can't change her. We'll have to wait, son. Time takes care of these things."

Despite his talk about fighting for one's rights, for fairness and justice, Papa allowed this cruelty to continue in his own house. The word formed on Heina's tongue and fell out of his lips: "Coward," whispered in a voice of half wonder and disbelief.

"It was your decision that caused this mess," Papa shot back with a harsh edge to his voice. "You remember that."

Heina had run from the kitchen biting back tears. He grabbed his keys and jacket, slammed the door behind him, and took off at a fast walk for the Klejdzinskis', stopping there to tell Friedchen it was better that she didn't come to the party that night. She sat on her bed, rubbing her hands softly over her rounded belly. She looked at Heina and glanced back down at the bedspread. She seemed half distracted all the time now, as if busy trying to figure a way out of their predicament.

"Do you think if I hadn't gotten pregnant, she would have given us her blessing of marriage anyway?" Friedchen asked softly. "Is that it?"

Heina grabbed her hands and pushed his face into her warm palms. He shook his head, still hiding his eyes with her fingers. "She's crazy. Anyway, Papa loves you. They both love you." He looked up. "And we're getting married, no matter what she says."

He stayed as long as he dared at the Klejdzinskis' apartment, and then ran with his jacket over his arm through the streets to the SPD hall, where the ceremony was ending. He had called Papa a coward on the very day Papa was honored for his bravery as a labor leader. Was Papa a coward, or was he being a good organizer, working with the conditions available, waiting for Lina to soften, letting Heina the adult confront his own problems? Heina felt sick, watching his father and the other men receive their certificates to polite applause.

Now, hours later, Heina carried the cool, green bottle of champagne out to the garden, half hoping that something in Mama's heart would move. He handed her the bottle over the heads of laughing couples, and she wrapped her fingers around its neck, turning to listen to a story, enfolded in conversation, not even making eye contact with Heina. She was in her element, the center of the social occasion. She popped the cork and asked Franz Rupprecht to read the poem on his certificate.

Franz, a thin man with light blue eyes and a close-shaven head, stood and cleared his throat. He read out, "*Purpurrot als Bundeszeichen, Fahne, wehe uns voran! Wollen uns die Hände reichen, Dir zum Treuschwur Mann an Mann!* The deep scarlet of our tribe, flags—lead us on! We reach out our hands to swear our oath to you!"

An older man who'd been active in the Workers' Council slapped Heina on the back and handed him a glass of strong schnapps with an aroma of bitter herbs. Heina tossed the liquid back into his throat. He didn't drink often, and to him the stuff tasted vile, but it would serve to blot out this evening, the stars and the candles and the horrible sound of Mama's false laughter.

Sometime later he found himself, definitely drunk, sitting on the front steps of their house next to Jupp, who nursed a beer and hummed.

"You're lucky Mama likes you," said Heina, his tongue loose. Maybe he could break the spell of lies Mama had wrapped around this household. "Our mother, the city council candidate, so forward-thinking, but so backward that she won't let a pregnant woman into the garden!"

Jupp stopped humming. Friedchen was Jupp's friend, too. If

only he would say something clear, a word to prove he could see through Mama.

"Mama loves us both equally," Jupp said. "She wants the best for you, even if she doesn't know what that is."

Heina shifted his feet and knocked a beer glass into the bushes. Jupp couldn't bring himself to criticize Mama outright. This was tyranny, and Jupp jumped right in line! Heina wiped his forehead with his shirtsleeve.

"I don't know what to do. Maybe I'll do like Mama did, just run away from home. That's what she did, you know. I feel like I'm melting inside. I—"

Jupp grabbed the front rail and pulled himself to his feet as if he couldn't stand to watch Heina fall apart. Jupp put his hand on the doorknob and whispered, "You've got to be a man about this, Heina. You're about to be a father."

7

Unions

Heina's fingers followed an endless path along the smooth gold ring in his pocket. He drank hot coffee as he stood in front of the oven and listened hard, hoping for a creak of the floorboards from his parents' bedroom. They knew about the wedding ceremony, but Mama had wordlessly decreed that Heina's impending marriage did not exist. Heina glanced at his watch and whispered out into the hallway, "Jupp!"

A shoe clunked against the floor, and the noise echoed in the quiet house. Jupp appeared in the doorway, clutching a hairbrush, his jacket, and the offending shoe. He dumped the bundle on the kitchen bench and presented Heina with a new leather-bound family book, the secular version of a family Bible, which held blank spaces to record marriages and the birth of children.

"Thank you, Jupp," Heina said softly, surprised Jupp would think of something at once so practical and so sentimental. It would also save them an extra fee at city hall.

"No, it's from Papa," said Jupp. "He gave it to me last night and said, 'Like father, like son.'"

"Did he seem glad, or angry?" Heina asked. Jupp shrugged, less interested in deciphering Papa's hidden messages. I don't know whether Heinrich bought this book or made any subtle signals of peace, but I hope he did.

Heina shut the book and ran his fingertip along its dark and oiled spine. The surly silence in the house seemed to demand a pious guilt, but Heina felt clear-headed and eager. After all, Papa and Mama's wedding had been conducted in this same solitary manner, with Lina's parents horrified that their baby would marry a socialist. True, Papa had avoided the scandal of a seven-months-pregnant bride. Mama's ire either sprang from these bourgeois conventions or stemmed from the fact that the process had not gone according to her plan.

In the cold anteroom of the courthouse chambers, Heina stamped his feet for warmth. Friedchen smoothed her dress over her round belly and grabbed for Heina's hand. A draft of cold air blasted from the outer lobby door. Emil from the socialist youth group stepped inside, holding a bundle wrapped in brown paper and brushing the snow from his slicked-down hair.

"Na?" said Heina in greeting. Emil pulled the paper from a beautiful small winter bouquet, sprigs of evergreen, deep green holly, hard red and white berries, all bound with a red ribbon interwoven with threads of gold. Heina smiled at the surprise he'd planned for Friedchen, black-market flowers in exchange for court filings for a farmer down on his luck.

"Wie Weihnachten," said Friedchen. It looks like Christmas. She held out her hands, the apples of her cheeks turning pink and plump with pleasure. Even with the dour response from their parents, this was truly a celebration. No one could take that away from them.

They entered the chambers of the justice of the peace. The official, a bored and sleepy man with curly gray hairs growing elaborately out of his ears, rumbled through the brief ceremony, smacking his lips between sentences as if he had just rolled out of bed. Thankfully he didn't cast a single judgmental glance at Friedchen's middle. He probably united souls ten times a week. When he recited the part about the wife obeying the husband, Friedchen and Heina smiled at the silly old language.

They placed the bright and heavy rings on each other's fingers. How responsible and strong his left hand looked, as if he had grown up over night! He curled and uncurled his fingers, feeling powerful and adult. They leaned over the dark wooden desk to scratch their names with a fountain pen onto the marriage certificate, dated November 24, 1928.

Heina opened the new family book and wrote their names on the first page, side by side. He skipped over the opposite page, which had spaces for die Trauung, the ceremony. As I saw seventy-five years later, he'd left blank most of the entries for the wedding. He did not list the parents of the bride and groom. The wedding, and the marriage, would be theirs, not owned by parents or a horde of relatives with the power to sanction or disapprove.

My mom, who immigrated to America and married at eighteen, would continue the tradition and become the third generation in the Buschmann family without her parents at her wedding. Although it would have been fitting in some ways for me to follow the pattern and get married on a cliff or in Las Vegas, Mom and Dad attended my marriage ceremony. But the legacy of isolated weddings made me feel awkward to play the role of the traditional bride.

A day before the ceremony I sent activist alert e-mails to members of the community-labor coalition in Columbus. An activist replied with an e-mail to ask, "Don't you have anything better to do right now, like getting ready for your wedding tomorrow?"

We hung white Christmas lights from the trellis in our backyard and lugged crates of liquor. I tried not to think about all those eyes that would watch me the next day as I walked down the aisle in a public garden and celebrated later in our backyard. I would wear a lovely twenty-dollar wedding dress, but I had to block out the imagined critical thoughts and comments from our relatives, who might whisper when they saw that the bride wore bright red with sparkles and beads, and spaghetti-straps that revealed a tattoo.

The roses in the public garden hummed with electric fuchsia, and a fluorescent pink Super Ball sun fell slowly behind the trees. I moved carefully and slowly so I wouldn't catch and tear the fabric of my dress. How strange to attend to the smallest details of this body, which I normally treated as a five-foot-three-inch coffee carafe. Licking my lipstick, adjusting straps, voice shaking, I avoided the looks of admiration and love. We recited our homemade vows, then my dreadlocked, red-headband-wearing husband and I walked down the aisle to the guitar strains of Led Zeppelin's "All of My Love."

If I found myself up in front of a crowd, it was normally either to teach or to yell at a demo. A protest demanded a wild and hoarse burst of anger, often met with stony silence. I could make a stink and be ignored in return. Here in this public garden, the white-hot agony of positive attention from friends and family burned into me an unaccustomed, uncomfortable sensation: that day I was beautiful. And I wished for Friedchen and Heina these simple pleasures of a backyard barbecue, friends and relatives raising glasses of beer, hours of blissful, forgetful laughter, and photos of Friedchen as nothing more complex than a shockingly beautiful, very pregnant stunner.

Two months after the wedding Friedchen moved with Heina into his parents' house. The three-story house was divided into apartments for as many as seven families over the years, mostly renters, and it's unclear whether Heina and Friedchen lived with Heina's parents and Jupp on the first floor or whether they moved up to the small third-floor loft. I imagine them on the third floor because of my own limitations; I can't imagine a new couple sharing such a small space with in-laws, but it was common. As my mother described these *eng*, or tight, living arrangements, it begins to make much more sense why Germans of the time period had the stamina or need to attend meetings and party functions every night until 10:00.

I hope dearly that Papa hugged Friedchen and said, "Wilkommen" as she walked in with her suitcase. Mama Lina, I imagine, was unpredictable, laughing with Friedchen in the hallway one day, and the next yelling upstairs about an imagined household slight.

Pregnancy had remade Friedchen's body. Even her face, with her bold Polish cheekbones, rounded out like a plump German girl. Heina caught himself daydreaming about how he would take their little son to demonstrations, explain to him the ways of the world, point out the coal tipples in the neighborhood to describe how the Buschmann family helped build those mines.

In mid-January Friedchen might have woken up and groaned, "I am so huge, I don't know how I'll make it through another day." She turned away from Heina and swung her legs around the side of the bed, pushing her weight upright with both hands.

Heina grabbed his pants and shirt, then forced himself out of bed to start a fire in the stove. He walked downstairs to the entryway of the house, which joined their third-floor apartment with the second-floor renters and his parents' apartment on the ground floor.

He picked up the January 11, 1929, copy of the *Volksfreund*, the *People's Friend*, folded in thirds and resting inside the letter-drop. Maybe there'd be a review of *All Quiet on the Western Front*, the new book about the Great War from a soldier's point of view. There was already talk of the government banning the book. Heina scanned the local news, the meeting notices, looking for a good editorial to read to Friedchen over breakfast. An article about the local SPD caught his eye, and he sat down on the step to read a report of an annual party assembly the previous Sunday, one of the dog and pony shows where the local SPD heads trotted out all of their various accomplishments and beat their chests.

But political maneuverings signaled from the newsprint: "A report from the youth group was missed." Report from the youth group?! They'd never received an invitation. Heina scanned the rest of the article, and adrenaline and anger tuned his mind to a sharp focus. He fished a pencil stub from his pocket and drew a heavy vertical line in the margin. The article listed election results and the names of members of a new youth committee appointed to clarify the "youth question." In other words the party leaders had enacted a bureaucratic coup, hidden in polite language with passive verbs.

The new youth committee listed in the article did not include Papa or any of the other men who had helped establish the youth home. Instead this new committee was composed of starch-collared conservatives who, to a man, suspiciously resisted any independent thought from the youth wing.

Jupp stepped in with a sack of warm rolls under his arm. "What are you doing hunched on the steps like that?" he asked Heina.

"Machacek, Von Heu, and Vogel. Those drones are the new youth committee," said Heina. He handed the paper to Jupp, who shook his head as he read.

Heina opened the door to the first-floor apartment. "Papa!" called Jupp. "You've got to see what the party's up to!"

Papa's house shoes scuffed along the tile floor. "Was, denn?" he said. He took the paper and read. "They'll be the death of us!" he growled, and Heina relaxed into an almost giddy sense of expectation. With Papa on their side, they'd figure out a way to get back at the leadership. "Three million unemployed, and they decide to waste time playing games and squashing the young people."

I found that news clipping in Heina's folder of papers, and I smiled at the signs of an active, vehement reader with a pencil: the question marks, exclamation points, and the few illegible words in the margin, along with broad scratches of pencil lead, some so heavy with ire that they shone a glossy slate against the rough gray paper. When I first found the clipping I assumed I would never understand the specific context or meaning of the scribblings. Months later, the story unfolded when I put Heina's personnel file in chronological order alongside the contents of his activist scrapbook.

This article sparked off a furious battle of letters between the youth group and the local SPD leadership, one small part of a pivotal power struggle that would shape Germany's future. The scrap of newspaper showed Heina's rage as his party and his nation turned to the Right and targeted the Left.

Activists hide these ugly internal battles even from each other. Heina's file of letters contained evidence of the heartbreak and anger he felt toward so-called comrades and elders. The jabs and accusations in the letters proliferated as the weeks progressed, and the polite addresses became more flowery and formal to couch the venom. The opening salutation "Honorable Comrade" could take on sarcastic and bitter undertones, even in print, with subtle degrees of mockery when followed by a host of questions about one's motives and intelligence. The phrase could mean, "If only you really were my Comrade" or "Stupid Comrade."

Drawing from my own activist experience, I imagine a stew of conflicted emotions brewing in Heina's heart. Maybe I have left myself too open to personal pain in the thrashing tides of change. Dread over an approaching battle or the sinking feeling of betrayal and disappointment would surface for me on a daily basis in the midst of a walk or cooking a meal. These flashes reminded me that my activist work stayed with me constantly as my subconscious mind chewed on the problem of the day. Heina might have lain in bed at night, convinced he would break away from the SPD, only to awake from a nightmare hours later and resign himself to patching things up—enduring the feeling that there seemed to be no reasonable or acceptable solution.

On November 23, 2002, I swerved through pelting rain to a rally and speak-out targeting Wal-Mart's discriminatory and antiunion activities. I'd worked for months to organize this, and I could barely force myself to turn the steering wheel. Running on too little sleep after grading too many papers, I tried to forget about a rejected mortgage application that seemed to judge me for my unimpressive income. I needed to refocus. The activists would arrive any second, soaked and faces red from the cold, with the slogans dissolving from their pulpy wet poster board signs. I hoped they would bring glowing stories about the delegation of clergy members who had asked for a meeting with Wal-Mart managers. I had fifteen minutes to set up pizza, get the press packets together, figure out an MC. I pushed open the metal double doors to the union hall.

"Back from the rally already?" asked one of the union officials, waiting for the busloads of protestors.

Guilt surged. My schedule had been too tight to even make it to the rally. "I organized the fucking thing," I growled. This was clearly inappropriate and also an exaggeration. I'd helped to organize it. The growl came from deep in my guts, built-up rage at two years of dealings with these union officials who never seemed to remember my name, despite the hours of cheap labor and community-coalition work they got from me.

"Man, I'm sorry about that," I laughed. "This has been such a horrible day for me." Would they understand a bad writing workshop? Definitely not. I smiled, I brought them pizza. But I'd never rate as a comrade. Comrade—what the hell was that?

A week later came my labor union dressing-down. At a table at a Bob Evans restaurant over a wilted salad and a cloud of cigarette smoke, the union's lead organizer told me in no uncertain terms that the word *fuck* must not pass my lips in the union hall. A faction in the union that opposed the community-labor coalition had seized upon the four-letter word (and my attitude) as a chance to threaten our tiny office in the corner of the union hall. That four-letter word passed through the chain of command all the way to the union president, relayed by chain-smoking union reps, each of whom swore and told off-color stories as freely as breathing, each of whom had been happy to have me when I could make calls and turn out warm bodies for their pickets and strike actions. I knew *fuck* was not the problem. A thirty-one-year-old woman who looked eighteen was not allowed to swear like a middle-aged guy with a big shiny belt buckle. What did I think I had: balls?

Obviously I'm no stranger to fury. In that moment at the union hall, I felt as though I had channeled Lina's disappointment and resentment. Lina got roped into the cruel hope of a new world, standing with Rosa Luxemburg and the other women on the front lines. Then later she watched as the SPD traded this painting of Liberty holding freedom's banner for a rosy magazine-cover illustration of women as the keepers of home and hearth. Lina kept pushing, even ran for office. And lost.

But for Lina, and for me, not every flash of rage and its consequences can be wiped away with the salve of another round of political action. For me, and I imagine for Lina, rage wells up from the lode of excess frustration at life, carrying a bitter potential to harm. Like Lina, I need more comfort than I have found in the world so far. I tell myself the truth: struggle will not feed my body or my soul. My social justice lifestyle has meant that at that moment I couldn't afford to shop anywhere but Goodwill and the clearance rack. I wanted my lilac aromatherapy hand lotion *and* my national healthcare. I wanted struggle *and* appreciation.

When I look at the photos taken at the anti–Wal-Mart speak-out and reception, I see my eyes dark and flashing. In one photo I lean forward in serious conversation, pulled into a sharp concern about a decision, while activists around me eat pizza and laugh. My temper flares more quickly in political meetings as I get older, and I can't decide whether this is clarity or whether it is simply toxic frustration. I need something outside of politics to soothe the disappointment, the way Heina turned to his walks in the woods for sustenance. I know too well how to become a Dragon.

Ten days after Heina read the infuriating article from the party leadership, the Hüls SAJ met on January 23, 1929, at the youth home. Heina invited Friedchen to come to the meeting, but she shifted under the weight of her hugely pregnant belly and broke her gentle demeanor with a look of pure sarcasm. "Heina," she said. "I can barely make it out to the kitchen." Heina winced. He was an idiot. He shouldn't even go himself. He promised her he'd be only an hour.

It was sleeting outside, the sky a thick gray. Otto would undoubtedly be in bed with a cold. Would anyone show up? The other SAJ folks must realize that someone else had to take the lead on this fight. If no one but Heina could lead, they might as well fold this group. Heina lost himself in a surge of doubt about the party leaders and the blasphemy of socialism that the SPD had become. The youth groups were digging a coal mine with teaspoons.

The knob of the youth home's front door rattled loosely, and the roof above the entryway needed patching. To Heina's surprise, however, six members had already gathered around the table, including Otto.

Heina spread out a copy of the offending newspaper article on the table. His heart dipped into hopelessness. "You all know how ridiculous this has gotten," he said, sighing.

Otto rubbed his chin. "We can't stand for this, obviously."

Friedrich, ever practical, reached into his pocket for his pen. "Where's the paper? Let's figure out what to say."

"These little dictators," said Karl, shaking his head.

"Dictators!" said Heina. "That's what they are. We won't stand for this dictatorial treatment."

Friedrich's pen nib scratched on the paper. When the room quieted, he waved his hand. "Come on, more. This has to be full of fire if it's going to get the attention of the regional headquarters."

"And of course we'll send it to the youth headquarters in Berlin . . ."

"Ollenhauer will flip!"

Heina, I know what kept you coming back: the bursts of shocked joy. So many people described you as shy, gentle, and quiet, and it's been a struggle to reconcile this with evidence of lifelong political confrontation. I have to assume that, like me, you dreaded the next gathering, right up until your stomach dropped and you opened your mouth. Then the words came out, and you listened to get inspiration from your own voice. People in the crowd nodded, raised their fists, encouraged. Somehow, the elixir of inspiration was distilled once again out of thin air.

When I was invited to speak about the labor movement to a group of young environmental activists a few months before the Wal-Mart rally, I used all my tricks to get past my nervousness. I put my hair up and added earrings and a V-necked black T-shirt to my uniform of jeans and sneakers. I decided I would flirt with this group, try to win people over by being a little nice to look at. A bare neck, a nice smile, caffeine, and adrenaline always seemed to put words in my mouth, and I know a little about falling in love with the charisma of politics.

On the elevator up to the third floor to the group's office, I worried that I would put the staff to sleep with a droning lecture about wages and the working poor—blah, blah, blah, poverty. After fifteen years of the activist life, a small and evil part of me wanted to tell them to go get good corporate jobs. Then at least they could pay back their student loans and buy a few CDs. Proceed down this do-gooding path to hell, I wanted to say, and it will get you a life of secondhand clothes, no vacations, and substandard dental work.

I knocked, and the director opened the door. I smiled, and my public persona took over. I wasn't faking; this is what shy people in any line of work do to turn themselves into extroverts for a few hours before they collapse. In the long scrubby office packed with several desks, a chalkboard displayed a note for free guppies, and the postered walls exhorted us to save the forests. I took a breath, and my introduction about our community-labor coalition spooled out of my mouth. It sounded like gibberish as it floated past my ears. We call this a "rap," and these door-to-door environmental fund-raisers knew the practice of relying on an essential prepared message.

I saw a few glazed looks, so I switched gears and told a story about an action that pitted striking steelworkers from Mansfield, Ohio, against the mill owners. The steelworkers gathered on the curb outside a board of directors' meeting at a hotel. Trying to get attention for injuries and safety violations in the plant, the workers squirted tubes of fake blood on the pavement, staggering around with bandaged limbs in a ridiculous street theater piece with ominous undertones. We howled with laughter at the rubber fingers and hands, red with fake blood, lying on the asphalt like worms after a rainstorm.

My rap faded into the Q&A, and the students asked good questions. I did my best to make the connection between my subject and their lives. It wasn't difficult to explain the desire for healthcare, enough money to live on, and the chance to leave work at the end of the day with life, limb, and sanity intact. I told the students about our next rally, and the stoned-looking girl with blue eye shadow and the electric tie-dyed T-shirt clicked her ballpoint and scribbled a note on the corner of her folder.

I said my good-byes to the group's leaders. Outside canvassers lounged by the curb, waiting for the van to take them out for a night of door knocking. A few of them stood in a circle, kicking a hacky sack beanbag back and forth in graceful arcs. As I walked down the steps the sleepy tie-dyed girl flashed me a peace sign and said, "Thanks." Walking down the road toward home, I held my hand over my heart. My rib cage felt warmed and lit. Maybe I could pin it to postadrenaline relief or endorphins, but a school presentation or a few laps in the pool never had this extra dimension. Color—pomegranate, nectarine—is the only way I can describe it. Those moments of connection are my vitamins, my fruit and vegetables, and maybe even my connection to the spiritual, when I do more than I believe I can.

Heina returned from the meeting and read the letter aloud to Friedchen. The group had combined his firm language with a few sly and mocking words from Jupp, all packaged in Otto's fine phrasing. Friedchen shifted uncomfortably in the chair and tried to focus on his words, but the baby had sunk deep in her pelvis. She felt lost in a hurricane, with fierce winds whipping at her body, the political on the outside and this child on the inside, both threatening to pull her apart. My aunt, Ingeborg Buschmann, was born four days later, on January 27, 1929.

I know nothing about the birth, but I imagine Heina waiting in the kitchen while the midwife tended to Friedchen.

"What if she dies?" he asked, pacing and watching the plaster as if he could see through it.

Mama was unwilling to give words of comfort but unable to keep quiet. "Don't worry. She only *thinks* she's going to die. Odds are she won't."

Half an hour later the midwife came out in her bloody smock, and a wave of nausea gripped Heina. Had she cut Friedchen to pieces to get that baby out?

"A girl!" said the midwife. She asked Lina for more hot water.

"And Friedchen?" he asked. "Is she okay?"

"Of course," the midwife said. "She needs some time to recover, but she'll be fine."

The women poured water into the large pot on the stove, and Heina sat down, lightheaded. Friedchen lived. He'd become the father of a girl. He'd imagined a boy. A girl? But why not? Half the babies on earth were girls. And now it was a real baby, not a daydream. Should he go in? He was rooted to his chair. Friedchen needed her rest. He felt an edge of fear at a new animal in the house, new life. What did it mean, to have a girl in this house? Would this creature be sweet and sensitive like Fried-chen, doomed to be mowed down by his mother? Or would this little girl turn fierce and sharp-tongued like his mother? Women were incomprehensible.

Heina assumed Friedchen would feel better immediately, and that the fat-cheeked baby would sleep. Instead the baby woke every few hours through the night with shrieks. Three days after the baby was born Heina began to relish the thought of going to work and the quiet of his office. Friedchen rose at 5:00 a.m. and pulled Inge from her bassinet, trying to hush her. Inge screamed, her face red and contorted.

"What does she want?" Heina snapped. "Is this normal for a baby to scream like that? Maybe there's something wrong with her."

Friedchen, her face gray from lack of sleep, turned to him and said loudly, "I hear this all day and all night. Maybe it's you she wants." She held the wriggling bundle toward Heina. The baby flopped in his arms, and he held her against his chest as he'd seen Friedchen do. He willed himself to relax, to think calm thoughts and direct them at the baby, but the baby opened some hidden reserve of lung capacity to scream even louder.

Friedchen's eyelids reddened as she fought back tears. "Your mother is hearing all of this," she said. "But of course she wouldn't think of coming up to help me."

The baby arched her back, stiffening in Heina's arms. He held the baby toward Friedchen. "Here, I'm going to drop her. I don't know what to do."

"Please do something useful, then," Friedchen said. "Go get my mother."

Heina dressed for the cold, relieved to escape yet ashamed to have to walk halfway across town to find a woman willing to help his wife when his own mother was just downstairs. What could he say to Lina to change her acidic disposition? He'd told himself a grandchild would warm his mother's heart, but Mama Lina seemed to want credit for everything she endured that was connected to Heina's "mistake."

Friedchen's mother walked back with Heina in a soothing silence. When they reached the corner near the house, he told her he had a quick errand to run. Reluctant to face Friedchen again, he walked down the street the four blocks to the youth home, his automatic destination. Maybe he was hoping for a little calm, a chance to light a fire, look at the building, to check the mail and tidy up. Heina flipped through the stack of mail, mostly newsletters and advertisements for the new popular theater group the Red Rebels. He drew another envelope from the stack and tore it open: a response from the local SPD leadership. He moved near the window to read, never imagining that his American granddaughter would hold her breath and read the same letter seventy-four years later.

The ultraformal language in the letter dripped with sarcasm. The writer claimed to be shocked that the SAJ hadn't attended the annual SPD meeting, with or without a personal invitation. Then a personal attack: "When a leader of the SAJ, who for a long time has been of adult age, is active neither at his union nor in the party, one doesn't have to guess how such viewpoints develop." Beneath the abstract German verbs, Heina saw the implication that he spent too much time on youth organizing, didn't give enough sweat and blood to the party—and that his instincts were fundamentally counterrevolutionary. After he'd busted his skull getting a youth home built, ensuring a place in politics for young people, the party only complained that he was not also a shop steward for the clericals *and* running to every single SPD meeting.

The letter continued: "The People need fighters, not suspicious persons who seek their fun with the youth group," and ended with, "We know the SAJ doesn't want to do anything silly like proclaim its independence from the party and live in a cave, so we can only hope that the SAJ develops itself to serve the larger movement."

Heina laughed. These bureaucrats—rapping him on the knuckles like scolding schoolmasters. Heina locked the doors and walked the streets of his neighborhood for an hour, letting the snow cool his hot head, muttering responses to the cold air as the impact of the letter's sentences reverberated in his memory.

"Sweetheart!" he called hoarsely as he entered the apartment, shrugging off his coat, "you're not going to believe it . . ."

"Sei ruhig!" whispered Frau Klejdzinski, standing in the bedroom doorway with the alarmed eyes of a new grandmother. Hold your peace! "The baby is finally asleep." Heina looked into the bedroom. The baby dozed, cradled in Friedchen's arms. Friedchen looked up and formed the word *endlich*, finally, with her lips.

Heina sat gingerly on the bed, then pulled the letter from his pocket, attempting to unfold it without crinkling the paper too loudly. "Look at this," he said. "It's unbelievable. Here, I'll hold it so you can read."

The smile faded from Friedchen's mouth, and she looked at him as if she were nauseous. "Heina, I have no room in my head for politics. I've got nothing left."

Friedchen scraped the bottom of her reserves, and the German economy echoed her desperation. Wall Street had crashed in the United States the previous October, and some lefties said it signaled the end of capitalism. All the crash had brought so far was hunger and the end of U.S. loans. Chancellor Brüning decided to raise funds for war reparation payments by cutting unemployment payments and social services for the poor, which sparked a depression. Thankfully the SPD had roused itself to protest. A Marl SPD history booklet revealed that the neighborhood SPD group ran a "poor kitchen" out of the youth home, providing soup and day-old bread to unemployed workers who had been denied welfare benefits, and Uncle Klaus and my mom both remember hearing many stories about the many hours the Buschmann family and the local SPD spent working at the poor kitchen.

I imagine the crumbs and the sliced turnips, and I picture a weekend in which a mother with two young girls, terribly thin, had snapped at Heina after he told her there was no more bread, "What do you know about starvation? You probably have a party bigwig's salary and a cushy job!" The woman's daughters might have looked up at him with wide eyes as he ladled soup. What could he do—tell her his salary had been cut by a third in the past year? He knew that at least he received a paycheck, which put him in a different world.

Heina's personnel file reveals that in these hectic and anxious months he was also appointed to the Ruhr area youth leadership committee. I imagine a typical morning in which Heina woke at 5:00 a.m. to drop off the youth home keys with Konstanze Hoffman, who organized the meals. Then he missed the early train to Düsseldorf for the regional Socialist Worker-Youth meeting. Hassled and lost in thought, he stood in the registration line and muttered his last name to the woman handing out delegate packets.

"Here's your schedule," she said. "And you've been added to the slate of nominations for area elections—you're due in the candidates' caucus in twenty minutes."

Heina made his way toward the meeting room. As he found a

seat in the auditorium, the young man sitting next to him turned and said, "There's a raging battle on the SPD about to start."

The facilitator pounded the gavel, and the auditorium erupted in shouts for order, with delegates raising their hands and making their way forward to be added to the speakers' list. The first speaker, a young man with round glasses, dashed up to the podium and read a resolution so quickly it was barely comprehensible. Heina leaned to the young man next to him and asked, "What did he say?"

"The independents want to push the SAJ leadership to take a stronger stand against the Nazis, and they've attached a no-confidence vote on the youth commission leadership." The young man with dark, serious eyes paused, surveying Heina's face. "What do you think about the Nazis? Are we going to have fascism in Germany?"

"Germany's not Italy," Heina said. "Hitler isn't connected to the military the way Mussolini was, so I don't think he can pull off a putsch. Sooner or later people are going to see that the Nazis are just like marionettes, some flighty distraction that the capitalists are using to scare people." I give Heina these words because such arguments were batted back and forth frequently in the pages of leftist newspapers before Hitler took power.

The young man turned to look at the stage, pursing his lips as if vaguely dissatisfied with Heina's answer. Heina winced to see that the young man had a fresh cut along the side of his neck. The young man glanced up at the podium, then ducked toward Heina to whisper furiously, "I think we're not taking the Nazis seriously enough. You've heard that horrible slogan, right? *Willst du nicht mein Bruder sein, so schlag ich dir den Schädel ein*," he said, repeating the singsong rhyme of the Nazi thugs: "You don't want to be my friend? Then I'll smash you in your head."

Heina opened his mouth to reply, but the facilitator, now red in the face and sweating, pounded the gavel on the podium thunderously. Heina jerked his head up and realized that the whole auditorium had been abuzz with similar side conversations. "The no-confidence vote against Comrade Ollenhauer has been brought to the floor. Will all certified delegates supporting the motion please raise your cards to be counted . . ."

SAJ history tells me that the attempt to steer the youth toward more direct anti-Nazi work, contained in a no-confidence vote in SAJ head Ollenhauer, failed 98–28. I wish so badly to know how Heina voted, exactly when he raised his card to be counted.

My uncle Klaus tells me that Heina was close enough to the national youth leader to have hosted coffees with the man at the Buschmann home, but maybe Heina had the clarity to see that the SAJ had not taken a strong enough stand. Or maybe he held his card in support of the elected leadership. Ollenhauer got up to thank the crowd, oozing forceful charisma, as if he'd just won a unanimous election rather than surviving a pointed challenge to his leadership. I wonder if Heina felt, like many, that the SAJ needed someone who could make your skin tingle with the force of his words. Everyone from right to left said Germany needed a strong leader, a *Führer*. The Left was asking itself where it could find Germany's Lenin, and the Right was waiting for a new Bismarck, someone strong-willed, to step in and take charge.

One of the sweetest inheritances I found in Heina's folder of papers was a simple to-do list scratched on rough brown paper, illegible except for the days of the week—*Montag, Dienstag, Mittwoch* . . .—in a column, each followed by a note, a word. I imagine Heina sitting for a moment, overwhelmed with the rush of promises and the march of hours, by the stress and joy of his son Heinrich's impending birth, sketching out a plan to remember it all and contain the chaos. I picture Heina keeping this list in his pocket for guidance: Tuesday—was that the Citizens' Working Group against Inflation? No wait, alternating Tuesdays was the coalition meeting between the communists and the SPD . . . I imagine him standing on a street corner as he stopped to pull out his cheat sheet.

Workers on midday break jostled around him in every direction. The raging inflation meant that a paycheck plummeted in value between its printing and the end of the same workday. Workers learned to use their lunch breaks to buy sausage and potatoes rather than wait until evening for grocery shopping, when the wages would be devalued as the currency dropped further each hour. As a child I heard stories about this inflation and formed strange pictures of a country long ago where it took a suitcase full of bills to buy a loaf of bread. Decades later my uncle Klaus pulled a stack of billion mark notes from a dining room sideboard drawer, a curiosity of zeroes and flourished engravings.

Heina squinted at the pencil scrawls on the rough piece of paper. Tonight was the youth coalition meeting. He steadied his hat on his head. Had he told Friedchen he'd miss dinner again? This morning before he'd left for work she'd looked at him as though she didn't know him anymore. The small slip of paper in Heina's pocket felt as heavy as a handful of coins. There was no group he could justify withdrawing from, but anxiety churned in his stomach. Was she angry at him, or was it the early months of pregnancy making her foggy and sad?

He'd tried to distract her at breakfast this morning while she wiped Inge's mouth. "Come with me to the Bochum meeting tonight," Heina said. "Some of the kids who started that youth paper, the *Red Fighter*, will have a table, and Kurt Schumacher is speaking. He's going to stand up to the party right-wingers."

Friedchen spread ersatz butter on a thin slice of bread and set it on the edge of the plate. She'd learned so many ways to stretch

Heina's salary, like cutting the bread as thin as paper. But Heina
... well, he wasn't the type to notice these things now—not while
gangs of Nazis roamed the streets of Berlin, smashing windows
of Jewish shopkeepers to celebrate the 1930 election. But hadn't
it also been insane their whole lives? When would it stop?

Heina bit his lip, getting a clear message from Friedchen's silence, her empty plate. "I'm sorry. Is something wrong?"

She shook her head no, instinctively, but then looked at the
tablecloth, trying to think of a way to say it without hurting him
too badly. "I hear about Kurt Schumacher constantly," she said.
"And how often do you talk about your own daughter? Have you
said her name half as often as his?"

Heina put his elbows on the table and put his face in his hands.
Had his parents faced these moments? If anything, Mama would
rather stand on the barricades than cook. But he hadn't wanted
to marry an iron rod like Mama. He'd desperately wanted a human being, a real woman who would show him affection, not
just lecture him about economics and strategy. Now he had her,
and he was botching it up.

"I'm sorry," he said. "It's just—well, it's just because of the
area leadership position, all these extra meetings. I . . . I won't run
again next term. This is the worst of it—it's a major change for the
SPD coming down the road, and we'll both feel good later knowing I put my all into helping reform the party." The words sounded
desperately empty. Heina, I put these thoughts in your head only
because I've uttered similar promises to myself and others. I've
worn those excuses so thin that my husband laughs at them now:
This is the bad week, I promise. Next month will be fine and I can relax.

The kitchen blurred before Heina's eyes. If only she would
rage at him—he deserved it. He felt terrible for hurting her, leaving her alone in this house with Mama, who made snide comments about the Hammond girl Heina should have married.

He took her hand. "I promise we'll look back at this and laugh, knowing we pulled through together."

There must have been moments of peace, of course. I imagine a Saturday in mid-September 1931 when a blanket of activity covered the Ruhr, but there was nothing on Heina's calendar or lists that he absolutely had to attend. He relished Friedchen's surprise when at the breakfast table she asked him, "What's going on today?" and he nonchalantly said, "Nichts!"

"Do you have shopping you need help with? Or we could go into Recklinghausen," he said. Friedchen blushed as if he'd asked her for a date. He cut open a roll for Inge and spread it with margarine and then a thin slice of liverwurst.

"No butter!" Inge squealed.

"You have to have butter," he explained. "It seals the bread." I heard this argument as a child but never understood my aunt Inge's firm philosophy about the composition of a heavy breakfast roll.

A soft tap-tap floated up from the stairwell, and although Friedchen looked at Heina, he shrugged and ignored it, hoping it was the coal delivery, which Jupp could take care of for once. Heavy footsteps sounded up the stairs, followed by a knock on the door. Heina caught Friedchen's eyes, a silent apology for the interruption. He dusted crumbs from his lap and opened the door.

Rudi Heiland stood in the doorway, his bright brown eyes glowing and his round face mottled with red. "Rudi!" Heina said. "*Guten Morgen.* Have you eaten breakfast?"

Friedchen called hello to Rudi from the kitchen. She had always liked sincere Rudi, son of legendary local SPD political leader Guido Heiland. Rudi held his hat, full of apologies. He waved at Inge and made faces at six-month-old Heinz, both of whom were immediately transfixed, as always, by his bright eyes and inviting face.

"Come in and have some coffee," Heina said, leading him into the kitchen, but Rudi hung back.

"Heina," he said. "I'm terribly sorry to bother you, but I have to talk to you. Ridiculous on a Saturday, I know, but . . ."

Heina motioned for Rudi to take a chair. He still saw Rudi as the breathless goofball on the soccer field from years ago, but now he looked so grave. Had someone been killed?

"Heina, don't look so pale—it's not life and death." Rudi folded his hands and put his elbows on his knees, leaning forward. Only twenty-three years old, Rudi seemed aged with concern. "My father—I can't imagine what he'll do," he said, then stopped. He twirled his hat between his hands, looked up brightly. "Anyway—I'm quitting the SPD. I had to talk to you to see what you thought."

Heina's stomach flipped, a free fall becoming more and more familiar as comrades departed for left-wing parties. What was that stab in his heart? It was selfish loneliness. Rudi, of all people.

"Why?" Heina asked. Then he rubbed the back of his neck and had to laugh despite himself, breaking the tension. "I mean— that's no tough question, is it?"

The SPD had voted again last year to fund the capitalist war buildup, buying into the argument of the grizzled and paranoid military leaders that Germany faced imminent invasion from the west or the east. Now even the youth group leaders had swallowed the fear-mongering as they stressed discipline and obedience in this mindset of fear.

"You understand," said Rudi, his coal-bright eyes glistening as he leaned forward and looked at Heina. "That's why I'm joining the Socialist Workers' Party. I look in the mirror in the mornings, see that damn SPD pin on my lapel, and I tell you, it takes a lot to keep down my breakfast."

Heina glanced toward the kitchen. Each morning conversation with Friedchen, the quick murmurs over the newspaper and quiet sentences as they fed the children, touched on the SPD and the rumors of a new opposition party. Friedchen supported this new party, the SAP, yet another left-wing effort to rebuild. She said she would join herself if she had time and was still active in politics—especially after the SPD had expelled its left-wing members in August. But Papa Heinrich's belief that it was easier to change "the devil we know" rang in Heina's ears.

Friedchen quietly set two cups of coffee on the table between Rudi and Heina. Rudi smiled and eagerly grabbed his cup, sloshing the steaming liquid over his fingers. He set the cup down on the table and reached for his handkerchief to mop up the mess.

"Look at this, Friedchen—I'm a bull in a china shop," Rudi said as he pushed coffee around on the tabletop.

"Don't worry about it," she said. "I'll get a towel."

"No!" he said, jumping up to run into the kitchen ahead of her. He returned with a rag from the sink.

As Rudi wiped up the coffee, Friedchen crossed her arms and smiled. "You've got my vote anytime, Chancellor Heiland," she said.

He bowed and sat down, still holding the wet rag. "Good! That's the women's vote all lined up, then." They laughed, and Friedchen held out her hand to collect the dishrag.

"Your father is going to be furious," Heina said. Rudi's face fell, and Heina knew it wasn't the right thing to say—even though it was true. He backpedaled. "Our fathers come from a different era. The party needs to be flexible, but right now we can't even debate these questions." As Heina spoke, agitation stirred in his chest. He heard his own voice admitting he wasn't happy in the SPD. If that was true, shouldn't he do something?

"So you'll leave with me," Rudi said, angling the words up an octave at the end, a hopeful half question.

Heina broke off eye contact and took a long drink of coffee. The word "yes" rested on his tongue uneasily. If he uttered it and meant it, the next dreadful steps were clear: he would laugh with fear and delirium as he agreed to sign a SAP card. He would sit and talk for the afternoon about recruitment and the wave of organizing needed in the neighborhood; these steps were almost automatic. Once Heina would have jumped at the invitation. But strangely, his years of battling with the SPD leadership had made him more attached to the party. Maybe he couldn't bear to admit that the heartache over those struggles had been unproductive.

"Ahh, Rudi," Heina said. "My dad always says if we cut up the SPD, we've got no power left."

Rudi nodded emphatically, fighting to show no trace of regret in his eyes. "Of course," he said. "I understand. Don't hold this adventure against me, my friend."

Heina invited Rudi to stay for breakfast, but Rudi was already late for an appointment. Rudi's footfalls sounded hollowly down the wood stairs. Heina shut the door and leaned his forehead against the wood. Was this what it was like—getting old? Heina had the sense of standing on the sidelines, watching as others moved to the front. Heina straightened his shoulders, flexing the muscles in his arms as he turned toward the kitchen. He was not old at all, barely thirty, and just now taking on the responsibility of being a man. Someone had to stay.

Thirty-seven years after Heina's death, I stood alone in the place where he raised his children, now home to the next two generations of his family. For weeks during this German research visit,

I'd hungrily eyed the high bookshelf spanning the broad arched doorway between the living room and the dining room. The top shelf held a row of my great-grandfather's coal-mining lamps, with rusted chimneys and glass globes. Beneath these stood a row of books that hadn't been touched in years, covered with a thick, silty layer of dust.

I wanted to see the volumes, but I didn't want to bother my aunt and uncle with still more mental and physical rearranging of furniture. Throughout my visit Uncle Klaus laughed at my hesitancy, my constant *Bitte* and *Danke* and fear of imposing. He said, "Sei nicht so Bescheid!" Don't be so . . . *Bescheid*. A strange word: I thought, as he said it, that it meant shy, withholding, nervous. Polite. And yet I felt so clumsy in reaching around the German handshakes, the stiff lips, the closed stories. Later I looked the word up to learn that it means "official decision," with notes of firmness and distance. It made me horribly sad to see my own German distance arise in those places when I didn't know how else to act.

With my aunt and uncle off on an errand, I saw my chance. I slipped off my shoes and pulled a heavy green upholstered chair to the center of the living room. I stood on the chair and reached up toward the hardback volumes. Someone—my grandfather?—had organized the books with the novels on the right-hand side of the shelf and the political works to the left.

I took down a volume and flipped through the pages, feeling Heina all around me in the intimate moment of sharing a book. Was he looking over my shoulder, maybe laughing to see his American granddaughter standing sockless on a chair in his former bedroom? His signature, now familiar with its faded fountain pen blur, graced the book's first page. I looked up again to scan the range of titles. I wasn't surprised to see the dusty volume of Marx's theories on political economy, which sat on the shelf like a squat beer stein, but I wasn't prepared for the life story of Stalin or a book of excerpts from Lenin's essays. I reached up for the thin volume of Lenin and felt my grandfather trying to scream something at me from across the distance between his death and my birth, but I couldn't make out the words. I didn't understand whether these books would have been the possessions of any good SPD member, or whether these were signs that my grandfather looked toward the communists with a more complex reaction than closed-minded contempt.

It was ordinary shyness that made me hurry through this treasure. I didn't flip through each page of each text, looking for penciled notes in the margin, the possible errant news clipping or note tucked between pages. Of course they were there. I tell myself I don't need to know whether Heina Buschmann agreed with Lenin's position on newspapers as a party-building apparatus. But I care now that I was too *Bescheid*, too polite, to ask so that I might see the exact shade of red that ran in Heina's veins.

Maybe I was afraid to know too much. I want to make my grandfather into someone who would question party doctrine. But if he was rabidly anticommunist, many historians would describe him as part of the left-wing paralysis that ushered in Hitler. Maybe that's what all this is about, the American granddaughter's search for a pure German forefather to assuage her own sense of familial guilt about being German, or American, at all.

I took furtive, quick pictures of the title pages of these books. Back in the United States I got the photos developed and saw the titles on the faded book covers blurred into clouds of white and red, out of focus and illegible.

Inge stood eye level with the table, her blond bangs and blue eyes showing above the tabletop. "Almost three years old," Heina said. "Such a big girl!"

Inge ran around the side of the table and stood next to her father. "Tomorrow," she said.

"No, your birthday is in six days, January 27, 1932. Six more times going to bed."

Friedchen carried Heinz out of the bedroom. The baby wheezed thickly. "*Mein Gott*. Why is he breathing like that?" Heina asked.

"A bad cold," Friedchen said. "I don't know what's wrong. I took him to the doctor last week, and he said it would pass. I'll put a hot poultice on his chest to loosen him up." Her forehead creased as she ran her thumb along Heinz's soft cheek. Friedchen had the same cold, and her face was pale from the strong nausea sweeping over her—pregnant yet again. She wiped her hand across her forehead. Heina felt an urge to get up and wrap his arms around her. Inge tried to balance on tiptoes to reach something on the table, fell, and burst into tears. Heina picked her up and grabbed his lunch. He walked over and rubbed Friedchen's back.

"He gets his terrible lungs from his father," Heina said. Friedchen looked up at him, bleary-eyed, asking him wordlessly for help. "What can I do?" he asked. "I have to go to military training today for the Iron Front." The SPD Reichsbanner militia had merged into the Iron Front, a more militant group with communists and independents ready to battle the Nazis in the street. "Do you want me to have Mama take Inge for the day?"

Friedchen's gentle eyes cut into him. "Have your father take her to the miners' co-op with him," she said. Then she brightened her voice and addressed Inge. "You'd like that, wouldn't you, *Schatz*? Going to the co-op with Opa?"

Heina took Inge downstairs to her grandfather and walked toward the local Iron Front gathering, which met at a firing range near the woods on the west edge of town. Jupp was already there, joking with new members who practiced loading pistols. The lifetime military men in this group, mostly conservatives from the Reichsbanner, stood at ease in well-worn jackets, hands comfortably cradling weapons, thumbs threaded through suspenders. Another group of young leftists like Heina had joined the Iron Front this past winter. In these times even die-hard anti-militarists had to admit that weapons might be necessary if only in self-defense. Histories of the Iron Front describe how local groups rarely had enough pistols or rifles to go around. I imagine the younger recruits drilling for an hour in basic military formation using broomsticks and branches. The men formed stiff rectangles and lines. Heina may have wondered whether this orderly stiffness would help against the Nazis, who often ran amuck in SPD demonstrations, arms outstretched and clubs swinging.

After the drills a young man named Felix yelled to the crowd to meet near the supply truck to talk about propaganda work. "Comrades!" said Felix. "We're chalking next weekend in Dorsten, because there's a big Nazi gathering there. We'll need you to take the last night train in and meet at the SPD hall, and then start out on the streets at around 3:00 a.m. The basic designs are on this worksheet . . ."

Felix passed around designs of logos with the "Three Arrows," which stood for the Unity, Discipline, and Activity of the Iron Front, to be drawn over the swastikas the Nazi had painted everywhere. Chalking actions, along with traveling political choruses and new posters with bold graphics, had been amazingly successful in drawing young people to the Iron Front. Felix described the planned militant bust-up of the Dorsten Nazi meeting.

Heina may have been confident until now that the Nazis were harmless buffoons. Some lefties in these prewar times offered complicated, theory-based proofs about why the Nazis had no base in the working class. And plenty of SPD folks still believed

the communists were the real threat, even after the Nazis formed
a powerful coalition with the military and other far-right parties.
The SPD turned Janus-faced, fighting Left and Right, backing itself into a corner but too timid to offer a real concrete alternative.

An hour later Heina walked up the street toward home, wondering whether or not to apologize. *Sweetheart, I'm sorry I'm late
again, but you know it was for a good cause . . .* He stopped himself.
No need to make her feel guilty on top of every other burden.

Heading around the shrubs near their yard, he nearly collided
with Papa. The older man stood in the street, stock-still and bare-
headed, staring up into the sky. "What is it?" Heina asked. The
night air, the cold, the stones all burst into sharp focus. Heina
held his breath. "Is it Mama?"

"It's your boy," Papa said, expressionless. "He's gone."

"Gone where?" asked Heina. "To the hospital?"

Papa stared. The world stopped turning and there was nothing
in Heina's head. He dropped his coat and hat on the sidewalk, ran
up the stairs, and threw open the apartment door. Friedchen sat on
the kitchen floor, her head leaning against one of the table legs.

"What have you done?" he yelled. "Where is Heinz?"

She was never one to yell, but the tone of her voice stopped
him cold. "What have I *done*? I was *with* my son when he died."

She dissolved into tears. You had to be ready to lose children;
they weren't yours, really, until they'd made it past their first
birthday. Until then, especially with all the pneumonia and the
TB, it was never safe. But her sweet boy . . . he was not gone. Was
not. Could not be.

Heina, her sane, rational, loving Heina, may have berated her.
"Why didn't you take him to the doctor? Where is the doctor
now? What did they do for him? How did you not know he was
so sick?"

Heina dimly saw Friedchen sitting on the floor, but all he could do was formulate questions. He knew that if he stopped talking for a second, he would lose his mind. Night crept into the apartment. There was a knock at the door, and Friedchen was collected and taken to her parents' apartment. Inge was somewhere, too, being cared for. But if Heina left that kitchen chair, the world would slide like a thin ice floe into the depths of the sea.

So he sat, not eating, not sleeping or undressing. He willed away his thoughts and sunk himself into reviewing every memory and every moment with his young son. Several times during the night he convinced himself that the whole thing was untrue, then got up and went into the bedroom to check the empty crib. He laid his hand on the cold mattress, as if the warm skin of a child could be felt beneath this emptiness.

Hours later yellow light came in the front windows. Heina knew the many things he had to do: inquire about funeral arrangements, find Friedchen and apologize to her for his ghastly, insane lack of strength. And, of course, he had to face his parents, to see in their eyes the contempt that would come with letting a grandson die, the grandson named Heinrich after Heina and also after his father.

There will never be another Heinrich Buschmann. That name has been ripped out by the roots. Heinrich went to the tap and splashed water on his face, drank from his cupped hands, and comforted himself with the thought that he could die any number of ways now, easily. He could step in front of a Nazi truncheon at the opportune moment, fall from a streetcar. Those were the ways out for the cowards, but the end could be also made to look very brave and useful, so that no one would know or be ashamed.

Pairing history and family chronology reveals a brutal crush of days. I imagine that the small and sick comfort after Heinz's death was that the world seemed to be showing its worm-eaten guts, and they matched Heinrich's thoughts. Mama despised him, he knew, for being so weak as to get so attached to a child, but he didn't care. She had never lost a son, never tasted the depths of this bitterness.

After baby Heinz's funeral, the SPD had surged further rightward to support Hindenburg's campaign in the March elections. The old general's sole selling point seemed to be that he was not Hitler. The SA and SS were briefly banned in April due to pressure from socialist Prussia, the chancellor was ousted because of financial scandals, and the new chancellor, Von Papen, began actively courting the Nazis, hoping to bring them under control with the paradoxical strategy of giving them more power.

By May Friedchen's third pregnancy had begun to show. In quiet and sane moments Heina began to chip away at the huge monolith of Heinz's death. It needed to mean something, to make sense. Was it his fault? If he had stayed home from the Iron Front meeting that night, he might have noticed Heinz was fading . . . but could he work miracles? Friedchen had done everything she could. Part of the blame must rest with the economic crisis and political chaos, the pay cuts that meant they couldn't buy vegetables or pay for a hospital stay. Walking in the woods, Heina felt the painful twinge of his heart thawing. Politics, a system for understanding and containing the world, once again prevented him from going mad.

That gratitude, however, was sorely tested by the summer. The SPD mobilized its forces before the July 1932 Reichstag elections, but the Nazis loudly promised to rescue the working class from its misery. At the height of the election buildup, on the morning of July 20, 1932, a coalition of right-wingers in Berlin launched a takeover of the government in Prussia. The SPD national paper had threatened violence, a general strike, to reclaim socialist Prussia by force. Throughout Germany people gathered on street corners, waiting for the call from their leaders to strike.

In Marl-Hüls, I imagine the stacks of morning papers arriving like bursts of lightning exploding on contact with dry grassland. Workingmen stood holding their newspapers and clutching fists nervously in their pockets, smiling at each other, giddy and unsure. Young boys volunteered to run to the SPD hall, the union locals, to see if word had come down from the national offices. In the midst of this half-carnival atmosphere, Heina waited, positive that today would mean no work, that the beautiful feeling from the revolution eleven years earlier would return. He remembered that boy riding with posters balanced on the handlebars of a borrowed bicycle who believed the world was about to be made new.

One report explained that the call for a strike would be delayed. The SPD locals told their members to report to work. The evening papers announced with cagey and muted fear that the Left would lose a strike if it were launched now; we'd be crushed. There are too many unemployed, the communists would turn on us . . . Fear, fear, fear.

Street violence among the Iron Front, Nazis, and the communists escalated to a feverish level as unorganized tension broke forth. Decades later historians would pull this key moment, this left-wing deadlock, from the muddle of daily events to clarify the knot that tightened with each day: the SPD leadership in Berlin watched the streets for rank-and-file signals of revolutionary desire, but the grassroots workers had been told only to obey, to keep discipline. The good Germans, trained in party organization, restrained themselves as they waited for a sign from on high that did not come.

Four days after the Prussian putsch Friedchen went into labor. Heina, down in the yard under the cherry tree, heard her ragged screams through the open window. His mother came outside to stand with him, trying in her hard and practical way to offer useful advice. "Don't name the baby Karl-Heinz," she said. "It's bad luck to name a living baby after a dead one."

He shook with a fatalistic fear, convinced Friedchen would die, and at the same time nursing a strange hope that the birth of this child signaled hope that the world would turn in a positive direction, a reading of tea leaves to prophesy that the Nazis could be crushed.

What did Heina do in the week after his second son was born—his son Karl-Heinz, named despite his mother's warning in an indirect attempt to have another Heinrich? I imagine he was terrified to leave his wife and child, but terrified not to. Did he go out to distribute leaflets with the local election committee? He must have.

On July 31 the Nazi Party earned 230 seats in parliament, 37 percent of the vote, with the Communists getting 14 percent, and the SPD electorate ever shrinking. That fall, as Heina's blond son Karl-Heinz learned to smile, one in three Germans were on welfare, and the suicide rate in Germany was triple that of Britain. The Nazis and the Communists, a bizarre pair of bedfellows, united to support a Berlin transit strike, and when the SPD failed to support the strike it lost still more adherents. One historical account mentions that people passing each other on the streets replaced the normal greeting of "Guten Tag" with "So kann es nicht weitergehen"—It can't go on like this.

On January 30, 1933, Hindenburg appointed Hitler chancellor, after interviewing him twice for the post and finding him unimpressive and mentally deficient. This time, however, a close group of advisors pressured the aging and confused Hindenburg to rein in the raging beast of democracy. Many people in Marl-Hüls didn't see Hitler as much of a threat. The largest area

newspaper, the *Recklinghausen People's Paper*, reported as its banner headline that day that the ice was melting on Haltern Lake.

The day after Hitler became chancellor, the day after his Nazi
men opened their mouths with laughing delight at how easy it
had been to stroll into power, there was a knock at the door of
the Buschmann home, according to a story from my uncle Klaus.
Maybe Heinrich Sr. was home from the co-op for his lunch break,
eating soup slowly, feet resting half out of his slippers as he sat
at the head of the table on the L-shaped corner bench in the
kitchen. The banging of fists on the front door created a ripple
of waves in Heinrich's soup, and he put down his spoon.

"Lina!" he called into the yard.

Later that afternoon Heina returned from work to see a single
book lying face up on the front porch. Papa stood in the threshold with his arms crossed.

"The last time socialism was outlawed they weren't this
quick," said Papa. "Hitler, apparently, isn't wasting any time."

"What did they take?" Heina asked.

"I don't know—they only left minutes ago. They went upstairs.
It's a mess down here. Took a few books, and some they ruined.
A perfectly good set of Marx's *Capital*, but of course those idiots don't even know enough to take August Bebel." Papa Heinrich sighed. "It was papers they wanted. They took our address
book." Papa seemed almost relieved by this turn of events, as if a
hammer held above them had fallen without any major injuries.

In the third-floor apartment, Heina knelt to stack the contents
of a dumped bookshelf in the hallway. Friedchen had been away
at her mother's with the children, *Gott sei Dank*, but the Nazis has
staved in the door and emptied the desk and various drawers. A
few books were missing, not even the most subversive ones, and
they'd left the huge stack of old saj newspapers.

Heina turned over piles of papers. Where was his slim brown

folder, the one that contained most of his current political work? It held notes, to-do lists, addresses, and plans for upcoming SAJ activities. He imagined the folder still in the apartment somewhere, missed by the quick and careless eyes of the SA men. But every membership list, both the area SPD list and the local and regional SAJ contact sheets, had been taken. Heina sorted and stacked papers, fighting to ignore the thrumming of panic. He grabbed his hat and muttered, "This is clearly illegal. The SPD must act. This goes no further." He didn't dare to utter a half-formed thought: the names. His people.

Papa and Heina walked together to the home of Hans Schuyer, the SPD leader for Marl-Hüls. Papa seemed stern but unruffled, his cheeks reddened by the January wind. He coughed and laughed, recounting bits of stories from years past about house searches, lost jobs, and relocations, as if having lived through those times would offer assurance that they'd survive them again.

Frau Schuyer opened the door with a subdued nod, and from behind her in the living room came the noise of a loud gathering. An older comrade spotted Papa on the step and said, "You were slow about getting here, old man!"

Heina added his coat to the pile on the hall bench. Hans Jr., the party leader's twenty-two-year-old son, pulled Heina into the kitchen with nervous energy and sidelong glances.

"Did they get your house, too?" Hans asked.

Heina nodded, noticing a stray pile of papers still spread haphazardly on the kitchen counter, a drawer pulled out and set on the sideboard. "They got the SAJ lists," Heina said. "I should have hidden them better . . . or something. But my father doesn't seem so worried. Or else he is and he's trying to hide it."

Hans's younger sister, her hair pulled back neatly, came in with a waterproof canvas duffle bag and laid it on the table. "Everyone's here," she said. "They must have gone through thirty houses in Marl."

"What's in the bag?" Heina asked.

She reached in and pulled out the corner of a rich red fabric edged with gold tassels. Heina recognized it immediately—the Marl-Hüls SPD flag. "Also some books," she said. "We're going to hide them where they won't be found. Did you ever play that game Capture the Flag?" She smiled wide, showing her eyeteeth. "We'll win this round."

"Let's go bury it out at Gänsebrink," Heina said. "They won't know where to look." This sad but hopeful detail—a buried party flag—survived in the brief telling of Uncle Klaus's story, and for some reason I imagine the limber young people stealing out into the night with the red cloth, their natural destination being the park near the youth home.

Hans, his sister, a younger brother, and Heina left the close heat of the kitchen and the roaring conversation. Heina had the loosest coat, so he was elected to carry the tightly rolled bag under his arm. It calmed Heina to walk in the cool of the evening with a specific mission toward the youth home. This act, at least, was practical. And if Hitler lost power in six months, as many predicted, the youth group would have a wonderful unearthing ceremony, the flag would smell a bit musty, and that would be that.

Hans seemed to be thinking much the same, and he hoisted his spade like a baton and joked with his brother as they crossed the street. His sister, twelve and thin as a rail, moved her lips silently as if counting houses or bicycles. She peered into the windows they passed. As the roof of the tall school became visible above the bare treetops, she turned to Hans and asked, "Is Dad going to jail?"

As if by agreement, Hans and Heina scoffed and shook their

heads, explained to her all the reasons why the Nazis were bluff-
ing and making a show of empty power.

The next morning, however, after the bag had been buried
and the dirt safely patted in place, word began to trickle back
through the SPD network as friends met at the bakery and on
street corners. Schmidt was taken in for questioning and came
back with his nose broken, it was such a mess, you should have
seen his face; Herr Konstanz was taken early yesterday, with no
word since, and his wife is about to lose her mind—should we
hire a lawyer? I heard the next SPD meeting's been cancelled, no
use giving them an easy target; that whip-smart organizer from
Bochum came home with two fingers mashed beyond repair—
he's a miner, what is he going to do now? . . .

Over the next few weeks the gossip mill and force of specula-
tion led Heina and the Hüls SAJ group to guess that one of their
own youth group members, Paul Plottki, had led the Nazis to the
area socialist leadership lists at the Buschmann house, which
gave the Nazis fodder for the round of local house searches.
The name Paul Plottki, according to Uncle Klaus, was ever after
marked with bitterness in the Buschmann family. I wonder why
Plottki ratted out his comrades, apparently without much pressure. Did he intend to reap personal gain, or did he speak out of
fear? Maybe he intended to save himself, believing that the Nazis
would find him one way or another, knowing his name was on
a list, thinking his only option was to tell the SA everything he
knew. Maybe he had a family. Maybe he told himself that to keep
his child's father alive, he had to sacrifice the parents of other
children.

Local history records a huge rally on the market square in
Recklinghausen on February 4. The Nazi newspaper reports over
twenty-five thousand people in attendance at the rally, including groups of schoolchildren brought by their teachers. These

children: their eager eyes, the furtive grasping of hands so as to not get lost in the rumbling crowd, the scraping of worn buckled shoes on cobblestones, the sniffling in the cold air, the thrill of massive noise and shouting, the banners, the mothlike human surging toward whatever flame shows energy, movement, and power. Those teachers: was their attendance recommended or urged? Or were there fervent souls among them, bursting out of the school doors for the walk to the rally, convinced they were taking their classes to watch history being made, convinced their pupils needed to witness the birth of a new country, the strong country that they as true Germans deserved?

The account in the paper quotes one of the speakers on the platform, who uttered these words into the cold air: "The Individual is nothing. A name is smoke and mist. The Nation is our patriotic conscience, our calling and our God-given task. The Fatherland is everything!"

8

The Führer's Peace

There was undoubtedly rich, fragrant coffee in a silver urn, and possibly a thin torte glistening with fruit in the middle of the gleaming oak table. The owner of a major steel manufacturers blotted a spot of spilled coffee with a napkin. "Is there an agenda for this meeting?" he asked.

The man seated next to him, a senior executive at the chemical company IG-Farben, opened his mouth to speak. He paused, searching for words. "We know who called the meeting. That, for me, is enough."

The historical record confirms that on the morning of February 20, 1933, the heads of Krupp, the Auguste Viktoria mining company, and other corporate leaders were seated around the table. I imagine twenty minutes passed. Then Chancellor Adolf Hitler strode in, launching into a speech. His voice darted quickly, outlining a summary of his success at smashing the "swines" of German communism. He lingered on the rough consonants of the word with a pleased sort of rage, winding up the volume on his voice until the sound seemed to ring against the panes of glass. Abruptly, then, his wishes: the right-wing coalition needed to win in this coming election, by whatever means necessary. For the good of the German people.

Most of these men had met Hitler before, and I hope—pointlessly—that they noticed his insanity, his inability to hold a normal gaze; his eyes either drilled theirs with an unnatural intensity or looked above their heads as if addressing an invisible audience in a large amphitheater. He gave a quick bow, thanked them for their time, then stood and left the room. After a short pause, Hitler's future finance minister cleared his throat.

"It seems we need an election fund. I propose 3 million marks as an even figure. Anyone care to make a counterproposal?" The mine owner, a member of Germany's other far-right party, nodded and grunted. One by one, the other men agreed. History confirms Hitler's corporate support, down to the deutsche mark.

A week later, as the election neared, flames broke out in the Reichstag parliamentary building in Berlin. Some believed the Nazis had struck the match. Hitler used the event as cause to take swift action against "Bolshevik terror," and the Nazis immediately limited Germans' rights to hold meetings and publish newspapers. The next day forty-seven communists were arrested in Marl and charged with planning to incite terror. Articles in area newspapers claimed the communists had planned to break all of the street lamps, then loot grocery stores and set off bombs.

A Nazi Party member approached Guido Heiland at work, sliding a copy of Hitler's latest tract across the desk.

"Have you read it?" the man asked. "We could use someone like you, you know."

Guido—veteran of the Great War, the German Revolution, the miners' strikes, the Ruhr occupation, and countless other struggles—didn't know his last major battle in Germany had begun. With the early March sunshine in the window, this conversation seemed innocuous. Maybe he could argue with this fool and pull him back from the brink of utter stupidity.

"My friend," Guido said, voice rumbling and brusque, "believe me, I've read Hitler's work. And I have several problems with it. For starters, he doesn't understand the economic issues facing German workers, and he's trying to distract us with this racial bullshit . . ."

That evening Guido rounded the corner onto Schillerstraße with his hands in his pockets, head down, deep in thought. He jerked his head up at the staccato slap of boots on cobblestone, and his hat tumbled into the gutter. Marl history describes some details of this attack, but I have to imagine others: I picture a large force of seven SA men, boots and buttons carefully shined, descending like a single beast. Guido could have been ready, could have taken them, if there hadn't been so many, if they hadn't been primed on adrenaline.

They left him on the pavement, blood smeared across his face, curled into a ball. Five or six spectators stood on the sidewalk like chess pieces, unsure whether Heiland's body was bait in a new kind of trap. Would the first who crouched to help this man be marked a traitor? One young man took off running toward the Heilands' house.

The next day a policeman stopped Guido's son Rudi as the young man, his face creased with worry, left the hospital. This cop, a longtime acquaintance of the family, glanced over his shoulder and then leaned quickly toward Rudi's ear. "Your father will be dead soon. He needs to leave."

Rudi took in a long breath and held it. The cop's dark eyes shone with fear beneath his hat's plastic brim, the hatband marked with a silver swastika. "Danke," Rudi said.

Within twenty-four hours the Heiland family packed Guido into a borrowed car. Thick bandages covered his jaw, a splint held his leg, and a cast enclosed a hand that had been completely crushed and would be crippled for the rest of his life. Guido's daughter smuggled him over the border into Holland. Wincing in pain, watching the trees whip by the speeding car and wondering about the safety of the family he left behind, Guido wanted only to recuperate and then come back for revenge. He could not imagine that he'd be gone for twelve years.

Here my imagination fails to illuminate a path into the terror of the Third Reich. I will try to remember that my grandfather couldn't imagine the Third Reich either. He saw those days and years spooling out ahead and behind him in a madness of details, with escalating force but no indication of when or how it might all end. The hindsight of a history book seals events against this utter uncertainty.

Shock and horror crept in imperceptibly as tolerance levels were slowly breached. At first there might only have been a sense of embarrassment and resignation: a far-right politician elected with the help of corporate cash and an expert PR machine, pandering to and exploiting people's fear and their religion. Not so unfamiliar. Disgusting, but comprehensible in its banality. Then the confusion: should the Left have worked harder to support a moderate or centrist candidate? The public couldn't really be this stupid, because the public . . . well, we believe in the people. So the Left must somehow be at fault. Anyway, our Führer is a simple nut, stupid and bumbling, barely able to form a coherent sentence! Favorite bits of insanity, outrageous quotes, were traded with head-shaking laughter. Hitler's team, however, was sane and calculating enough to send out his message and grasp power using the gears and

levers of a democracy that felt itself on shaky ground, nudged
on all sides by fear.

At first Heina and his comrades might have rolled their eyes
and maybe laughed with a weary cynicism: have we drastically
overestimated our own countrymen? Didn't these people—especially the workers—see that these promises were completely
empty, that Hitler would not be bringing peace and economic
prosperity? And what was it with the swastika crap, these banners and nighttime torch marches? Are we really animals, scared
and riveted by fire into throwing off millennia of civilization?
Heina and his group, after all, were living in a parallel country,
insulated a bit from the raw edges of fear with their deep Red culture and community. The book burnings and bannings were also
not a surprise, a propaganda move borrowed from the 1890s, the
last time socialism was declared a public enemy. But who were
the average citizens in the photographs, taking such glee in feeding the flames?

Still, you roll your eyes and think with a definite hope: this is
evidence that things have gone too far. Every surge rightward becomes a kind of bitter satisfaction, and you take hope from the
belief that your fellow citizen will be eventually repulsed when his
own sense of innate decency is violated. You have ultimate faith
in this sense of decency. I imagine, despite the insanity of 1933,
a perverse hope that this brief blot on the country would act like
smelling salts or a smack in the face, that every day would unearth
more scandals, and that scandals might be the tonic, the medicinal
cure, to leach out the poison and bring this country to its senses.
You might take hope in the wretched news because there was no
other solace, thinking that at least things couldn't get worse.

In Bochum, to the south of Marl, in towns all over the Ruhr that
March, SA members dragged thousands of communists and so-

cialists into warehouses, jails, and basements and beat them. In Recklinghausen, the Nazis won eighteen seats on the city council, and the SPD won four. The communists received six seats but were then barred from the meeting hall. Marl accounts reveal that SPD members were let in the doors to the city council but not allowed to vote.

On April 1 posters went up in and around Recklinghausen urging Germans not to patronize Jewish-owned stores. A huge banner hung across a main street in Recklinghausen with the command, "Germans, don't buy from Jews. Whoever buys from Jews is a betrayer of the people." Newspaper ads justified the boycott by claiming Jews had exaggerated their mistreatment in Germany and had tried to turn the world against the Germans. Later that month Hitler requested four years without parliamentary oversight in order to run the country as he wished. Members of Parliament agreed, hoping a strong hand and ultimate authority would give Germany what it needed to survive this economic crisis. During the next few months people across the political spectrum slid, crept, or leapt toward the Nazis, out of opportunism or fear.

Walking to work through the crowds on Viktoriastraße, Heina might have felt disgust and rage as he tried to imagine how that smug man waiting for the streetcar, for example, honestly believed Hitler was best for Germany. Heina glanced up as he reached the courtyard in front of his workplace, which had always been named City Hall Court. Today it was Court of Adolf Hitler.

Hoping to save their skins or burrow into the new regime for safety, the German labor unions endorsed Hitler's official May 1 labor celebration and marched under a Nazi banner in Berlin. "Shit, no, not the miners!" said Papa. But yes, even the miners. Did the leaders think they could win at Hitler's game, or were they as trusting as children? The answer didn't matter. On May 2 unions across the country were shut down, their offices ransacked, and their leaders imprisoned.

Later in May Hitler announced that he would address the Reichstag with his plan for maintaining peace in Europe. "Boycott the speech!" cried a few SPD delegates, including Heina's hero, the young Ruhr reformer Kurt Schumacher. "We need to be there to disagree. We can't pull out and abandon the government to these goons," argued the SPD majority.

The day of Hitler's "peace" speech, only three SPD delegates chose to boycott: Schumacher, his comrade Mierendorff, and a female schoolteacher named Toni Pfülf. The rest of the SPD delegates filed in, only to hear, "Sorry, no time for responding statements." The call rang out for a vote in support of Hitler's peace resolution. *What to do? We knew he wouldn't carry it out . . . Have to vote yes, don't we, because this will show we were on the right side. Hold him to his word when he breaks it . . .* and other such fantasies. The SPD then voted, with the rest of Parliament, to endorse Hitler's empty peace resolution. Those in attendance remembered that a few SPD delegates even stood and joined in as the assembly sang "Deutschland, Deutschland, Über Alles!"

Three weeks later the boycotting delegates took their own stand. Schumacher and Mierendorff launched an illegal network against Hitler. Toni Pfülf, the young and idealistic activist and schoolteacher, hanged herself in her basement.

Toni's life and her choice are memorialized in Germany by a few street signs, but I couldn't find record of any monument. I want to ask Heina how he would feel about a space for lighting candles, for sitting and thinking about her kind of political desperation. Maybe a multicolored circle of wax candles or one tiny park. Or one room on this whole wide planet where the ruffling noise of traffic is muted, where the cell phone calls are blocked. Heina, did you despise her choice because you knew it was unavailable to you? What I really want to know, Heina, is whether you would think that I, too, am weak.

With all the options in the world, I stood holding a razor blade against my arm, alone in a grungy bathroom of an office space in Boston rented by a political youth project on the verge of messily shutting down. We had no money to pay ourselves. We had national action plans and allies and visibility and buzz, and despite all that crap, we were finished. I felt like it was partially my fault, in the sense that I could have figured out a solution if I were a whole lot smarter.

The razor blade was the only thing on the shelf besides a roll of toilet paper. The yellow globe light above the mirror was apartment-complex anonymous, and this plain fixture seemed to shame me for not being able to take advantage of the building's blank potential. I held the blade, not even wondering what it had been used to cut, why it was rusty, and why the former tenants had left it in this bathroom. I ran the blade against the pale inside of my forearm more than once. Through tunnel vision I saw lines of red, and the prickle of flesh sung with clarity. I didn't need medical care, and this was no suicide attempt.

Here's what matters: I felt trapped, downed in a dark office with a project bigger than I could control or manage. Hindsight whispers that in that moment I should have walked, well before I told myself that the problem was me. But hindsight is the easy part. I quit soon thereafter, but I didn't run away from politics or its seemingly unavoidable effect on my body and my mind.

Within two years I found myself at a socialist conference on a college campus in Michigan. My name had been put forth as part of a new national leadership slate. If I'd known you then, Heina, maybe you could have sustained me in that freezing college auditorium. The speakers' voices resonated with intricate logic and finely pointed rage to argue their cases before a vote. I slouched in my metal fold-up seat and cried, baffled at the intensity and the ire. We were accused of plotting a coup, which was news to me. I'd been added to the slate because I was young, female, and reasonably active. The votes were tallied, our slate was elected, and applause erupted.

I wiped my face and ran out of the auditorium to the road, then walked the far perimeter of the campus. I cried out loud in the heat, under the sun, telling myself in frustration, "Jesus! What's your problem? Do this!" With a red and puffy face I forced myself back into the building. I took a seat in a classroom as the new national leadership committee made its lists of urgent tasks. Even a time-management genius couldn't help me figure out how to shave minutes from hours to shoehorn this huge new responsibility into my life. But I agreed. I said yes. Then I bolted without saying good-bye. I tossed my sleeping bag into the cab of my pickup truck and gunned onto the highway.

Heina, I think my desire for politics, for leadership, for action, led to a sort of breakdown later that fall. It just doesn't all fit into one life, even if you push. I told no one besides my family. Without health insurance, after a week of being afraid to get in my car because I was too tempted by concrete embankments, I found a psychiatric emergency room, described my symptoms, got medication for anxiety.

Let me humbly propose a taxonomy of political depression, and tell me what you think. The moments I've told you about have been personal, my inability to fit myself into what was asked and to regulate the daunting balance of "no" to "yes." Then, one layer above, there is the larger sense of hopelessness when comrades betray you, which might have pushed Toni Pfülf over the edge. This is combined with the third stratum of depression, resulting from the cruelty of events, the way they can snap shut and close off escape routes.

This choking dead end descended when the Twin Towers rushed toward the earth in an endless loop, and the people ran, covered in ash, screaming. The future spooled out on the CNN ticker running beneath the images. We turned off cable news only to sleep. Hitler appeared in the wings like a movie prop: everyone from Bush to Saddam Hussein was painted with his name, a hot-button weapon still capable of eliminating thought decades after his death. Then the antiwar demos were organized, but I did not go out for a month. I sat on the couch and watched the news. I knew I could stand at a peace vigil holding a candle until my hands were flecked with burns from dripping wax, and it would not make a shred of difference. The rippled tidal wave set off by the rush of collapsing steel and concrete screamed over us, and I could only tuck myself into the fetal position and wait. That month I read about SPD members in Hitler's Germany who could not muster the strength to be active, and I understood that paralysis.

Each morning when Heina opened his eyes, I imagine that for a split second he was ageless, untouched. Then the realities of his life seeped in along with the light: one of his sons was dead. Politics was a waking nightmare. He swung his feet to the side of the bed, got up to fetch warm rolls from the bakery for his two living children, then rode his bicycle to work in Recklinghausen. Official swastika banners hung in windows at the police kiosks and shops.

Maybe Heina read about Toni's death in the Ruhr Echo, the illegal communist paper. A suicide brought the shiver of recognition as he remembered the colorless fingers of dread threatening to pull him under in the days after Heinz's death. He might have felt the need to stay away from the curb, brushing his sleeve against the bricks of storefronts, avoiding the temptation to jump in front of a streetcar. It was the most selfish of fantasies. A German man—and a revolutionary—would never admit to indulging in such weakness. If one's life was to be lost, at least let it be of some use.

That was the problem: determining the use of a life. He'd been surrounded by a vibrant spectrum of Red community, from fuchsia to scarlet to milky pink. Now that velvet protective cloak had grown threadbare and disintegrated. Most of the party leaders had emigrated. They drank coffee in Prague and Amsterdam, charting positions and issuing pronouncements from positions of safety, trying to operate the German working class like a hand puppet. Only a brave few, like Heina's hero Kurt Schumacher, chose not to flee.

Returning from the bakery one morning, Heina stopped short in the front hallway, almost tripping over his brother. Jupp sat on the floor, pulling straps on his hiking pack.

"There's a weeklong trip to the Hartz Mountains. It's going to be great!" Jupp said. "I'm sure I told you about it." He tightened a strap and lifted the pack onto his back. "By the way, old man, I need you to walk Else to work while I'm gone."

"For God's sake, Jupp," Heina sighed. Else, Jupp's girlfriend, worked at Julius Friedlich's dry-goods store on Hülsstraße, and Heina knew that this extra errand would make him late to work all week.

"The Nazis follow her if she goes alone," Jupp said. "They shove her and call her Jew-lover, because of the damn boycott."

"I'm sure she at least gives them a mouthful," Heina said.

"You have to love that about a woman," Jupp said. "A snapping tongue, just like Mama."

The next morning Heina kissed Friedchen goodbye. As he

neared the bottom of the stairs, Karl-Heinz let out a cry. Mama opened the stairwell door and yelled to Friedchen, "A baby wouldn't cry so much unless there was something wrong!"

Heina urged himself into battle. Do it, he said to himself, tell Mama to hold her tongue. His lips clung together as he slipped on his coat, hoping Mama could sense the rigid waves of anger he projected in her direction. He could launch a war and then Friedchen would have to withstand Mama's daylong retaliation. Maybe it was better not to provoke her. On this imagined morning, I see Heina falling into a trap, one that should have been illuminated by the stark light of his politics. Those who would divide life into separate realms of "his" and "hers" preached that the home—the kitchen, the children, the hearth—was the women's battlefield. I know that for some reason Heina felt powerless to intervene. Either he was afraid of his mother, or he had not read his August Bebel closely enough. How much blame can I assign this man, born in 1902, for not making his head a liberated space with regard to "the Woman Question"? Since we're talking, Heina, I will point out to you that the home is a workplace (see Friedrich Engels), and your wife needs a union. But if I play the smug granddaughter, I will have to fan out the cards of my own experience and reveal the many ways in which my home has been shrouded in layers, veils, and gauzy ribbons of false consciousness.

I never took my *tante* Else seriously. She would later marry Jupp, and even as a child I learned that Jupp's side of the family was associated with "something bad." How did I know this? A tension, frequent half-formed allusions barely explained to a four-year-old, a shrug in the garden outside my aunt Inge's house during visits. My mother would shake her head, try to explain what was impossible to communicate but was still real: something suspicious about Jupp, something during the war. A fracture between Jupp and Heina, barely visible, would widen during the war years, leaving them unwilling or unable to talk to each other for the rest of their lives. Long after Jupp died, my voluble *tante* Else with her snapping eyes and rambling stories pedaled on her bicycle to my aunt Inge and uncle Günther's house to visit with the American relatives. She talked constantly. I think I might have developed a fondness for her if I hadn't been instinctively loyal to the distance my mother claimed. Only as an adult did I learn that this tug away from Else was the hand of Heina, urging my mother to stay true to an old battle of ideology. Despite this iciness, I learned much later that Tante Else dove right into politics in an admirable way. As a shopgirl, she refused to quit her job at a Jewish-owned store. I don't know much more than that, but Else continued to do what she could even as the Nazis threatened to close the store. A local Marl history supplies the details about Herr Friedlich's shop, and I cheer for Else now as I imagine her refusing to be cowed.

Heina stopped at Else's house, and they walked the path near a small stream that led to the shopping district on Hülsstraße. Else talked nonstop, explaining that she hadn't gone camping with Jupp's group because she was working to save extra money now that her father's hours had been cut. Heina half listened as he watched the light filter through the treetops. Walks with Friedchen were so quiet and soothing, but Else's bubbling energy was perfect for Jupp's personality. They passed through a thicket of trees toward the shopping area.

The crude slashes of a large swastika ripped like wounds across Friedlich's storefront. Herr Friedlich leaned heavily on the glass, rubbing at the smeared paint with a rag. Heina offered to help, and Friedlich turned to him with a grim and searching expression.

"You're hired, if you'll be here every morning. It grows by it-self. Must be the moonlight." Herr Friedlich crossed his arms and gestured with a nod across the street. "I don't know what they expect me to do," he said. "Close up shop? Board up the windows? I'm more German than those rats."

Else hurried inside the shop to avoid the brewing confronta-tion. Heina followed Herr Friedlich's gaze. Three young men leaned against a wall opposite the shop. A soft "click" sounded from the next doorway down, and as Heina turned an SA man lowered a camera.

"Eyes to the pavement, worm, or we'll get you," said one young man. Without thinking Heina glanced down, then stiffened his neck to hold his chin aloft. He clenched his fists. There was little chance he could beat even one of those thugs in a fight, much less three. He turned to say something of cold comfort to Herr Friedlich, but the man had already gone inside.

Another in the group, a red-cheeked boy, pointed at Heina and said, "I know that guy. He's SAJ. Claims to be all about the work-ing class, right? There he is, in bed with the Jews."

Heat went to Heina's head and words rushed out of his mouth in a shout. "You thick-headed goons! Is this monopoly capital?" he spat, pointing at Friedlich's shop. "Who owns the arms fac-tories and the mines? Not Jews, not Friedlich! Can you even spell the word economics?"

"We'll string you up by your economics, egghead," one of them mumbled.

"That's Buschmann, that's who that is," another said. "His dad works at the miners' co-op." Heina's face flushed. They knew him. But what did it matter? Let them draw swastikas on the miners' co-op and then see what happened.

Several housewives with baskets over their arms stopped to stare. Heina turned quickly and headed toward his streetcar stop. A large Nazi Party poster from the past election hung in tatters on a brick wall, still showing the stark images of a blond muscled worker striding above the huddled caricatures of a banker, a Jew, and a fat SPD official. These were the fairy tales, the Brothers Grimm stories, that adults told each other, and now we are all trapped in the storybook and can't follow this dark path through the woods.

A week later Heina walked past the bank in the main Hüls shopping district, and a blur in a shop window tugged at his peripheral vision. He doubled back to the bank's large storefront. Behind the glass was a placard that announced, "Betrayers of the German People—Patrons of Jewish Stores!" Above the placard hung rows of photographs, including a photo of Heina, brow crossed with a scowl, his mouth ajar in shock. Although I have no idea whether Heina was photographed, Marl history documents this as a favored Nazi propaganda tactic to induce fear.

By the end of June the Nazis declared the SPD and the socialist youth illegal, and in July all non-Nazi political activity was banned. Communists had already formed secret cells, but many SPD members reeled in uncertainty. A few, like Papa's friend August Kastner, a Marl SPD leader, served as vital links in literature distribution, but these visible figures were soon arrested.

I half wonder if Heina experimented with withdrawal, vowing to forget about politics to exercise some control over this process of slow strangulation. Maybe he read novels in the evenings and gave up trying to analyze the Nazi newspapers for shreds of reality. Perhaps he tried to stop noticing the implications of Nazi directives at work. Maybe he attempted to focus not on politics but on people: the kindness of the butcher, the smile of his son. He might have opened the Bible to read from Revelations and find wretched solace in a description of the apocalypse. He found that his mind needed problems to analyze, and he envisioned writing allegorical stories with deeply hidden political messages. He slipped back and forth in this sleepy landscape between thoughtless comfort and a sense of meaninglessness.

If this did happen, it did not last for long. One night in bed Friedchen nudged his calf with her toe. "Heina," she asked, "are you awake?"

He grunted.

"I feel like you are letting yourself die. I feel alone," she said in a quavering voice. He turned toward her, trying to see her eyes in the dark. How did one do this, he wondered, remain selectively alive?

I am sorry to tell you, Heina, that the shushings and strangled spike of the word *Hitler* have not yet been silenced in the house you helped build. In February 2003 I sat with my cousin Oliver, another of Heina's grandchildren, over crumbs of lovely German *Brötchen* and cups of drained coffee in the third-floor apartment where Heina and Friedchen might have had breakfast as a young family. My cousin cleared his throat and carefully handed me a section of the newspaper, folded so that I could read the headline: "U.S. prepares for war." The clock ticked.

"Do Americans approve of this?" Oliver asked, his brown eyes pained. I scanned the text. A second article described antiwar demonstrations, seven thousand people in Düsseldorf, seven hundred in the small town of Dorsten. "It is so much like Hitler, this preemptive strike," Oliver said. "Bush wants world domination. Iraq hasn't attacked the U.S."

I told Oliver I'd been to demonstrations in Washington DC the year before. We knew war was coming; we formed affinity groups, marched with puppets and drums. We held aloft peace signs, shouted, and burned our faces in the sun. At that march our contingent ran together with a larger Palestinian rally, and together we called for world leaders to respect the boundaries and rights of nations. A few of the large signs displayed bobbing swastikas, which danced in time to the jumping crowd. Many of the Palestinian marchers declared Ariel Sharon of Israel to be another Hitler. "If the Jews Want a Homeland, Give Them Rhode Island," read one sign. I remember freezing on the pavement as the shouts echoed around me, and the decades seemed to unhinge. Palestine was occupied land, I knew, and rage made sense. But I had to fall back, away from that contingent. It was a bit too chilling to be marching in a roaring crowd with that symbol held aloft.

Oliver tightened his lips. He gave the tight, downcast German shake of the head that meant words failed him. The buzz of strong coffee seemed to squeeze my heart, and tears sprang to my eyes. Oliver left for work. I went down three flights of stairs in the subdivided Buschmann house to check my laundry in the basement. A load of wash sloshed in the machine, the motor's monotone echoing against the thick concrete walls.

My family members took shelter in this cellar from the bombs. They crouched against the thick cement walls and listened with all of their animal instincts between siren blasts for the whistle of metal rushing through the sky. Mom had told me there was once a root cellar down here with a winter's load of potatoes stored like coal in a huge wooden bin. That was how this search for Heina felt: a bin full of eyeless roots, raw, mute. I wanted meaning, another cache of letters and photos, tucked away in mildewed leather cases and stacked on rusting shelves, or a secret symbol scratched by Heina onto the walls.

I had artifacts but not enough explanation. The other day Klaus had revealed several boxes of slides made with some long-dead photo technology that imprinted pictures in soot between two panes of glass. Images of World War I tanks, men in uniform on bleak landscapes, and painted pictures of Lenin and Trotsky had furled and half dissolved as the cellar's moisture came in contact with the glass. Heina was a stockpiler. He saved Third Reich coins in a round metal tin for Camilla hand lotion, a cheery yellow and green design with a drawing of a daisy on the lid. Somehow I inherited this tin when I was in high school, probably from my mother or from a German visit. I felt its ominous significance and kept it tucked in the back of my sweater drawer. The swastikas stamped on so many pieces of pocket change frightened me with their ordinariness. Mom told me Heina also kept his copy of *Mein Kampf* long after he was required to turn it in, long after most Germans discarded the past to begin the process of separation. Heina knew that we forget to brood on what we cannot see and touch.

The washer thumped to a stop and I pulled out cold denim. The gravity of exhaustion pressed into me, as if it was heavy lifting to nudge Heina from the peace of death with my questions. I followed the stairs up to my room, a square at the front of the house that had once been my mother's bedroom and before that a fifteen-by-fifteen one-room apartment occupied by a mother and her daughter. At the window I watched the dark clouds move across the sky. Freezing sleet coated the orange tiled roofs and the bare trees. Standing in my mother's old room, looking across the street at the familiar view of the bakery and the shuttered windows, I felt a flash of what I can only describe as occupation, as if Heina in all his various ages was passing through me in a procession without chronology. I tasted heartbreak and wondered if I was projecting my own, or feeling it seep from the walls of that house.

A bare fact fleshed out with imagination and fear:
The Marl-Brassert open-air market on a September morning

was peak time for the end of the cherry harvest, so even if you didn't have money, you could walk by the stalls and that old man would yell, "Probiere mal!" Try one!

The man rolled a newspaper cone, filled it to the brim with cherries, and tucked the corner over that heavenly load, then handed it to a woman in a fancy coat. He handed you a sample, and you'd take a cherry, nodding gratefully, feeling the slick skin against your tongue, the deep red meat. You could suck one cherry pit all afternoon to remember that taste.

Don't look hungry or play the beggar. Bring a basket with you, as if you intend to do the full week's shopping. The baker might wave a slice of rye in your direction. Bring your little cousin with you, because the butcher Rosenberg always gives out slices of fat sausage ends in return for a pinch of those baby cheeks. Frau Rosenberg had such a weak spot for kids, especially the under-fed ones with the gray under their eyes. She gave out so many free sausage samples it was a wonder she and her husband made any money. I was just at Rosenberg's yesterday, such a beautiful chop I got, and on sale, too . . .

From the corner of your eye you see a commotion, people running from the far side of the market near the church—what is it, a wild dog back there? You take steps away, put your little cousin on your shoulders for a better view—what can you see from up there? It's the Rosenbergs . . . What's happening? It's their stand, the sunshade's been torn down, ice from the coolers spilled onto the cobblestones, sausages and cutlets on the ground, a crush of people soundlessly rushing to get away from this sight. Six or ten men growl in brown uniforms, clearing a path in the crowd.

They drag Frau Rosenberg by her long gray hair, her braid is undone and she's kicking against the ground, breasts heaving as she squirms and the SA men push her against the stones. You run with your cousin pressed to your chest, and the little girl is shaking and crying against your body. Let her forget this, let her not ask the question of why, to which you would have to answer, "Because they are Jews. Isn't that silly? That is all."

But your little cousin doesn't ask why, because she has already learned in her short time alive that those questions will bring stern scowls. She works on being silent, and at home you wash her face with a wet rag and pry the mashed bit of warm sausage from her fist. The Rosenbergs are two of forty-seven Jews in Marl. Local history collected after the war will record this event, but you do not hear the details, do not know that they were forced to sell their shop for 300 marks, a pittance, and to flee. You only know they have disappeared.

On September 30, in the same month the Rosenbergs were dragged down Brassertstraße, Heina returned a questionnaire from the Nazis, the second one to demand his political and racial pedigree. Once again: Which now-banned political activities did you participate in? "SPD, Iron Front, Reichsbanner," he wrote. Once again: Can you attest to your status as an Aryan? He penned in "Ja" with a swirl of emotions that must have included shreds of rage and selfish relief.

Heina, your granddaughter would one day hold that form and see your responses. Even seventy years later, I was breaking the law.

I didn't know to look for these documents. I had made my appointments and requested forms and files at the city archives, but the archivist had said the Nazi-era documents were gone. In the place where Heina had spent his entire career, there was no record of his existence other than a few phone directories. I returned from those daylong searches disheartened and mystified. The Germans loved paperwork. What was going on?

Three weeks into my research trip, a friend whom I won't name

came to Uncle Klaus's house for a visit. She took a sip of her coffee, then pulled a file folder almost three inches thick from her
shoulder bag. She flashed me a German poker face: a controlled,
enigmatic half-smile paired with wild, laughing brown eyes.

"This folder," said my uncle Klaus, smiling broadly, "doesn't
exist."

In English that doublespeak would have been clear, but it took
me a full minute to sort through the verbs. "Oh," I said finally. "I
get it. There's no folder."

"It's his personnel file," said the woman, who had a friend
at Marl City Hall. "These folders were all supposed to be destroyed," she said, "and all the rest of them were." She opened
the front cover of the thick cardboard folder and explained that it
had been "borrowed," saved by a friend who knew Heina.

I held out my hands to receive the weight. The first tissue-thin
pages, with ornate engraving and fountain-pen script, listed the
details of Heina's clerical apprenticeship at age fourteen. Each
page held dates, names, records, actions, pay stubs. It slowly
occurred to me just how incredibly precious these papers were.
The record of his life. Ridiculous: nearly missed, nearly shredded, saved in a moment of curiosity or in defense of the past.
The room around me seemed to fade as I was immediately pulled
down into the German phrases, the blurry typeset and printed
forms, the smattering of umlauts, the expanse of meaning that
promised, between the lines, to deliver my grandfather. My fingers itched for a notepad and my boxy yellow and blue German-
English dictionary.

Tiny swastikas dotted the letterhead and signatures on every
sheet in the middle of the stack. I ran my fingers across Heina's
signature on those old Nazi forms, which demanded again and
again that Heina assert whether he was a member of the Nazi
Party. Nein, he replied.

"Look," I said to the woman, who peered over my shoulder. Heina was asked to attest to his former political affiliations four times in between '33 and '39. Each time he listed his former membership in the SPD, the Reichsbanner, and the Iron Front. The forms themselves, with their repetition and insistence, spoke of a grinding administrative process, an accumulation of official evidence that could later be used to threaten non-Nazis with their own signatures and pasts. You could have argued, Heina, that joining the Nazi Party would have protected your family. You could have bowed to the pressure, but you never did.

"Interessant, neh?" asked the woman, with the same half smile. Interesting: a devastating understatement, delivered with the German delight in subtlety. Yes, interesting. Klaus's eyes shone.

In November 1933 the street violence and arrests—combined with election fraud and public demoralization—paved the way for a sweeping Nazi election victory of more than 92 percent of the vote. The next month Heina might have coldly surveyed his options and decided he was in danger. Maybe a sympathetic Nazi Party member in his office approached him and said, "Heina, I like you, but people are talking. You need to make an effort here, or I can't protect you." Or maybe Heina decided he needed to see people in meetings once again, even as a member of a local Nazi group organized to feed the unemployed. Another possibility, backed up by the last remaining SPD documents before the war, includes the brewing strategy of sending socialists undercover in Nazi organizations to make contacts. On December 1, 1933, Heina signed a card and joined the NS Volkswohlfahrt, the Nazi welfare committee. One month later he joined the Nazi union for public officials. Maybe he agonized over signing on to any Nazi-related group, or maybe he realized there was no other choice.

At some point I believe he decided to regain contact with so-

cialists by taking part in an illegal meeting. Many socialists organized nature hikes to meet in the woods, and the record of Marl-
area socialist work shows specific plans and networks springing
up almost immediately. Although I don't have any evidence for
Heina's participation, it was not an uncommon step for a socialist in the early years of the Third Reich, especially before the
waves of arrests devoured many of the activists.

"We're going berry picking, Mama," Heina called from the
foyer. "Will you watch Inge and Karl-Heinz for the morning?"

Lina sighed, then put down her book and removed her reading glasses. "At least it won't cut into my reading time. All we
have left in this house is novels, anyway." Then she smiled at
Karl-Heinz, his white-blond hair and bright blue eyes. "Come
to Oma," she said, with a smile she never bestowed on adults.
"You look just like your papa when he was a baby, white-haired
as a little old man."

Inge swung from the knob of the side door, and the door
creaked in a slow arc. "Ich gehe mit," she said, her high-pitched
voice echoing in the hallway.

"You can't go with us, Inge," said Friedchen. She bit her lip,
searching for a reasonable explanation for a four-year-old. "This
mountain is too steep, and you'll get tired. We'll bring you the
best berries, and we can make a torte."

Inge let herself fall from the doorknob and then ran out onto
the porch. Lina scowled. "If you two don't know how to teach a
child to mind . . ."

"Papa!" cried Inge, racing back in, her blond braids bouncing. "I want a spider flag! If I can't go with you, bring me back a
spider flag from the mountain."

Heina glanced at his watch, then at Friedchen. "What is she
talking about?" He leaned down and put his hands on his thighs
to get closer to Inge's eye level. "What do you mean?"

Friedchen started to speak, and then caught her breath in her throat, making a noise of exasperation. "She's been doing this all week."

"The spiders! The red and black ones!" Inge cried. "Why does everyone else get one?"

Heina stood up abruptly, realizing what she meant: the swastika flags draped from half of their neighbor's balconies and windows. "No," he said, voice flat and stern. "You can never have one, because only bad people have those."

Inge scowled. "Frau Hennig isn't bad. She's nice. She gives me flowers. And all the other children . . ."

"When will you be back?" Lina asked. "I have the women's Red Earth choir this afternoon."

Out on the street they waved to their children in the window. Friedchen leaned in and hissed quietly at Heina, "You can't say those things. She's four."

He stopped in his tracks and turned to glare. "Are you saying we shouldn't teach our children that the Nazis are bad people?" He swung at a shrub with his metal berry bucket, sending a rain of tiny leaves onto the sidewalk.

"Heina, listen to me. She's too young. And it will scare her. Do we want her to grow up frightened, so that she thinks bad people are everywhere?"

He leaned in still closer, hissing through his teeth. "They *are* everywhere."

Friedchen sighed and looked off down the street in the direction they were supposed to be walking. "We're going to miss the group," she said.

He turned on his heel and started walking quickly, so that she had to rush to catch up. "When is she old enough to understand?" he asked her in a soft whisper as they moved to avoid a man passing the opposite way on the sidewalk. They waited until he was out of earshot before continuing. "I knew capitalists were bad when I was four. My father—"

"Heina," she said, a low and soft tone of sudden sympathy in her voice as if she were trying to comfort him or calm him down. "Your father didn't have to worry about his children denouncing him. Imagine what would happen if Inge got a Nazi for a kindergarten teacher, and she was overheard talking to her classmates about the bad Nazis. We'd be done for."

They were silent on the streetcar out to the edge of town. They walked to a parking lot where a truck waited. A few comrades gathered around the truck, careful to nod in a subdued way and keep their voices low. Heina had lost track of who was communist, socialist, or environmentalist, and those differences didn't seem to matter now anyway. Only when the truck accelerated, following a gravel road out of town toward the hills near Haltern, did Heina feel his chest loosen. As the rolling terrain of green brush and low reddish heather unfurled before them, he spotted a mine tipple's peak in the distance. This is the land of the Red Earth, Germany's proletariat, and here we are sneaking into the woods so that we can see other socialists face-to-face, he thought. Pathetic, but necessary.

Conversations and laughter lifted above the roar of the motor. The truck's wooden sides rattled furiously in their metal brackets. One of the comrades described last month's sales. Every month they picked berries and then held an informal political conference in the woods. They sold the berries at the Monday farmers' market, covertly raising money for families of political prisoners beaten or taken by the SA.

The truck turned and parked in a small lot near the trailhead, and Friedchen jumped down from the back of the truck. For a second the sight of her braids swinging as she laughed, and the smell of woods and fern, cast Heina back into 1922 when he was a wide-eyed and energetic twenty year old with bound-less time and hope. He jumped down off the bumper and then reached forward to grab her hand. She looked back, smiling and surprised, and their morning fight was forgiven. Heina followed Friedchen up the narrow trail, lulled by the clump of boots, let-ting himself imagine they were kids again.

The sound of a comrade's voice behind him distracted Heina from the memories. "I heard from a comrade in Düsseldorf about that railway worker. On the way to work last week—the morning rush, can you imagine—people were almost tripping over a goddamn corpse laid in the square off the market."

A woman up ahead made a noise of disgust. "He was beaten to death, with a sign around his neck that said, 'A communist who gave up his freedom yesterday. Shot while running away, ha ha.' Unbelievable."

A hiker ahead on the trail muttered the beginning of another rumor. Months ago each story like this had heated Heina to a glowing rage, and he'd felt a twitching in his hands as if he wanted to run into the street and pummel the nearest Nazi. But months of solid anger led to a kind of sleepiness as if he longed to stop thinking for a moment of relief. He would lose himself in remembering old campouts, or in thinking about the streets of Kahla, the red bunting and clouds of pipe smoke at an SPD congress meeting when he was a boy.

Other comrades had become so drained and hopeless that they'd stopped responding to verbal invitations about secret po-litical meetings. Instead they'd sit in the corner pub, spending their energy on chess games or old Goethe novels as if desperate for any form of pleasure and mental stimulation. It was too late now to escape the country, but some were opting for what com-rades called "inner emigration." They were forced to greet each other now with shouts of "Heil Hitler!" in the street and at work, but if a comrade fought to keep mentally alive, you could see it immediately in the sarcastic crinkle of an eyelid, the overenunciation of Hitler's name, a thousand tiny and untraceable clues to let others know that this was just an offensive but temporary façade.

The group stopped at a widened part of the path and wandered into the underbrush. The fat green gooseberries plinked like raindrops against the bottoms of the metal pails. Heina grabbed the translucent berries one by one, at ease for a moment, but then his imagination began to work on the idea of the communist rail worker whose last living moments had been drowned in a flurry of fists.

Four clerks and an apprentice in Marl had already been fired for their politics. Heina had just received an official questionnaire, which was still lying blank on his desk. The four-page form asked each employee to list all past political activity as well as the names of parents and grandparents to certify Aryan heritage. He hadn't mentioned the survey to Friedchen. He wasn't even sure, given the Nazis' complicated racial theories, whether she qualified as Aryan, being half Polish. He glanced over at her, wondering what she was thinking. She leaned away from him, talking and laughing with a woman with dark curly hair. Heina sighed and looked down into his pail, then realized he'd been crushing the berries between his fingers.

The laughter of his friends slowly warmed him, and he was glad to hear that a secret SAJ meeting in the woods outside Bochum had gone well. Communist youth had formed a tactical agreement with the SAJ to do shared illegal activity. The communists had come up with some brilliant ideas, like leaving leaflets against Hitler on the assembly lines at a Krupp factory, letting the conveyor belts distribute the information anonymously to the workers. They'd also nominated a few comrades to go underground to breed resistance in the Work Service Corps, Hitler's solution for the rampant unemployment.

The group walked down from the forest in the afternoon light. They poured berries into large pails and climbed into the truck bed. When the group arrived at the first drop-off point, two comrades got out and went around to the truck cab, then left in separate directions. The truck made its final stop at a parking lot near the youth home. As Heina and Friedchen jumped off, the driver called out, "Friend, you've forgotten something."

Heina walked back to the truck cab, trying to remember the driver's name. Then he realized he'd never been introduced. The driver motioned him closer. "You can take this if you want to, but no harm done if you're not interested. From Amsterdam. Just make sure you leave them in a public place where there's no risk to yourself." The man raised his bushy blond eyebrows under his watch cap and touched a flat packet of papers next to him on the seat.

Literature! A real distribution operation! A surge of adrenaline and joy brought a smile to Heina's face. He stuck his hand up toward the truck window.

The driver said calmly, "Stand on the running board, and lean in with your elbow while you open your jacket." Heina did as he was told, and the driver slid him a tightly folded oblong of thin paper, barely bigger than an envelope. "There's fifty. Unless you absolutely need to, don't tell your wife. No one else in the group knows you've got them, either. That's for all of our protection."

Hope and excitement may have drained into anxiety by the time Heina lay in bed that night and wondered how to get rid of the flyers. Maybe he waited a day or two, the package covered with work papers at the bottom of his briefcase. Early in the morning he might have walked to an unfamiliar bakery for morning rolls. On the way home I imagine him stepping into a phone booth.

He unwrapped the packet's paper covering, dropped the leaflets on the shelf beneath the phone, and then exited, walking quickly up the street. He heard footsteps behind him, a shout of, "Excuse me, sir, you've left something here at the phone!" Damn the helpful, efficient Germans. He broke into a run. No baby carriage, just lonely fear. Heina, whose babies struggled to survive, would not tempt fate with his flesh, his child.

I understand why Third Reich resistance movements aren't featured in many history books. The numbers of participants were proportionally very small. It would be dangerous, too convenient, to give the highly mistaken impression that every other Heinz and Fritz was a freedom fighter, which would amount to denying the sweeping support, both active and passive, the Nazis enjoyed. Hans and Sophie Scholl, leaders of the tiny "White Rose" Christian resistance movement, are always mentioned in U.S. high school textbooks. But I did not learn about a complex network of other anti-Nazi groups until I dug for months among primary sources and German-language texts.

My hands shook as I sat at a long wood table in an archive in Amsterdam and opened a box to lift out original copies of the communist *Ruhr Echo* and stacks of other faded leaflets. Some flyers had touchingly hand-drawn mastheads, pen-and-ink slogans, a crudely drawn hammer and sickle or a roughly sketched star. Those symbols—signs of the communist and the revolutionary—seem to cancel eligibility for shared memory and for honor.

I know from family stories that pamphlets, papers, and leaflets like these passed through my grandfather's hands. Beyond that all I have is faith, along with the phrase uttered by my uncle Klaus: "Auf dem Fahrrad," on a bicycle. Heina traveled the Ruhr on bicycle, delivering illegal papers, said my uncle Klaus. Mom nodded. Yes, she had heard that, too. On a bicycle. I rest my faith in a few mannerisms, the way Mom and Uncle Klaus both shrug, quickly backtrack, when they are unsure. They clam up, look at me with silent brown eyes, sorry they have such gaps in their knowledge. But they both said this sentence with a clear confidence, an absolute conviction. My mother added that she was sure Heina put himself in great danger, that he could have been arrested and sent to the camps. But both Mom and Uncle Klaus uttered the same sentence with a clean lack of pride or personal investment: it is just the way things were. It is fact: they cannot elaborate, but this much they know. A time capsule, small and carefully sealed.

I imagine, based on nothing but my own guesses, that Heina had to work up to those bike rides, that he had to first wrestle with his fear. Imagine the improbability of obtaining an SPD paper smuggled from Prague, or *Neue Vorwärts* or *Sozialistische Aktion*, published in Antwerp or Brussels, knowing that this small rectangle of paper had required a chain of anonymous connections and risked lives. This paper was maybe smuggled in with the help of resistance leader Kurt Schumacher and many others, delivered, according to historical accounts, to a bread factory in Duisburg run by Reds, who gave it to Red delivery drivers to be distributed in Dortmund along with warm loaves, the stack parceled out one by one into mail slots.

Or maybe the packet is left in a phone booth, and you are informed by a signal: a flowerpot on a comrade's windowsill has moved from left to right. You snatch it up, rush with this burning packet in your coat to a windowless room in your apartment, as eager for connection as if you are seeing a lost love again after months apart, as if about to receive a small dose of sanity. You turn the precious pages to read an article denouncing the rival set of SPD émigrés in Amsterdam, quoting positions and grandstanding. Throughout the paper you read the inked slogans: German Socialists—Rise Up! Defeat the Nazis! But the practical advice is lacking: where do we meet? Who is still free? What arguments will counter demoralization and hopelessness and fear? What will work? Give me a weapon, tell me the appointed hour and place, and I swear on my life I will be there.

Nine years after the youth home opened for meetings, nine years after Heina tapped a nail into a fresh white wall and hung up the red saj banner, the Nazi sa claimed the building as a conveniently isolated site for interrogations. Uncle Klaus tells me Heina received advance warning of the youth home's takeover. An ss member, maybe someone who had known Papa in the mines, might have stopped by one night and, over coffee, made a pointed allusion. Or maybe Jupp, the well-liked charmer, heard rumors from a friend of an acquaintance.

Family stories tell me this: what mattered to Heina were the books. He smuggled a bookshelf full of socialist tracts and bound classics four blocks away to the family home. He carried the books up two flights of stairs and tucked them in the attic, beneath the eaves and behind a bookshelf. Mom remembers hearing that story about the specific placement of the books, though I'm not sure whether the memory includes a hint of a question: What words on a printed page would be important enough to risk the lives of your family members? Book spines, book covers, and paper lay waiting for the full span of the Third Reich above the heads of the Buschmann family. Maybe the volumes provided a sense of shelter for Heina, who gambled that the Nazis would be satisfied with the house search the family had already endured.

The youth home itself was no longer a shelter, according to Marl Third Reich historical accounts. Willi Butz, a former mem-

ber of the Reichsbanner militia, was dragged into the little Serbian wood house and beaten by twelve SA men. Willi might have
rolled over during a lull in the SA men's kicks to press his swollen face to the cool wood floor, feeling the trickle of warm blood
and thinking about the time when he met others here for the
Reichsbanner group portrait.

The SA men dragged other Reichsbanner and SAJ members to
the youth home; Heina would have been an obvious target, but
there's no way to know. And those SA men—once miners, once
hungry, or else career-minded careful men, some familiar with
cruelty, some only unassuming—opened their mouths to yell in a
raw babble as they took turns with their victims, who writhed on
the floor. These SA men felt the sweat of this new work dampen
their backs under their uniforms, and they shed their jackets and
hats. Some of them must have felt truly victimized, wronged,
by these Reds. As knuckles cracked with punches, some of the
SA men must have felt proud to defend their own children and
wives from Russia's Red hordes. Afterward, feeling the cool air
on their scalps as they kicked the last man and sent him running,
bloody, they felt the shiver of a close call, how narrowly Germany
had avoided being taken over by these terrorists, these spies.

The horror of being outnumbered twelve to one in a room in a
forest where no one could hear you scream must leave a permanent mark on one's psyche. Photographs of Heina taken before
the Third Reich show a headstrong, smiling young man with
shoulders back, eyes blazing with idealism. In photos after the
war, he is seated near head tables at banquets and dinners hon-
oring the old SAJ comrades. His shoulders turn inward as if to
shield himself. In one photo Heina's body leans toward August
Kastner, a comrade seated next to him who survived the concentration camps. There is a soft and shrinking reverence in Heina's
eyes, an apparent need to be close to men like Herr Kastner, as if

their survival sustained him, as if something in their eyes held a clue to something that kept him sane.

I walked to the youth home alone one sunny and cold afternoon in February 2003, and in the silence I felt Heina's presence under the radiating branches of the tall pines. I crisscrossed the plot of ground once claimed as Red Earth, where the youth group members pitched their tents under the stars. The old Serbian log cabin was long gone, first renovated after World War II and then knocked down and replaced. I peered in the windows of a one-story white stucco building with sliding glass doors, now a meeting hall for the Workers' Welfare Association. There were potted plants on a window ledge inside the building manager's apartment, which meant that at least someone came here often enough to keep the plants alive. I picked up a rounded pebble and a triangular chunk of blackened cement from an old foundation or wall and put them in my pocket. There was no small plaque, no tiny sign with letters in raised bronze, to tell visitors that this was once the first youth home in the region, established by Heinrich Buschmann Jr.

Heina, I wanted to touch your name in weathered metal. As it was I felt whole and warmed by your presence. I am glad, now, for the pure moment there, before I went back to my books and discovered the Nazis' use of that place.

I don't know exactly how white-blond Karl-Heinz, Heina and Friedchen's second son, died. But I will imagine for the sake of selfish mercy that his death was quick. Maybe bacteria from winter meat gone bad in 1935 overwhelmed his weakened immune system. In the midst of fears about impending war, of questionnaires and Aryan certifications and beatings and house searches, six-year-old Inge was once again, horribly, an only child.

Inge was sent to Friedchen's parents during the numbing January funeral. She wouldn't see the black procession and the tiny casket, but she had already seen the worst—a vomiting, moaning brother, the unsmiling doctor, then the hush. The door slammed as her papa left to walk and walk at night under the cold stars. Heina cried, gasped for air, remembering only for seconds at a time that no one could afford medical care, that Karl-Heinz's death didn't reveal a special mark of doom on their threshold. That night it felt as if he himself had killed the boys. He now had more children dead than living. Heina might have felt himself harden on that cold night walking alone, might have made a clear decision to avenge his sons and the conditions that caused their deaths. With whatever it took.

Karl-Heinz was two and a half years old, the age of walking, talking, and questioning, the age a baby becomes a person. The way he laughed and turned his head and squinted his eyes showed glimmers of the specific man he would have become. What did Friedchen do to stay sane?

I imagined motherhood and failed to intuit the truth. I imagined my way into Friedchen's head before my son was born and believed it would be harder to lose Karl-Heinz than baby Heinrich. I guessed that if you had more time to get attached to a child, the loss would sting much deeper. I imagined that as a child aged and passed some critical point in consciousness, he or she would be transformed from an anonymous baby into a specific person who would leave a greater void. But my son, Ivan, was a writhing, screaming personality the moment he was handed up to me, slimy with vernix and still warm from my insides. Five weeks later he looked at me with brows cocked and lip curled. Though his brain wasn't fully organized, he responded with temperament and tone already baffling in complexity and unpredictability. From that first meeting, it is too late to change the fact that you have touched and known another person. Friedchen knew the loss not of babies but of full people, half visible as if seen dimly through a misted window.

In his first weeks Ivan slept most soundly on my chest. His legs wrapped around my ribcage, his body curled, his lips parted to leave a circle of drool on my shirt. His fingers clutched my collar and found folds in my skin. His hair fuzzed as he buried his face into me, knowing what he would forget: we are of a piece, sharing a smell, sharing cells, temperature, and pulse. Seeing his outrageous vulnerability called to mind, over and over, the easy work that torturers have with our soft skin.

Who let me be a mother? I am so small, the thrift-shop girl with her hair in her face. I thought giving birth would let me taste divine creation, invincibility. The splashes of blood and fluid, being ripped open by an uncontrollable force that wanted to get out of my body—all of it felt closer to death, even though I was never in danger. Later, newly released from the hospital, still raw flesh, I stood at the curb on some errand and held my smaller bit of new flesh, clinging to me, and I saw for the first time how I am destined for nothing, how any speeding car could cancel my heartbeat, pierce delicate membranes, and disorganize this carefully calibrated but unshielded life. I understand a bit better now how humans make such easy targets.

Jupp's girlfriend, Else, sat in their kitchen eating a slice of buttered bread and twirling her hair. Heina was sorry he had underestimated her; she was being very brave, even if she didn't understand all of the possible consequences.

"Those laws—" Else began with a wave of her hand.

"The Nuremberg Racial Laws," Lina added, turning from the cutting board.

"Right," Else said. "They're terrible." Else explained that her boss, Herr Friedlich, had been forced to sell his shop to his son-in-law. "People are terrified to go in there anymore. So us girls have decided to go out and see all the old customers, take orders, and then bring them what they want." Else pushed a pencil and piece of receipt paper toward Lina.

Heina stood at the counter making a sandwich for lunch, and he marveled at Else's ease with Lina. Maybe Lina held a grudging respect for a fellow hothead.

Lina put the pencil to her lips and then said, "Let me see. I need a dish towel, and . . ."

A few months later during that same warm summer of 1935, a crowd gathered on Hülsstraß in front of Friedlich's store. People in the crowd yelled, "Jews out!"

Herr Koopman—not a Jew but married to a Jewish woman—came out to see what the ruckus was. Men from the crowd grabbed him roughly and threw him through the glass shop window. Shards sprayed out into the street and bounced in the gutter, flashing in the sunlight.

The Nazis searched the Buschmann household a second time. I imagine Friedchen running with Inge into the back bedroom. One ss man was almost apologetic, shrugging and giving a half smile as if to say, "I'm only doing my job," as he shuffled through papers in a drawer and culled out meaningless household receipts. Klaus tells me the family had once again received advance warning, though he does not know its source. Heina and his father had turned the place upside down, throwing away or hiding anything that could be incriminating, including a few copies of illegally distributed papers.

I imagine Jupp raged at the violation of their house, fuming as he helped his mother stuff her recipes back in order. But a few weeks later he sat in the kitchen with his legs sprawled out cockily, smiling that winning smile.

Here is what I know: Jupp joined the Waffen-ss, Hitler's elite military guard, the torturers, the men who coordinated the beatings of comrades. This cuts a wound between Heina and Jupp that will never heal. This is the reason my mother was dropped off at the street corner near Jupp and Else's house for visits so Heina would not have to make eye contact with Jupp, long after the war.

In many ways membership in the ss marks Jupp as a monster, one of the henchmen directly charged with coordinating the Holocaust. The choice to join the ss was simply incomprehensible; the desire to understand this rift was part of what motivated me to write, and the part that I failed to understand.

In 2006 German left-wing author Günter Grass, one of my literary heroes, revealed that he had also served in the ss and then had kept the secret for over sixty years. Grass claimed he was conscripted into membership in 1944, at a time when the ss was desperate for members. He admitted that during the war he— now a giant of moral clarity and literary subtlety, then a teenager—had not understood that Hitler's mission was evil. The question of whether his age is exculpatory is one I cannot decide. But the admission is chilling, and it leaves me feeling as though some safe, sacred ground has been lost. Then I realize that in the territory of the German soul, or the soul of any aggressor nation, pure land cannot be found. And I am missing the critical piece of information about when Jupp joined. Jupp was thirty-five by the time the war started in 1939, not Günter Grass's thirteen. Because of the rage that leeched into every crack of my split family tree over this choice, I assume Jupp joined the ss earlier, for different reasons, but all I have are dangerous assumptions.

"I can't get work unless I join. Else's on the records as working at Friedlich's, plus I've got the whole 'Buschmann' thing against me," Jupp said, listing the reasons as he touched the fingers of his left hand. He turned to Heina and pointed at his brother's ashen face. "This is just like you joining the Air Raid Protection Society or the NS People's Aid, or any of the seventeen silly clubs you've gotten yourself into as a cover."

Papa sat, smoking his pipe and seemingly trying to stare through the kitchen table. Heina's heart raced. Papa should stand and break the furniture. Mama must throw Jupp out on his ear. Heina willed his father to react, then words spilled out of his own mouth.

"No," said Heina. "No—Jupp, this is something you can't do. You think it's easy now, but this won't keep you safe. What do you think the SS does for Hitler, make coffee and stuff envelopes?" His family was crumbling from the inside, as if his sons' deaths had been a precursor to everything else falling apart.

Papa took a draw on his pipe and coughed furiously, a racking sound that rattled the plates on the shelf. They all involuntarily winced as he spat into a handkerchief and then stuffed the cloth in his pocket. "Jupp," he said, "I know it's been hard to find work. But if you'd been desperate, truly desperate, we could have gotten you in at the mines. I know that's not the work you want to do, but it's honest work, at least . . ."

Jupp stood, his dark curly hair bobbing as he paced back and forth in the small kitchen. He turned to stand in front of Heina, jabbing the air with his finger. Veins stood out on his forehead, which shone with sweat. "I'm the reason you're not in jail," he said to Heina. "It was me that had Reichsbanner friends in the SA, and I got the news before the house and youth home were searched." Jupp leaned in close to Heina's face, dark eyes flashing. "If you fault me now for this, you're a hypocrite. You'll take the benefit of knowing a few Nazis, but you won't even let me pay the price to protect us all."

Lina stood with her back against the sideboard, arms crossed, a spectator at a boxing match. "The only thing for Jupp to do now is to use that Trojan horse tactic, the one the communists keep talking about—infiltrate the Nazi organizations to reach other socialists and communists." She looked through her half-moon spectacles at Jupp. "Think about it as a covert organizing drive, Jupp, as long as you feel this step was necessary."

Heina put his face in his hands. They were insane, all of them, acting as if Jupp had joined some paltry do-nothing neighborhood organization.

"I think Jupp could also be a great source of information about what the NS is planning," Lina said.

Heina put his hand in his pocket to reach for the rough paper scrap of his list, a neurotic comfort but the only reminder of life outside these suffocating walls. Jupp, free and easy with political discipline, believed his instincts would save him. This was Heina's best friend, his Jupp, that laughing, younger, and brighter version of himself, the other half, the one who tempered his solemn shyness. Heina stood and grabbed his coat and briefcase from the bench, hands shaking as he pressed his lips together. They would not see him cry. He left the kitchen in a daze, not bothering to push in his chair or say good-bye.

The net around the socialists in Germany drew tighter. Jupp and Heina's boyhood friend Rudi Heiland was arrested and sentenced to two and a half years' protective custody. August Kastner, the local SPD leader, received a four-year sentence and was repeatedly tortured. During the investigation into Kastner's supposed "preparation to commit high treason," the Nazis rounded up fifty of Kastner's local comrades for questioning and imprisoned most of his family. The SS brought many political comrades to the Recklinghausen prison blocks near where Heina worked;

a startling number of these people "disappeared," followed by notices in the paper announcing the suicides of more prisoners.

In the early spring of 1936, Heina signed up for a two-month stint in the *Arbeitsdienst*, or work service, a civil service and quasi-military training program. Uncle Klaus explained that Heina enlisted because he was getting passed over at work for promotions. "Passed over": it's impossible to know whether Heina saw this lack of promotion as merely inconvenient or whether he was worried, in the daily unspoken series of slights, that he was being shunted aside in the Nazi-run administration as a precursor to being fired or worse. Maybe Rudi Heiland's arrest or that of his father's old friend Kastner had spooked Heina, and maybe he felt he'd be safest away from Marl for awhile. It's surprising that a lifelong opponent of militarism would voluntarily enlist, but Mom guessed there was money, too, that the pay for enlisted men was higher than for those who would eventually be drafted.

On March 8, 1936, the day after the Nazis remilitarized the Rhine and blatantly violated the Versailles Treaty, Heina shipped off to the "Pioneer" military camp #5 in Stettin on the Oder River. He was given a uniform and a bunk in a narrow, long barracks. I imagine him staying silent on the trip toward the barracks, nodding when he could at fellow trainees, trying to locate and avoid the ardent Nazis in the crowd.

A photo of the Stettin barracks shows a long wooden single-story building and a large utilitarian garden surrounded with a high fence and barbed wire. Between the building and the garden what I assume are chin-up bars connect high posts. The barracks buildings form a U-shape with a large, empty square of packed earth in the middle, a vast space that must have been used for exercise and military drills. Toward one edge sits a tall platform, possibly a reviewing or surveillance stand. Beyond the camp stretches an expanse of cleared land, industrial buildings, and then the harbor.

I imagine the commanders at the camp waited for these recruits to change into their uniforms then ordered them to put away any personal effects. The commanders already knew from the roster who was an NS member and who was not. Maybe they ordered the men to turn over a patch of land on the first day, and Heina felt lucky because he was handy with a shovel. As he worked the hard earth, he might have hoped to be assigned garden duty. Keeping his head down, he avoided drawing attention to himself. That evening, however, the corps was ordered to run to the far well pump and back, and Heina's chest tightened as he pulled in air. He had hiked and played soccer since he was a boy, but a dead sprint for close to a kilometer revealed him as an office worker with lung trouble.

"Buschmann!" one of the leaders called out. "Your Führer needs top physical performance. Do you have that in you, man?"

Then there were the Heil salutes, the waiting at military attention while an officer proceeded slowly down the line, picking out tiny scuff marks and wrinkles on uniforms as a prelude to shouts of ridicule, punishments of extra physical exercise, endless laps, or digging pointless ditches that would then be filled. Papa was a military man, had lived through Verdun; now Heina wondered how his father had adapted to the mental tedium. After a few days Heina noticed himself falling into predictable traps, feeling fondness for the less cruel of the two officers, a desire to please, happiness when he mastered a maneuver or when his sweating and muddy group raced back and forth in formation across the field.

Three weeks after his arrival Heina sent a postcard to Friedchen's parents and another to his daughter, both of which were saved. The front of the Klejdzinskis' card shows Stettin's port on the Oder River filled with tugboats and cargo ships. On the back the printed postmark reads, "Your Voice for the Führer!" Heina wrote a few sentences in a blurred hand to say that three weeks were finished. "Now one is slowly fitting into one's collar," he wrote, a German figure of speech that means getting used to something uncomfortable.

To his seven-year-old daughter he wrote in a neat hand, "Dear Inge-mouse! Thank you for the lovely letter and for the beautiful drawing of a flower that you sent. It made me so happy and proud of my little daughter . . . I showed it to the men here, and they were so surprised. The photo you sent is a good one—you're smiling as always. I'm home again in fourteen days." Heina ran out of space at the bottom of the card, and his writing became pinched and small, continuing on the opposite corner, "With greetings, your papa."

After serving in the Arbeiterdienst, running clothing drives for the NS welfare agency, and signing up for three or four of the Nazis' many auxiliary organizations, after twenty years of service for the government, Heina finally got a nod to apply for a promotion to public administrator, a more secure and well-paid position than clerk. But there were problems. His personnel file includes a stack of repeated requests for his criminal and political records. His arrest record came back clean in the fall of 1936, and on November 13 he was asked to complete yet another questionnaire about his political history, to which he gave all the same answers. Two weeks later a Nazi county officer sent a "confidential" individual request to other administrators asking for more information on Heina's political work. Maybe as a result of this investigation, Heina next joined yet another NS auxiliary club, the Reichskolonialbund—in support of Germany colonies around the world. Heina began to collect various letters of reference on his own behalf, also included in the file, to attest to his qualifications. He was then asked to sign a pledge asserting his eternal readiness to serve the Führer.

He received notice on January 30, 1937, that he had earned a probationary review of three months. If he passed this evalua- tion he would be promoted. In May, as the sun broke through the gray of a German spring, he received another form asking him to attest, once again, to his membership or nonmembership in the Nazi Party. Once again he uncapped his fountain pen and wrote "Nein" on the form.

That same month signs went up in some stores in Reckling- hausen: "Jews not welcome here." Marl history relates the story of a Jewish schoolboy named Rolf Abrahamson who grew up in Marl. During these same months that Heina waited to hear about his promotion, Rolf walked back and forth between Marl and Recklinghausen, bringing groceries to Jewish families banned from the shops. I imagine Rolf as a round-faced boy with dark curly hair who saw this sneaking and subterfuge as adventure. He knew what stores in Marl to visit, how to spend the precious marks and buy cabbage and potatoes, to walk across the fields or ride his bicycle down the hill into Recklinghausen. Like a hunter coming home with a fine catch, he was always greeted at the door with smiles as women pulled his cheeks, proclaiming him a fine boy, a brave boy.

In the fall of '37 Heina walked a little more carefully, daring not to hope too much but allowing himself a sliver of happiness. Friedchen was pregnant, four months along already and begin- ning to feel energetic again. And he had finally cleared the last hurdle at work to confirm his position and a raise that would help the entire family.

I imagine Heina may have rewarded himself with another step

into the world of risk, possibly to balance the guilt he felt at his own security in the face of so much suffering. Maybe he attended a gathering at a former SAJ member's apartment to listen to a banned radio station from across the border. The whispers of a barely intelligible voice described the civil war in Spain, with antifascists coming from as far as the United States to fight Franco. "Imagine—that could be here, too," said his friend Fritz. Karl, whom Heina did not know, stared into the mesh of the radio speaker as if Spain itself could be seen through the thin fabric. When the program ended Heina stood and said he needed to be getting home. Karl followed him down the stairs toward the door.

"Listen, friend," Karl started softly, and Heina's heart sank and constricted. Fear and resolve. It was starting again. And that was good, wasn't it? There was no other choice . . . "We need a local point man for the literature distribution, and you're in a position that ensures excellent cover. We've lost quite a few people." Lost. Heina stopped, not making eye contact, not moving away. He could not turn and grab for the door handle, though half of him longed to.

"There's a former SAJ comrade of yours working in the mines. He'll come to city hall to seek advice on a tax issue," Karl said. "He'll be asking for advice on two properties—these will be the delivery points. If you are willing to accept a shipment at that time, tell him when he leaves the office that you're 'so sorry' you couldn't help him. Then, the day after the meeting, get up before it's light as if you're on your way to work and ride by the back of the Catholic cemetery. You'll find a satchel near the gate, the kind used to store garden tools. Take it and distribute the contents to the points mentioned."

Heina silently repeated the instructions to memorize them and search for weak points, so distracted that he barely muttered a good-bye. The heavy wooden door slammed shut behind him. Out on the concrete step, with fog covering the street in a heavy layer of silence, he reached for his bicycle. A cycle of constriction and elation seemed to pull his heart tight like wire being formed through a drawing press. The presence of fear felt almost as solid as a piece of furniture. Yet his life would be of use.

That night Friedchen pulled the goose-down comforter onto their bed. Heina sat on a chair, fighting distraction. "Friedchen," he said softly. "Friends got in touch."

She turned, the light from the streetlamp making a glowing haze on the white curtain behind her. "Heina, sei vorsichtig," she said, be careful. Her face was pricked with anxiety, adding a sharpness to her features. She seemed to concentrate on saying nothing else. He kissed her good night. Her breath evened and slowed, but Heina could not sleep. He turned on his side, facing out into the room to stare at the heavy wooden wardrobe with doors shut tight. Be careful. He should not have told her. Now she had worry of the heaviest kind, a situation of specific danger over which she had no control.

The next morning Heina's head swam as he fought to wake up. Friedchen drew in a sharp breath, then moaned as she swung her legs onto the floor. She whimpered as she stood. He rolled toward her and saw on the mattress the irregular dark shape of blood, too much blood. She ran into the bathroom and he threw on yesterday's clothes.

"I'll run to get the Schillers' car—stay right there—it will be fine, don't worry, it's nothing . . ."

She miscarried in the hospital waiting room. The nurses loaded her immediately on a stretcher and wheeled her away, leaving Heina on a bench. An hour later the doctor found him and told him simply, "It was a boy. Your wife will live."

A boy. The third dead son. It was beyond bearing. Heina got

up and pushed open the side door of the hospital, left the neighbors' car, left his wife, and walked home.

What is bitter is remembered. Heina knelt by the fresh grave of
his unborn son. He stared into space and said in a voice cold and
numb, "And the girl lives."

Heina's daughter, Inge, must have been there with him. She
has carried that sentence and repeated it her whole life, but even
at seventy-four her hurt is fresh. My mom cannot imagine Heina
saying such a thing, but I am partial to what children remember,
and I find it impossible to write this sentence off entirely. I do not
understand how Heina, despite his bottomless longing for a son
and the loss of three of them, could say this within earshot of his
daughter, even in deepest grief. Family lore reports that Heina
was so upset at this third loss that he did not visit Friedchen in
the hospital; this is another sin Inge sees as unforgivable. If it is
true, I cannot imagine a reasonable excuse.

And that sentence: "And the girl lives." I heard this story when
I was young, before I got to know Heina's life, and it made me
withdraw from imagining him. I wondered whether he would
see me as just another living girl.

After the loss of the third son, the cumulative sadness and
stress finally began to wear on Heina and Friedchen's marriage.
Inge, then eight years old, broke away from her father, whom she
saw as deficient. She has never changed her assessment of him. I
imagine the strands of political and familial pain are interwoven,
but I have no way of knowing. I do know that Inge joined the
Hitler Youth as Germany balanced on the brink of war. Maybe
the pressure of not belonging, not having the neckerchief and
the white shirt, not laughing with the right girls after school,
pushed her in this direction. Maybe Heina put up a halfhearted
fight, or maybe he gave in to the claim that all the other girls had

joined, that they learned songs and baked cakes. Maybe Heina let her have her way to try to make up for damage done.

In the League of German Girls's meetings I imagine young Inge felt a soothing sense of belonging. She sat cross-legged on the floor, listening to her group leader explain about the Führer, and the other little girls sat giggling, flirting with each other as little girls do. When Inge stretched her right arm high with the other girls, she felt as if she were growing taller, as if she might reach up and touch the sun. Everyone at home was so sad all the time, their faces pinched, and it had been that way her whole life, dead baby after dead baby with only a living girl. Here in the crowd of girls playing soccer, learning to make cakes, taking hikes in the woods, laughter and familiarity called up the warm memory of those huge rallies and gatherings she'd attended with her father ever since she was small.

But her father had stopped going to rallies and seemed half dead. Now she was alive; she could walk with her group of girls in a march and listen to the roar of the crowd. She felt as if she might burst with pride, as if the crowd were cheering for her, cheering for the mature young woman who was not afraid to step forward for her country. She tried at those marches to hold her arm as straight and proudly as possible in the Hitler salute as they passed the reviewing stand, even if it made her shoulder ache.

Her group leader explained about how Hitler wanted to make life easier for the workers, and that the war was for the German people. Inge raced home that day to tell her father that he was wrong about Hitler: the Führer believed the same things as her family. When she tried to explain, he waved his hand to stop her words. And so this old and bitter man had to be replaced. A few years later, maybe watching a group of the Hitler Youth boys play soccer with their shirts off under the hot sun, she would see her laughing, kind Günther, and they would fall in love.

tory photos of me as a five-year-old playing with Legos on the carpet, after the offer of schnapps, Günther asked our opinion about President George W. Bush's threats of war. We shook our heads and moaned.

"I have to show you something!" Günther sprang toward the bookshelf, bringing back a thick volume of German history in English: the transcript of the Nuremberg Trials from the U.N. Commission on War Crimes. Günther hunched close to the page, looking through his bifocals and following the text with his finger. "There are all the definitions for war crimes here," he said, "and according to this your Bush is a war criminal!" He raised his finger in the air for emphasis, then hefted the book to set it on our laps. "I want you to read that—then you'll know what Bush is really doing." Tears filled his eyes. "It's just like Hitler, only we didn't know then what was happening. I didn't know about the Jews! We were so young . . ." he said, his voice trailing off.

Back in the United States in mid-March 2003, I learned that I was pregnant. A few days later George W. Bush appeared on television to announce that the administration's halfhearted attempts at diplomacy had failed. Donny approached the television screen and stuck a Post-it note just under Bush's nose. We laughed and gasped for air through the rest of the presidential address, not able to look in each other's eyes to see the dread reflected there. A few days later the television showed the bright flashes of bombs, the start of the U.S. military's "Shock and Awe" air strikes. I wrapped myself in a bedspread on the couch and cried. We turned the channel to VH-1, and Donny and I sat there, numb and silent for three hours straight, watching a music video countdown of the top one hundred one-hit wonders.

Papa Heinrich opened his mouth and a cavernous croak escaped. He gasped for air as the scarred flesh of his lungs tore. His skin was mottled purple from the lack of oxygen, and his fingers gathered a stranglehold on a wad of the hospital sheet. Heina's throat twitched involuntarily as he remembered the choking from childhood, the desperation for air that would not come. He squirmed, unable to bear it. Tears fogged his vision, and he bit the inside of his mouth to keep his face impassive.

They'd been watching his father die for years as he spit black phlegm into handkerchiefs and bent over, wheezing, when he climbed the stairs. That was just Papa, who had smiled through the coughing fits, joked about the Cough ("This is the coal miner's pension!"), and never gave up his pipe. The last few months had been horrible, blood at the corners of his mouth when he coughed, a hacking so violent that ribs broke in his barrel chest and there was nothing the doctors could do.

"Papa, drink something," Jupp said, reaching for the pitcher on the nightstand. "The nurses say you're dehydrated." Heina wanted to reach over and close his hands around Jupp's throat. Did he really believe a drink of water could save the old man now? Jupp's hands shook as he raised the pitcher into the air, sloshing water onto the floor, and for a moment Heina looked beyond the ss man's shaved neck and sharp cheekbones to see the little boy biting his lower lip, afraid.

Lina stood near the bed, her hands resting on Heinrich's knee, and that gesture looked affectionate. But her back was ramrod straight, and she glared at Heinrich with something that an outsider might take for hatred.

"Why won't you drink, you fool?" she said in a hiss, furious at her strong man as she watched him choke. She was desperate for a fight, for that opposing force of her husband to rise up and push her back, make her complete. Lina took the glass from Jupp and set the rim on Heinrich's purple lip. She would make him drink. She set her other hand at the back of his neck, then tipped the glass so that water flowed into his mouth. As if he didn't want anything to prolong the misery, Heinrich pursed his lips. He swung his forearm from the bed and swatted the glass from Lina's hands. Water sprayed as the shards exploded up from the floor. She shouted and covered her eyes.

This moment, a shattered glass, is frozen strangely in family lore: she tried to make him drink, and he swatted the glass away. This final scene is delivered to a third generation, and I wonder why it has been chosen to be passed down while other details are forgotten. As I collected these stories and reconstructed the weeks leading up to Papa Heinrich's death, I was stunned to see the echoed destruction of shattering lives beyond those hospital walls.

I knew about Kristallnacht, the Night of Broken Glass, but I had no idea that the timelines matched exactly. That same night, November 9, 1938, someone lit a torch in Recklinghausen and tossed it through the broken window of the synagogue. Marl historical accounts say that the SA, SS, and Hitler Youth all took part as onlookers cheered. The head of the Recklinghausen fire department showered the roaring flames with gasoline, and a tractor rolled in to topple the synagogue's tall tower. How did those onlookers feel as they walked homeward in the dark, their clothes reeking of smoke and their voices hoarse from yelling? When they locked their doors and checked on their sleeping children, were they feeling proud that they had defended Germany from attack? Headstones at the Jewish cemetery were knocked over, spat upon, and painted. All over Germany these coordinated attacks on the Jewish population exploded in the dark with an army of eager men to carry out the task.

The SA men of Marl waited until late at night. First they spent hours destroying the Boldes furniture store on Josefstraße. It wasn't until almost morning on November 10 that they reached the textile store. Herr Abrahamson ran down from the family's apartment on Loestraße in the smoke. Aghast, he hurried in to hit the flames near the front window with a large roll of fabric. SA men grabbed him from all sides and beat him with metal rods until he was no longer moving. Neighbors watched, terrified but silent, as Herr Abrahamson's body was thrown into the burning shop.

Jupp must have been called to one of these anti-Semitic attacks. As he was an SS man, there would have been no rational excuse for his absence. Here is where I feel the irrational tug of selfish fiction. I want to write that he escaped duty that night to sit at his father's bedside. I am not attached to Jupp in memory or affection, but I am in blood, and the question of the acts he committed on that night opens up a grief so huge that I turn away from imagining his cruelty. I have given myself permission to imagine, but I have refused my own challenge here. I realize that in five years of living with this story, I have written Jupp as naïve, as hopeful, so that I might understand what it means to become a monster. But I have not written the monster.

Jupp, son of a socialist, thought private thoughts about whether or not this action was justified. I will put him in the Boldes store, splashing gasoline on piles of fabric, in a state of mania or denial. This outrage would wake people up, he might have thought, and the Nazis would never get away with it. And so, in his strangely folded thoughts, he was helping to bring down Hitler by helping Hitler. Or maybe he generated a righteous rage I cannot fathom or a sense of self-protective victimhood. The shop burst into flames shooting skyward. Jupp saw a family dragged out into the night. Maybe he saw Rolf Abrahamson sprinting away into an alley and, almost without thinking, shouted, "You there!" to alert another SS man.

These actions may have happened, but they fall flat because

I don't understand Jupp, the man whom everyone described as happy-go-lucky, a joker. What is important is not an abstract generational guilt but the tangible details: a man with dark eyes and curly dark hair, an impish smile, and other ghostly mirrors of my own body, holding a rod to beat a Jewish man's spine until it shatters. What this image demands is beyond discursive analysis. Instead it asks me to realize how close, how linked by blood, how possible, how real and bodily and somatic and charged with the electric reverberations of inheritance are these moments. I force myself to study Jupp's face again in the photos and see with a shock of recognition that I am physically much more the image of Jupp than Heina, down to the curve of the eyes, the alignment of nose to eye to mouth, in the same way that my mother's face surfaces eerily in every photo of Lina the Dragon, Jupp and Heina's mother. And this is whence I sprang. If you will claim it, live in it, you must claim and mourn it all.

The next morning the Abrahamsons, including thirteen-year-old Rolf and his little five-year-old brother, were brought to the Gestapo prison and detained for two days. Rolf might have felt that his first job was to comfort his mother, his severely injured father, and his brother. He was old enough to stop his thoughts, to feel the edge of terror when he realized that nothing would be the same—not his school, not his friends, not the soccer field or the boys on the street or the candy from the corner store, that everything good in the world, everything besides his family, was being pulled away from him. His family returned to their apartment and discovered the city had shut off their heat and electricity. After freezing like this for four weeks in late November, they fled to Recklinghausen to live with friends. At the end of this elaborately planned assault, there were no more Jews living in Marl.

The morning of November 10, newspapers were ordered to omit wide-sweeping articles about Germany's swath of destruction from the previous evening. Reporters focused on the "spontaneous" actions as small local events, stressing that only windows were broken and ignoring news about the beatings and murders. The arrests: describe them as necessary protection for the Jews. And above all describe in the text the "righteous rage of the German people, brought about by the actions of a clique of Jewish émigrés," and the "final destruction of the synagogue, which had been a blot on the town." I wonder whether Papa Heinrich understood in his last hours what his country had become. His lung collapsed, and he died that morning as the embers of the synagogue smoldered.

9

The Cataclysm

Heina leaned his forehead against the cool window glass. Mist-covered hills blurred as the train raced past a farm, roads, there and gone, good-bye, good-bye. He'd been terse with Friedchen this morning and had snapped at Inge. And for what? Now he was off to the front, and it might be their last memory of him. German troops had crossed the Czechoslovakian border that spring, then Britain and France declared war at the beginning of September. Heina knew he'd be drafted along with any male who could walk. In the weeks after he received his call-up card, Friedchen had begun to look at him mournfully, as if he were already wounded or worse.

The men tumbled off the train and waited in line, each shuffling forward with a Wehrmacht bag near his feet, scooting the bags along the dirty tile floor toward the sign-in desk. Heina repeated a word to himself in a whisper: "Noncombatant. Noncombatant." The sulfur stink of a match flare wafted from the back of the room, followed by a warm cloud of burning tobacco.

"Wonder where we're going," said a husky voice.

"Naja," said another. "When I got my call-up card this summer, I would have guessed Czechoslovakia. But we're going to Poland."

A pause. An audible drag and exhale. "You better hope that's as far as we'll go."

The men had passed around newspapers that morning on the Stettin-bound train, as enlisted men creased the pages and pointed to headlines, maps, and significant phrases. "Took us three weeks from crossing the border to take Warsaw!" "My wife is praying this is the end." "No, we can't go into Russia—what do we want with Poland, anyway? Fucking bad food and a bunch of Poles." "It's part of the old German Reich. Hitler thinks he's going to claim the German-speaking people everywhere."

Heina reached the front of the line. A thin, severe-looking man with a pointed chin asked, "Name?"

"Buschmann," said Heina. He spelled it. "Heinrich. Noncombatant."

The man looked up from his card file. "Noncombatant?" he asked. "That's not on your card. You're an enlisted man. You volunteered."

"Noncombatant," Heina said. "Training for medical duty. Medic."

The man sighed and pulled Heina's card from the file. "What grounds—political, religious? Are you a Jehovah's Witness or something?"

At a loss for words, Heina wondered what response would arouse the least suspicion. "Either-or," said Heina, hoping his downcast eyes and the lack of challenge in his voice would allow him to slip by.

"Take your card to the third office and have the assignment changed, then go to the back of the line at the end of the hall," said the man. "Next!"

Heina took his card, was assigned as a medic, and disappeared into Hitler's war machine. Here I lose sight of the thread of his life. I can't trace his movements or even guess where he was sent, what tasks he had to perform.

I imagine him rolling bandages, learning the basics of splinting a broken bone and stocking a med kit. He must have joked ruefully with the other medics about the inadequacy of the medical supplies. The medics bunked together for training. Doctors and medical students, seminary students and politicos shared whispered exchanges of truth and rumor. Then Heina was swallowed up among the soldiers, and they boarded trains for a destination I can only guess.

Maybe he was sent on the invasion of Holland that spring. He would have worked on the back lines, knowing the German socialist émigrés in Amsterdam were in danger. The German army stormed into Denmark that April and made quick work of France, Belgium, Luxembourg, and the Netherlands that May. On June 14 the Nazis took Paris. Heina learned the sounds of shelling and tanks. Back home, the SPD and the communists desperately knit together patches of resistance in the Ruhr as their key contacts disappeared into the prison camp system and as the distant SPD party leaders continued to oppose any united action with the communists.

In the warm month of June, sticky with the new blood of war, laws were passed to prevent "ethnic mixing." If a Russian or Polish man had sex with a German woman, he could be put to death. If a German man had sex with a Polish or Russian woman, he faced prison. In that same month a drunk mineworker from a neighborhood near Hüls chatted with Polish workers in a bar. For that crime he was corralled by SA men and set atop a high scaffold in the town square with a sign around his neck that said, "I'm a friend to Poles." Then the local residents pelted him with horseshit.

Four months later, in October 1940, Heina returned home a different man. He might have thought of his father constantly, knowing only Papa Heinrich would understand the madness he had seen. Abruptly, then, he was out of uniform, ripped from chaos into routine like a set change in a horrible vaudeville show. When he first saw the thick, stuccoed wall of the family's home, he wanted to kiss the cement.

Back at work Heina was asked to commit the violence of forms and papers. I have no evidence of this, but it would be ridiculous to assume that Heina's hands were clean. So I imagine that twelve houses in Marl changed hands barely a month after Heina returned home to his white shirts, his bed, his wife, and his civilian breakfasts. These twelve homes, like the Buschmann compound, were solid and warm buildings once owned and lived in by the forty-seven Jewish residents of Marl who'd been imprisoned, murdered, or forced to flee. Their deeds had been transferred by special edict, and I imagine that Heina had played his small part in that erasure, instructed to adjust and transfer tax records to the state.

He touched the top form: "Abrahamson, title and tax record transfer." He glanced up to see the backs of the necks of his coworkers, this one bobbing his head, that one with curls of hair around the ears, all bent over their tasks. The revolution was dead if a socialist raised his stamp over these forms. The seizure of property had already been completed, but the stamp would make it official.

Heina grabbed the form by the long edge and curled it. *Rip it in half*, he told himself. But he didn't. He was apparently not strong enough to tear a sheet of paper. *Get up from the chair*, Heina told himself, *and walk out*. And surrender one's family to fate. He could not do it. He said a prayer for each of the families, a wordless pause, and then moved each form beneath his signature stamp. A black abyss open beneath him, far worse than the fear on the front last year with shells exploding everywhere. At least at the front his body moved for the love of life, trying simply to save itself.

At lunchtime he pedaled home numbly. He parked his bicycle against the outside wall, praying he could slip through a meal in silence. He climbed the steps and opened the back door to the kitchen. A rich brown smell engulfed him: real coffee, not acidic roasted chicory root. He stopped, his hand still on the door handle.

Mama stood at the stove stirring the soup. "Heina, Jupp's got coffee!" she beamed. "I had to brew a pot. Don't let the neighbors smell it," she joked.

"Close the door, man. You're letting all the heat out," said Jupp from the table as he reached for a slice of bread. Friedchen sat next to Inge and buttered a roll. Heina slid next to Jupp's wife, Else, to occupy Papa's seat at the head of the table. Bitter and laughable, he thought, that he should attempt to fill Papa's place as family patriarch. Spoons clinked against soup bowls, the kitchen filled with sighing and chatter about Inge's schoolwork and her boyfriend, Günther, who'd just been drafted. They moaned and clucked tongues over Hitler's latest military moves, the bombings of civilians in London, the British retaliation with the air attacks on Berlin.

Jupp raised his coffee cup and took a sip, then dipped the cup forward as if making a toast. "At least we got something from them," he said. For a split second, Heina couldn't place the pronouns. Who was the "we"? The fascists? The ss? Jupp noticed Heina's look. "The coffee, brother," Jupp said, "A perk from the Nazis—who don't even know it's going down socialist gullets."

"They don't know, huh?" Heina repeated.

Lina brought over the black coffeepot and poured some of

the steaming liquid into Heina's cup. "What's that supposed to mean?" she asked.

Jupp set down his cup, smiling with a complex mixture of sarcasm and real humor. "Do you want me to be sick over this, brother? Do you want me to tear out my hair because I got us some coffee? Should I tell you a communist comrade gave me coffee in exchange for a warning about a house search?"

Heina looked down at his scarcely touched broth, the chunks of tough carrot and thin bits of meat in his bowl. "If it were true you could say it," Heina said. Dully, he watched himself as if from afar. You're picking a fight. You want an explosion, Heina, provoking it with false withdrawal, a feint.

Jupp reared back his head and laughed. Friedchen stiffened as she leaned close to Inge and urged her to eat. "Everyone has to be in quiet agony all the time, don't they?" said Jupp, wiping his mouth and then moving his lips together as if still tasting the coffee. "Is that your contribution to the anti-fascists?"

"I would never tell you what my contribution is," Heina said, feeling a pulse of rage and disgust at himself, at every living thing. "God knows where the information would end up." Of course today of all days he should play the saint, the day he'd signed away Jews' houses, to make himself feel pure next to Jupp.

Jupp opened his mouth in shock. Heina believed that Jupp would never betray a socialist or the family, but it was so easy for Jupp, who confidently declared the territory between his ears a pure socialist nation. The trust between them had eroded on a much deeper level. They had both plunged over the brink already, unsavable. The argument bristled between them, subtle and poisonous, on fifteen different layers of meaning, old resentments held since childhood, knowledge about each other's weak spots now deployed in battle.

Heina pushed the full cup of coffee away with his fingertips, and in the same moment Friedchen raised her own cup, took a sip. Mama cleared the dishes in silence, and Jupp pointedly stayed with Else in the dining room, easy and relaxed, as if to emphasize that he hadn't been rattled, hadn't lost, hadn't been wrong. Heina walked upstairs. Maybe a ten-minute nap would stop the ache in his head. Friedchen smoothed Inge's hair and sent her out the door to the Hitler Youth meeting.

Heina turned a corner of the railing and looked down over the banister at Friedchen. "And how was the Nazi coffee?" he asked.

Friedchen looked up at him. "Heina," she said slowly, "I didn't mean anything by it."

"Jupp didn't either. He has no idea what anything means," Heina said.

She pressed her hand to her forehead and gripped the banister for support. The walls pitched, either from nausea or sadness. She was pregnant again, predictably, a month after Heina had returned. He'd been away for a year, and a sliver of her heart said silently, *Go back then, if you're itching for more fighting.* It had to be the baby, a good enough reason for bursting into tears. "It can't always be war, Heina," she said, voice shaking. "I can't take it. It was a cup of coffee." She wiped her eyes on her sleeve and ran past him up the stairs, slamming the apartment door behind her. He sat down on the cold stair, stunned at his bitterness and hate, wondering if this was what happened to Mama, too, these surges of words that receded, leaving regret and shock.

Heina, I only see you in that moment on the stairs because I imagine myself there, overwhelmed with impotent anger. Relief for you came from walking miles in the woods. You explained to your children, "My God is in the forest," a sentence passed down to me that revealed layers and rings like a tree trunk's cross sec-

nearby, hundreds of people turned slightly from their whispered conversations or twisted their shoulders toward the sound. The light turned to the purple of dusk, and the trucks never came. Jupp was dismissed from his shift and told to report again the next morning.

On the truck back to Recklinghausen, Jupp hid his face in his collar, relieved to leave those thousand doomed people. He looked across the truck at Jürgen, another ss man who had once been in the SPD. After each shift or action they worked together, Jupp sought Jürgen's slow drooping eyes. They stared at each other as if to say, "Today was once again hell, and not something we would do by choice." They granted each other sympathy and thus paradoxically enabled each other to carry on with their duties.

I have invented Jupp, invented Jürgen, and invented a divided consciousness. I imagine that part of Jupp innocently wanted to do good or to understand what "good" still meant. This might be incredible naïveté on my part, the only way I can connect to a character who shares my genes and who joined the ss. I write this fiction, this version of Jupp, partially to explore how the notion of individual virtue and purity can paradoxically allow a person to function within and support an evil system.

I imagine Jupp couldn't sleep that night. He sat in the kitchen darning socks. Else asked what he was doing. He shrugged, uncharacteristically silent, pulling at the thread. He planned to give some of these socks to the prisoners. After darning five pairs, Jupp cut five of yesterday's rolls and smoothed them with a layer of ersatz butter. He slipped a roll into each pair of socks and tucked the bundles into the pockets of his warm wool overcoat.

Else puttered in the kitchen, closing the curtains and wiping the table, straightening their small but well-appointed apartment in the Buschmann house.

The next morning Jupp arranged the folds of his coat carefully over his legs, hiding the small packages. During his watch shift he could not reach any of the prisoners to give out the bundles of socks and bread. An old olive-skinned woman with long silver hair sat on the ground, crying. A man who might have been her son inspected her feet, bluish-black from the cold. The man tucked her feet inside his coat, and she began to scream in agony, then pulled away, moaning, "Let them fall off. Let me die."

After noon four huge cargo trucks rumbled into the lot and braked. The ss men at the back of the lot tightened their ranks, pushing the crowd toward the trucks. A loudspeaker squawked commands: "You are to leave your bundles on the ground. Your possessions will be loaded into trucks that will follow you to your destination. Move now!"

A scuffle broke out at the edge of the crowd between ss men and some of the younger Jewish men; words flared with the raking sound of feet on gravel, ending in a shot. The crowd bucked like a single body, surging toward the trucks, and people tripped over the bags left strewn on the gravel. Jupp stepped into the crowd, holding out a hand as if to lead a family onto a nearby truck. He slipped a package of rolls and socks into the hands of a red-haired man with sharp blue eyes.

The man accepted the package with a blank face and put it in his pocket, then began to walk away, guiding a teenage redheaded boy. Jupp felt a rush of small happiness at this temporary human connection. The man turned back to Jupp. "Bread, something for the journey?" he asked in a quick whisper. Jupp nodded. "You are the worst of demons," said the man, looking into Jupp's eyes, "trying to give me just enough hope so that you'll own my soul as well." He stared at Jupp a second longer, then turned away to follow his family into the dark of the truck.

On the ride back to the Recklinghausen barracks, my fictional

Jupp reviewed and relived the instances in which he'd helped Jewish prisoners, had found ways to sneak money and food into the cells of political detainees, all the gratitude he'd been shown that had helped him convince himself he was of service, of help, that told him he was doing something worthwhile. But it would take him weeks to bury those sentences, that glance, from the red-haired prisoner, months to enclose that memory within a hard shell.

By the time Jupp had stopped worrying about the red-haired man I've imagined, the prisoners had arrived at the Riga Ghetto. The people on those transports might have been unloaded when the train stopped three kilometers away from the camp. Everyone who didn't survive the straggling march was shot. I imagine that the silver-haired woman with the frozen feet didn't make this march. She'd died during the transport.

What is true is that thirteen-year-old Rolf lost contact with his mother amid the crush of twelve thousand people in the Riga Ghetto. Frau Abrahamson, judged unable to work, was shot and buried in a mass grave under birch trees, die Birken, the trees with the white peeling skin. Some people who survived the transport joined the ten thousand Jews crammed into the Warsaw Ghetto. Rolf was later sent to the concentration camp at Kaiserwald, then to Buchenwald for two months to break stones. Still alive, he completed this sinister circuit when he was shipped back to the Ruhr, to Bochum, to assemble grenades. The imaginary five pairs of socks from Jupp were shredded into bits or buried with frozen feet in the Polish ground.

The ss division in the Ruhr—with Jupp as one member—filled cells and basement interrogation chambers with political prisoners. Connections between communist émigrés in Paris and the underground in the Ruhr strained and then shattered, and a new link was needed. A communist named Leo Kneler, disguised as a Polish laborer, got a job at the CWH rubber plant on March 9, 1941. Kneler found sympathetic contacts at CWH and met with a communist comrade in Recklinghausen. He formed a circle of resisters, who met to discuss politics and organized to collect food for the Russian prisoners in the Marl camps.

A German historian, Detlev Peukert, mentioned Leo Kneler in a book about Ruhr-area resistance. I carried that thick paperback in my bag every day for three months as I slowly translated the words. The detailed volume contained indexes of place names, activists, and code names. A dozen times or more I thumbed back to the same index and traced down the listings, hoping that the letters of the page would magically slide back to reveal a secret passage, that through dint of my work and love of this volume, my grandfather's name would finally be revealed. The passage about Kneler was one of the most specific examples of resistance work in Marl. That page also helped me nurse and maintain the idea that I'd found another shred of my grandfather's wartime life.

Not all of Kneler's contacts were identified by name. One of the Marl contacts was an enlisted man—as was my grandfather—who was also identified as "antifascist" rather than communist. This anonymous man was tagged by Kneler as a *Zentrumsmann*, a word I thought meant someone who worked in the city government because the city center was sometimes called the *Zentrum*. The time periods also overlapped: Kneler was working in Marl when Heina was home from the war, and this made me wonder if the mystery man was Heina. It could just as well have been anyone, but I wanted to believe it was my grandfather.

For that reason I imagine a morning in the summer of 1941 as the sky turned predawn turquoise. Heina folded back the featherbed and reached for his wool pants, not wanting to wake

Friedchen. As he slipped on his coat, she walked into the kitchen, squinting in the light. "Where are you off to?" she asked, her hands in her hair, fixing her long braid. She pulled her robe across her pregnant belly.

He leaned in to kiss her cheek, partially to avoid her eyes. "Errands to run," he said. He wasn't going to lie to her, but he didn't want to tell her the truth.

She looked at him, deep and still, willing her face to reflect no judgment, no fear. But she knew this man, knew by the twitch around the delicate skin of his eyes that he was thinking ahead to a task requiring his full attention. She knew by the pants he'd chosen to wear that he would be riding long distances and needed to be comfortable. Good Lord, how could one not put it together in an instant . . . Still, no use making it worse for both of them. Resolute, wasn't he, maddening and so himself.

Heina wheeled his bicycle out into the darkened street, repeating under his breath the details of the drop-off and pick-up points. If he were caught Friedchen would not be safe. But it was no use to think like that. Fear would make him jittery and noticeable. Focus on the task at hand, do it well, with quiet and humble efficiency, the German camouflage. Pushing on the pedal, swinging his leg over the back of the bicycle, and then in motion, with the wind in his face as he maneuvered through the familiar streets, he felt a hint of elation. The air was slightly cool and wet for June, but the first light on the trees made him want to race, pound the pedals and feel air in his lungs. He steered over cobblestones that looked like shining hunks of coal, past the bakery with its windows blazing and the door open to let out the heat, then under a bridge and out onto the bike path toward Bochum.

The sun emerged from behind the far tree line, and the first early morning walkers and paper salesmen nodded and said hello as Heina sped past. Twenty minutes into the trip he cut over onto a deserted farm road that would lead to the automobile repair shop where he would pick up a large envelope of newspapers from Amsterdam. He counted rough stone markers that must have once been fence posts along the edge of a field, and birds shot up from a gnarled linden tree.

A guy named Leo, a communist working in the underground as a foreign laborer at the CWH plant, had set up this literature route, and he seemed to be on the level. The directions so far had been accurate and detailed. Heina had run into a former youth communist leader in Recklinghausen through some friends at city hall, and had then met twice over the past month with Leo and other former SAJ members still in Marl.

Heina recalled his first impressions of Leo, or whatever his real name was, sitting forward in his chair, gesturing with hands too large for his small body, his eyes shining as he talked about the Russians, who he said would resist the Nazi invasion to the last man. Heina didn't know the other man and woman at that meeting. When Leo brought up the nonaggression deal that Stalin had made with Hitler before the start of the war, the other man (very pale, with a nervous habit of bouncing his knees) rolled his eyes and asked sarcastically, "Can Mother Russia do no wrong?" They avoided an all-out argument about Soviet politics only because the meeting was short. Leo deftly parried the criticism with a humble shrug and then put the question about literature distribution to the three of them. Heina tried not to be offended when Leo said to him, "You're perfect for this. You've got a nondescript face, the kind that blends well into a crowd."

Heina pumped the pedals and thought about the wild impulse of a mild-mannered man that made him accept this mission. Was it silly that it had something to do with loneliness, with the feeling that he was a loose limb without a body? He and Jupp barely even spoke anymore. Yes, it was partially his fault, but he had no idea how to break through to Jupp. Now everything was fouled up, with little hope of an honest conversation. Heina felt desperate for comrades, for that trust he had always shared with Jupp.

The red tile roof of the Siegfried auto yard cut an angular line against the blue sky. Stepping into the deserted yard, Heina pulled the handle of a heavy sliding door and picked up a knapsack filled with potatoes that hid a layer of pamphlets and papers. Heina slung the pack on his back and took off for the busy streets of Bochum. Among crowds, weaving past families out for their Sunday walks, was the safest leg of the trip, where it was easiest to escape if he were followed.

Heina made two other stops on a looping route back to Marl, reaching into the bag to pull out smaller packets. One went into a mailbox of a decrepit toy store with blackened windows in Dorsten, and the second went to a farmhouse far outside Recklinghausen. His thighs ached as he pedaled up the gravel drive toward his last drop-off. He left the packet at the back steps of the house and shook with relief to be heading home with only potatoes.

Five minutes up a steep hill toward Marl, a police wagon overtook him and pulled roughly onto the gravel roadside, spraying stones. Doors opened in slow motion and slammed. A short policeman barked sentence fragments that swirled around him: "Questioning—on suspicion of—in the truck . . ." The bicycle flew into the truck, a jangle of metal, and then Heina landed hard in the back of the wagon, his shoulder catching one of the pedals. He stood and banged his head as the wagon pulled roughly onto the road and accelerated. Where had he been sloppy? Who had followed him?

At the station it became clear that the farmhouse, owned by a known leftist, had been under surveillance. Sitting on a hard wood bench in a holding area, Heina ran his hands through his hair and wondered if he'd see the outside again as a free man. Maybe Jupp could get him out. Good God, if he were charged he'd lose his job. You never plan on getting caught. How to get word to Friedchen, what they could charge him with, maximum sentences, and who else would be betrayed? He would say nothing . . .

A policeman came in and took Heina's identification card. Fifteen or twenty minutes passed, and Heina heard his name in the rush of a muffled conversation from the next room. Ten minutes or an hour, then the same policeman stood in the doorway, bored and annoyed, and motioned Heina with a flick of his fingers. "Go," he said. "We're done here." Heina grabbed his jacket and stood, too slowly. The policeman sighed and tossed Heina's card in his direction. "Enough!" he said. "Get out."

He rode home in a daze under the blazing searchlight sun. There was only one explanation for his sudden release: thanks to Jupp, the name "Buschmann" now served as a password to safety instead of a badge of rebellion.

Heina pulled his head down as the wind rushed past, barely able to see for the black spots of fear massing in his vision. Breathe. By all rights he should still be waiting in that cell. He was free. He reached for gratitude and felt only hot rage and resentment. His escape seemed to prove that Jupp had been bought. Irrationally, being freed on Jupp's account only hardened Heina's heart against his brother.

After pulling apart these sentences, I read them to Mom and asked her what *Zentrumsmann* meant. She replied that the word probably meant a political conservative, someone from the center-right Christian Democratic Party. In that case the man running the mission for Leo Kneler would not be Heina. I felt Heina twisting away as I tried to hold his collar, and I wished for a moment I hadn't been so persistent with the translation. Desperate for proof, I want documentation, Heina's name in a list, like a relic to touch when I lose faith in my own life. For that easy icon I would reach back into history and move Heina closer to the inferno of Hitler's camps. On these searches through indexes and lists of the imprisoned, I feel him pushing back at me from the grave, asking, "What would be good enough for you?"

The baby yawned luxuriously, with an endless stretch of tiny limbs, safely settled in her mother's arms. Heina let his heart open when baby Brunhilde arrived to fill the carriage on August 28, 1941. She was screamingly alive, tiny, red faced, with wisps of light blond hair. She was a flower, one of those babies who clings instinctively to your neck and wants only to be held, who fits into your arms and trusts absolutely. Friedchen was also drunk with love for this little summertime girl.

Heina caught himself lost in dreams as he rode his bicycle to work and watched the blur of sunlight on the grasses and cattails in the ditches. This child felt like a sign, as tentative but real as warm earth, that his life and the war might turn around. The Russians fought back furiously on the eastern front, and Reds of all shades secretly nursed wild hope. Walking to the bakery one morning, Heina saw the slogan F-F-F chalked on the wall of a cinderblock warehouse. He'd heard whispers at the air raid warden's meeting: the communist underground paper *Ruhr Echo* had launched a new propaganda campaign, urging activists to chalk the Fs, for *Frieden, Freiheit, Fortschritt*—peace, freedom, progress. That warm summer teenagers did the impossible, grew their hair and called themselves the Edelweiss Pirates as they hung out and drank and mocked the Hitler Youth. They chalked over swastikas and danced, giddy with the lure of busting open all the lies.

Heina heard the rumors and remembered that delicious surge of teenage electricity from twenty years before.

Or was the road ahead rougher and more ominous? The SA shot two Edelweiss Pirates. German troops took Kiev. And there were whispers of a coordinated war on the Jews throughout Europe, of transports that led to prison camps or worse. The newspapers published the list of new laws requiring yellow stars for the Jews. But there were no Jews in Marl anymore.

Iron doors swung open, and socialist activist August Kastner moved toward a high desk with his hands cuffed in front of him. A saucer-shaped lamp cast a circle of light on the SS clerk, who found Kastner's name on a roster, signed his release, and said, "You're free to go." Kastner had spent two years in protective custody for trying to start an illegal miners' union. He pressed his dry lips together and waited, knowing freedom would never be that simple. "Check in every two weeks with the police bureau in your neighborhood," the clerk said. "Notify them when you find a job, and apply there before you travel. If you at any point . . ."

In the midst of this droning list of regulations, another SS man strode in, shoulders pitched forward. Kastner waited, signed the release form, and stepped slowly toward the door, stalling to cross paths with this second clerk. "Excuse me, sir," said Kastner, stopping to glance briefly in the man's face.

Jupp Buschmann looked back and his businesslike expression broke into a full smile. Kastner, an old union friend of his father, had often joined them for Sunday dinners and sat at the kitchen table planning the next move for the miners' union. Jupp looked over Kastner's shoulder, waited until the other clerk had left the room, and said softly, "Herr Kastner—it's me, Jupp Buschmann."

Kastner took his time examining Jupp's face. "In an SS uniform, no less," he said dryly.

Jupp shrugged, a hitch of the shoulders as if to say, *We're all in this together.* "My mother says it's good to have someone on the inside. I've been able to get word to—"

"Your mother's a fool," Kastner said and turned toward the exit.

Jupp swallowed and composed himself, but a flush crept up from his collar as he hurried to the prisoners' cells. His lips twitched. *Kastner! That judgmental old man . . .* Jupp could list the names of lives he'd saved in this position. *Didn't that count for anything? This was what was wrong with the Left! This was exactly why they'd failed: never being satisfied with what a person had to give, always expecting so much sacrifice that you had to hate yourself for anything less.*

Jupp checked the prisoners' roster and opened the door to an interrogation room, where two other ss men sat sprawled in chairs in front of an older prisoner in handcuffs. The folder on the desk was marked with a handwritten note: "Communist, connections to Paris? Find local contacts . . ."

"Look, we can sit here and wait," said Weiland, one of the interrogators, "but we also have other things to do. The quicker you tell us your contacts, the easier it's going to be." Weiland stood and walked behind the seated prisoner, who turned his head to look. Weiland grabbed the man's hair and yanked backward, and the man tumbled off the chair onto the cement floor. Jupp felt an instinctive tug of revulsion at the violence, then that familiar numbness. The prisoner on the floor struggled to put his legs beneath his body and pulled himself up.

I imagine Jupp continuing his one-sided conversation with Kastner. *Couldn't Kastner see it was no use to have another man dead? What good would Jupp be as a pious martyr in a grave? Kastner—it was just like him to judge, not to even allow Jupp to explain, not to understand the constant stress he was under; it was just like Heina . . .*

Weiland grabbed the prisoner's collar and hurled him toward the wall near Jupp, who put his hands out to catch the prisoner. The prisoner collapsed weakly against Jupp's body, tears streaming down his face. *They hadn't done more than toss this guy across the room and now tears. Some of these damn politicos could talk but then they crumpled like paper dolls.* A wave of rage flowed down into Jupp's fingertips. He grabbed the prisoner's shoulders and drove the man's head toward the wall. *A momentary lapse, a defensive reaction, a second of misplaced frustration.* He would later feel ashamed, mull it over, confess to Else, and then add it the list of the regrettable things the Nazis had forced him to do. *He had no choice. What would Weiland do if Jupp had reached out to protect this communist guy? No, there was no way out of it.* The prisoner's blood marked the cinderblock wall in a small wedge shape, with a few strands of dark hair pressed into the red stain as it dried.

Friedchen held a bowl of cucumber salad toward Heina. "Take this downstairs. We're having lunch with the family," she said. Friedchen, pregnant for the sixth time and nauseous, could eat only bread and cucumber salad. She reached down and lifted their baby daughter, Brunhilde, into her arms.

Heina scowled, his jacket half off, and sighed. "I get an hour for lunch off work, and instead of eating quietly I've got to have some drama," he said.

Friedchen waited on the landing, her face blank. Heina patted Brunhilde's wispy blond hair and the girl cooed, turned her face into her father's hand. The baby's soft cheek made Heina's chest ache. How would it be possible to leave this sunny child? He'd gotten his draft notice a few weeks ago, and in September he'd head to the front. Inge's young boyfriend, Günther, had barely started his service when he was captured and sent to a prison camp in the Netherlands. By the time Heina returned—if he returned—Germany might not exist. He might end up in a Russian POW camp, he might . . . Brunhilde laughed, and Heina forced himself to focus on this instant: his wife, the stairs, Brunhilde's pink cheeks, the bowl of spring-green cucumber salad with sprigs of dill.

"Why are you so intent on having me talk to Jupp?" he asked as they walked down the stairs.

"He's your brother, Heina."

Else and Friedchen greeted each other. Jupp's voice rang out from the kitchen, something about the British air raids on Köln, asking whether the basement was adequate air raid protection. Inge ate quickly, her suntanned face expectant and hurried. "Late for a soccer game," she said and ran off on gangly legs. It was good she had distractions. Mama set a plate of potato pancakes on the table, and the greasy smell of onion and potato filled the kitchen.

"When's your call-up date, Heina?" Jupp asked.

Was Jupp trying to remind Heina that he was headed to the front lines while Jupp himself stayed here in Marl? Friedchen scowled a silent warning at Heina.

"September 3," Heina said. He would miss the birth of his child. He reached for the applesauce, busied himself with filling his plate to avoid Jupp's eyes. He chewed slowly.

Jupp, conscious always of the flow of conversation, sighed lightly. "Well, Mother," he said, "plenty of families have both sons called up. I guess the Buschmanns are lucky."

The wad of potato turned to glue in Heina's mouth.

Mama ladled cucumber salad onto plates. "I pity any mother who loses more than one child, like Frau Schneider down the block. Imagine, three boys," she said, twisting her lips into a knot of abstract sympathy. Friedchen coughed into her fist. Two boys. Babies, weren't they always babies, no matter how old.

Heina focused on the silver tines of the fork, on the edge of the knife, on the curve of the plate. "Are you planning for me to be dead already?" he asked, voice barbed with careful politeness.

A pained expression crossed Jupp's brow. "Of course not, Heina!"

"To even say such a thing," Mama scolded.

"There is no such thing as luck, Jupp," Heina said, swallowing, attempting to maintain control of his face, not even able to look at his brother. "Did Marx write about luck as a social force that creates history? Luck is what people tell themselves when they don't want to ask why things *really* happen."

Heina, I know you were called to the eastern front, to that wide swathe of murder and destruction. But what coordinates on the map marked your path and destination? You know where I want you: permanently holding anti-Nazi flyers, frozen in plastic like a paperweight, surrounded with colored glitter that reflects the light. Look, a happy activist, a smiling saint. I don't want to know that you looked up from your medical supplies to see the ragged outline of a mass grave. I don't want to know about the talk and whispers at night around campfires about the bodies in the ditches. I can feel you pushing. I can hear you, Grandfather, though I can't make out the words. You have volumes of stories to tell me.

The soldier's tongue writhed like a pink fish and flitted behind the ragged hole in his cheek. Heina bent down into the camp medic cabinet for the stitching kit, taking a moment to breathe and clear his head. He'd gagged while inspecting the soldier's torn cheek, a strange reaction after seeing mangled bodies and much worse.

"You're fixing me up so I can be shot properly," the soldier said. Air whistled through the hole as he spoke.

The soldier, apparently a deserter, had been found in the Ukrainian woods that morning as a few men from the Sixth Battalion's camp tramped into the underbrush to relieve themselves. The soldier told them first that he'd been separated from his unit and was shot during an evacuation action at a ghetto in Lublin, but he couldn't explain why he'd passed out in the forest with his weapon a few feet away.

"I'm sorry," Heina whispered as he pierced the man's cheek with a needle, wincing as he drew the black thread behind the hole and began to pull its edges together. The soldier sat motionless, but his eyes darted and rolled. He seemed comforted by Heina's touch, by the needle, and his shoulders slumped downward.

"One thing I know: if you're going to blow your head off, take a moment and straighten your weapon first," said the soldier, laughing in a monotone. Heina knotted and clipped the end of thread. A failed suicide. Heina wiped the blood and spittle from his hands.

"You're a bad shot," Heina said, smiling gently. "Why do that?"

The soldier's stoic face dissolved, and he opened his mouth wide to sob, his lips pulled unevenly by the stitches. "Two hours west of Warsaw there is a huge pit filled with bodies. We had to shoot and shoot and shoot, back of the head, base of the skull, kids, miserable old women, these women with these eyes, and the blood everywhere, the screaming, and then—good God, it was August, the hot sun after three days and still not being done, the stench—" The soldier, with his rubberlike face pulled in terror, reached out to grab Heina's hands. Heina yanked away and stood up, toppling his stool. The man reached both his hands out toward Heina, palms up, hungry for contact. "Please."

"What? What do you want?" Heina stood as if he might bolt. Listen, the trees seemed to demand, relieve this man's soul.

"I promise I won't tell you the details. I have to tell someone what I saw. You have to tell other people—"

A huge space in Heina's heart opened, the vast wasteland where he stored the horrors he'd seen. There was, of course, room for more. He nodded. "I can do that," he said. He reached for and righted his stool.

The soldier didn't resume his litany. Instead he rested his elbows on his knees, hands clasped together, and looked at the earth. "I'm not religious. But what do you think about a man's soul . . . a man who was forced to do those things but who did not want to? Where will my soul go?"

Heina flinched, muscles tensed. "I don't know about the soul, friend. I don't spend much time thinking about it," Heina said. That wasn't entirely true, but Heina scrambled to close a wall between himself and this desperate man and the vision between them of Jews shot and tumbling one by one. Heina stared at the soldier's hands. The soldier began to weep, torso collapsed over his knees. Despite the effort to stay back, Heina's hand flew forward and came to rest on the man's shoulder.

"What does it mean, that I pulled the trigger again and again? If I wasn't willing, it isn't the same, is it? It isn't the same!"

Comfort the man, demanded the trees. *Say it's not the same.* But Heina kept his mouth closed. *Bite your lips,* said a razor within Heina's mind, *so that even if you die you won't go down a wretched liar.* The man's howls attracted the attention of the guard standing outside the tent, who handcuffed the man and dragged him down the path toward the center of camp.

Alone in the tent, Heina hunched over the metal trays of rolled gauze. The white gauze must have reminded him of raw dough, because in an instant he was standing in the bakery in Kahla, smelling and seeing the rows of dinner rolls his father pinched into shape and slapped onto a huge metal sheet. The brain did strange things, desperate smokescreens and shields. Then the real smells came back: the distant stink of a hastily dug latrine pit nearby, the smell of sun-warmed and musty canvas, spilled gasoline, and the unfamiliar tang of Ukrainian wheat and hay, the metallic and sharp scent of the black soil.

Papa—for an instant Heina forgot the man was dead. Papa would know how to survive this. He would either have leapt into the pit of confusion with that soldier or roared at him with clarity. Unable to act, Heina was dead inside or near that point. A memory of Papa seemed to scoff: writing your own death certificate was another form of cowardice.

Heina knew he was not dead yet. Dead was like the rumors of the Lahava Ghetto in western Bylorussia—"liquidated." Dead like people in the Tutzin Ghetto in the Ukraine who were said to have fought up to the minute of their deaths with sticks, bottles, and ancient weapons from the First World War. Soldiers arrived two days ago with murmurs of all the Jews in Germany shipped somewhere to the east, about a plan for massive violence. And tomorrow the Sixth Battalion would march south. They'd meet with another unit at the southern end of the Ukraine and continue further. At the end of the march there would be bloody feet, boots too big and too small rubbing holes in the men's flesh. And more death.

Blond braids flying, Inge ran, swinging a day pack for the Hitler Youth hiking trip. Up ahead a crowd gathered at the corner near the pub and the Auguste Viktoria mine entrance.

Friedchen yelled, "Inge!"

Inge looked back toward her mother and rolled her eyes with frustration. Friedchen yelled again, more harshly. Rifle barrels and SA caps bobbed above the crowds on Viktoriastraße. Inge looked back and tilted her chin sarcastically at Friedchen as if to tell her to hurry and not be such a worrywart.

Had Friedchen ever been this fresh with her own mother? Surely not, though she'd had a different way to give her mother headaches. Instead of the swastika and League of German Girls pin, Friedchen had had her youth meetings, the red songbook, and her reform clothes, those simple loose smocks that her mother had called flour sacks. And here up on the left was the bar where they'd had the first SAJ meetings to plan the youth home, the meetings where she knew for sure she loved Heina . . .

"Guck mal—Look at these creatures!" bellowed an SA man from the street. Beyond the row of SA men, a group of gray shaved heads appeared. Russian prisoners in shackles shuffled from the camp on Römerstraße to the mine. I know these daily marches took place and read about this specific route and the crowds, chronicled in local history. I also know that Friedchen's brother Willi worked guard duty at that POW camp, and I imagine him in a watchtower on third shift, surveying the two thousand prisoners. "Worms in the soup," I imagine he'd said about the camp. "Dysentery. The prisoners don't last long, and when they can't work they get sent away to die. Some prisoners go to the rubber plant for training, then they're shipped to the other IG-Farben plant—at Auschwitz."

Friedchen struggled to see faces in the march and focused on a strong young man with red cheeks, then a pair of unbowed shoulders, then a third prisoner with shoes on his feet, a fourth face unbroken by sores. That one will survive, she told herself, playing a desperate game of pretend. Inge twisted forward through the crowd to get a better view, and Friedchen grabbed her shoulder roughly. Inge turned around with shock on her face, blue eyes wide. "Stay by me," Friedchen whispered, pulling Inge close to her. "There's no reason why you need to be near the street. Why do you need to see that suffering?"

"Untermenschen!" cried a voice in the crowd. "Subhumans!"

Friedchen didn't want to see the face of that yelling idiot, probably a supporter of Recklinghausen's mayor, who'd recently announced that area Jews had been "evacuated" for their own safety.

Inge pushed through the thinning crowd and turned left on Viktoriastraße. Friedchen lagged behind, then called to Inge that they would take a different route toward the city center. Inge turned, scowling, and followed Friedchen down a side street close to the labor camp.

"This isn't even the way," Inge said. "You're going to make me late."

"This is like the camp where Günther is held," Friedchen said, motioning to a high fence strung with barbed wire. "I want you to see it."

I imagine a Russian foreign worker leaning against a building ahead. Marl history tells the story of the foreign workers, who received a meager wage and could leave the camp briefly between shifts—unlike prisoners captured in military campaigns. Barely fed, the Russians made treasures to trade for bread and bits of food, begged for side work from people living near the camps, creating a delicate web of connection between this work-prison and the residential area, which older folks today still call the Römerlager, the prison on Römerstraße

I imagine a sparse, dark beard covered the Russian's jaw. He smoked a tiny stub of rolled cigarette and nodded as they approached. Inge veered away, and Friedchen slowed her pace. The man held up one finger and put his other hand into his jacket pocket. He pulled out an elaborately carved wooden box and held it toward Inge. She stopped and stared, her hand reaching forward.

"For bread," he said in heavily accented German. Such trades were common, and the wooden handiwork is still saved by many German families.

Inge looked at Friedchen, reached toward her knapsack, and hesitated. She put her hand inside and took out one of her two lunch rolls. The exchange was made. The man tore off a bit of the roll and placed it in his cheek. He nodded in thanks and turned back toward the camp.

Inge touched the cover of the box and held it toward Fried-chen. "He gave me this box just for a roll!" Inge said, pleased at her bargain.

"He was probably hungry," said Friedchen.

Inge studied the box, maybe thinking about Günther, who had assured her in letters that he was safe because he knew English.

"I don't want you coming out here by yourself," Friedchen said as they walked, hoping her daughter would remember the man's desperation.

A gray-faced soldier cut in front of Heina in the mess line, el-bowing Heina's chest to reach for two slices of hard bread. The soldier's lean and weathered face was somehow unanimated and seemed slapped together from discarded features. Heina turned to Roland, another medic and former SPD member. "He looks half dead," Heina whispered.

Roland said, "I wonder if we'll get that look." They filled their tin cups with the brown watery liquid that passed for coffee and took seats at a long table. Clipped conversation flowed around them.

Their unit had been joined yesterday by Section IIB of Ein-satzgruppe D, a special unit under Commander Ohlendorf that had swept southward on the invasion of the Ukraine. Most of these Gruppe D men didn't say much, but within a few hours of IIB's arrival rumors charged the air—talk of mass graves and days filled with the task of shooting Jews, thousands of them, at Riga, Babi Yar, the killing grounds at the Ponary Forest in Poland

. . . The knowledge of these acts seemed to seep from direct skin-to-skin contact with these soldiers.

"Medic! Over here!" A gray Sauer van pulled to a stop on the rut-ted dirt road. The cab door swung open, and a voice called from inside, "Help this soldier! He's been hurt in a fight with locals at the prison."

Roland and Heina darted out of line as soldiers tromped past. Roland dropped a medic bag at the roadside and shouted, "We've been ordered to move out, sir." Heina craned his neck, searching for the commanding officer.

A man fell from the truck's cab with his hands pressed to the side of his neck. Ribbons of blood splayed between his fingers, spatters of red on his jaw and his uniform, his eyes clouded and unseeing. Heina ran toward the man and tripped on the tire-track ridges in the mud. He reached for his pack: a deep cut, the jugular? Heina fumbled for gauze as the man collapsed. The truck's engine fired, and a crash of metal echoed as the truck lurched. The gauze under Heina's hands soaked with red. Where was Roland? There, useless man, standing stock-still behind the truck. "Roland, I need help now with pressure . . ."

Roland stared. The truck's cargo door had flown open, and inside the dark rectangle of its hold, strange angles and curves appeared: clothed limbs, pale faces. The smell of exhaust, vomit, and urine billowed out. A limp forearm fell and dangled from the mouth of the cargo hold.

Heina's fingers tightened around the man's neck, and warm blood seeped. Inside the truck: the shine of two eyeballs, frozen wide and reflecting the white sun, the face of a shocked young boy, a metal glimmer of a buckle, a ripple of dark hair. Bodies, newly dead, entwined as though they'd knotted themselves in agony, now hauled like a load of stones.

Heina loosened his grasp on the soldier's warm, wet skin. The soldier's drained face moved, tongue swollen, mouth burbling, hands fumbling at the collar. The driver leapt from the cab and grabbed the edge of the cargo door. He slammed it shut, but the door smashed against the hanging forearm and shot back open. Soldiers on the road broke formation and some stood to gape. Others pushed roughly past, eyes ahead. The driver kicked at the dangling arm, pushed it back inside the truck, and closed the cargo door. An officer jumped from the truck's passenger door, shouting at the marching unit in disarray: "Soldiers, back to your positions!"

Numb, Heina bent and took the pulse of the man lying at the side of the road: dead. He pulled the body into the ditch and uselessly closed the man's eyelids. Soldiers scrambled back into formation, and the gray truck shuddered onto the roadway.

"It had a false window painted on its side," Roland said.

Heina wiped his bloody hands on his thighs. "That throat wound—" he said. He imagined a struggle, a concealed knife, a kicking and dragging and blood as the door slammed.

In the slow tromp of marching, words floated, the rumors and talking untraceable as men muttered, hardly moving their lips. The Russians called that van the "Soul Killer," one of three such vehicles. Exhaust was funneled into the back chamber, delivering death in ten minutes. It was used to empty orphanages, schools, ghettos. The officers said the van was built out of concern for the soldiers because it was easier and more efficient than shooting Jews and prisoners one bullet at a time.

Family stories place Heina in the Crimea at the end of the war, where the Soul Killers closed their doors and delivered death. I imagine Heina learned this much and more as the German troops moved south toward their unraveling. I imagine his days, dealing with wounded men brought to the L-shaped minihospital set up between two medic trucks. The German troops razed the villages of Russians and Crimean Tartars, moving south down the rocky hills of the Crimean peninsula against fierce resistance. Heina wrapped burns and stitched up knife wounds, treated human fingernail marks clawed into soldiers' faces and backs.

"Quit your bitching," Roland yelled to the line of waiting and moaning soldiers. "I don't care if you're in pain. We take the most serious first, so you can just sit there and bleed into the fucking dirt." Roland sat down on his campstool and turned to face an abdominal wound. What were they supposed to do with this one? He would bleed out a few liters of blood on their cot and then die, whether or not they tried to bind him together.

Heina picked dirt and shards of wood from an officer's mashed eyeball. The officer stayed very still, as if he were getting a haircut, and even tried to make conversation. "Don't say where you heard it," the officer said, "but we're facing the advance troops of a Russian counterattack. Hitler said it wouldn't happen, but they're coming for us. The Reds, though, they aren't disciplined, so we've got a chance . . ."

Hands and gauze soaked, Roland tilted his chin to get Heina's attention, then nodded over toward the medic kit with a wicked smile. This was Roland's sick joke: a bottle in the med kit marked "antiseptic" that he'd filled with gasoline. Heina pretended not to see and turned back to the gory eyeball, swelling shut. He cut strips of tape, lined them up on his tray, and taped a pad over the eye.

Hours later Roland sat smoking while Heina drifted in and out of sleep, sitting on the ground with his knees tucked up, his head resting on his forearms.

"If we were men . . ." Roland said.

Heina raised his head. "What? We'd be out there with rifles?"

Roland held the small cigarette stub delicately against his lips and inhaled, deepening the lines in his cheeks into vertical creases. He crushed the butt in his palm to save the remaining threads of tobacco. "No," he said. "We'd have used that gasoline by now on some of the wounded Nazi fanatics. Or poisoned the painkillers. Or . . ." Heina worried that lanky, blue-eyed Roland might lose his mind before the end of this deployment. Still, talking about sabotage was the only memory of humanity they had. It was unclear what out here qualified as a moral act, or whether the question was idle philosophy.

"I'm a terrible medic. My work should count as sabotage," Heina said. "Think of all the Nazis I've killed through total incompetence."

Roland closed his eyes and leaned his head against the side of the truck. Heina stared at the brown gravel, the low oval-leafed plants curling in the cold toward the ground. He feared death so far from home. He couldn't do anything bold like pour gasoline on a commanding officer's eye. Resting his head on his arms, Heina saw the image that always rose before sleep: the gray truck with the fake window painted on its side, the door swinging open, the limp arm and the face of a staring young boy.

On April 6, 1943, Friedchen gave birth to Klaus on the dining room table, in the same room where I learned my family history. Maybe a midwife coached her as she bore down against the contractions. Her husband was countries away, dead or alive, fighting a hopeless war.

Klaus's birth opened a new chapter in a story plotted with illusions of race and genes: the second wave of Buschmann children, the dark to replace the light. Though no one knew it, blond Brunhilde was doomed. My uncle Klaus made his way into the world with blond hair and the slate-colored eyes of European newborns, but his hair and eyes later turned coal-black. Mom would be born with the same coloring, followed finally by Werner, the dark youngest brother. Someone told Mom as a child that the first three children after Inge were two light boys and a sunlight girl. Mom remembers thinking that when those light children passed, the finer blond energy of her parents was used up.

Maybe because her parents were exhausted and sad, she was told (or imagined) that only the dregs of baby-making material were left for the darker, baser children. No one would say this directly to a child, would they? But children pick up on the rules that bind adults. Mom always knew that her existence depended on the death of her older siblings, that she was a replacement child born in postwar distraction, out of sadness. What shocks me is the racism in the story, woven deeply as a fairy tale, into a household that supposedly struggled against judgments based on imaginary bloodlines. When I first heard that story, too young myself to understand the context, I felt its sting on my own olive-skinned face.

They couldn't hold the peninsula, but Hitler told them to stay.

"We're moving forward, men," yelled General Schmidt. Veins pulsed in his forehead as he waved frantically, motioning to the south, toward the bay. Soldiers widened their mouths, dumbfounded.

A lieutenant tossed weapons and ammunition into the open lockers of a supply truck. "Impossible," said the lieutenant to General Schmidt. "The Russians have the neck, the Perekip land bridge, and they'll squeeze us off. They're creeping around from Kerch in the east. We'll be trapped."

"German battleships will sail in from the south, we'll be saved by water—"

A furious cackling erupted. "If you believe that! We don't have enough men to keep Sevastopol!"

Gunfire echoed off the cliffs. Roland had been killed the week before, shot in the stomach when Russian troops circled and cut off half their unit. Now escape was the only thing. Heina leapt forward into the supply truck, intent on siding with the retreating lieutenant.

In April 1944, with the Russians almost upon the German troops and no way to retreat, Hitler gave the order to run. Soldiers waited on the beach, straining to see through the smoke, clutching their weapons and firing shots behind them up the slope. They followed orders and watched for the German ships to rescue them. But the ships stayed in the harbor through incompetence, a misunderstanding, or by design, and twenty-six thousand men were taken prisoner.

Where was Heina? My information unravels for the last eleven months of the war, with Heina lost in the chaos of the eastern front. I imagine soldiers traded stories and pointed out the sites of massacres as they retreated back through Poland. They were burning bodies of Jews and others at Auschwitz, more than you could ever imagine. The Allies had bombed the Ruhr. If you hated Hitler, you cheered inside with the sickest sadness to know that the only way to rid Germany of the Nazi cancer might be for the whole country to die.

Heina might have moved north with the remains of his unit. When Germany called for a full retreat in the face of advancing Russian forces, he might have sewn up soldiers wounded in the Russian victory at Stalingrad. He might have moved east with the unit that beat down a Polish rebellion or the armed Jewish resistance in the ghettoes of Bialystok, Czestochowa, or Lvov, or the armed resistance at the Treblinka camp. Those Jewish fighters were later "liquidated" along with the people from ghettos at Minsk and Lida.

At a certain point in 1944 the German eastern front began to

dissolve. Heina might have merged into a unit responsible for
the eastward death-march evacuation of Auschwitz as the Nazis
tried fruitlessly to hide evidence of the camps and the cremato-
ria. Heina might have wrapped the frozen foot of a soldier who
would thank him, get up from his cot, and two hours later gun
down a starved Jewish woman from Poland named Magda who
loved, above all else, the music of Tchaikovsky and the glinting
of the sun on water. As Heina survived, his hands contributed
to the last frayed attempts of the Nazis to scrape together a few
more months. Then there was a burst of confusion, the attack of
a Russian unit, and maybe he was running somewhere, behind a
front, and suddenly overtaken.

I imagine a path led him up a hill, and the bushes pulsed in the
wind, looking strangely like plants underwater. Time stopped,
and each leaf moved in a fanlike wave. Two soldiers ran ahead
of him. One dragged his gun in the dirt, shot in the arm, a red
rivulet widening on his shoulder blade. In the ocean roar of gunfire, Heina flew forward as if his legs were on fire. He did not
seem to gain any ground on the two slow-moving soldiers. If he
could reach them, it seemed he would be delivered to safety. The
warmth spread down his leg, down, down into his ankle, and
then the horizon flipped and the plants and rocks came up to
meet him. His mouth opened, choking and making noises, and
his hands flew down to his thigh, grasping tightly, drawing away
as if burned, and he waved his hands in front of his face and saw
them covered in streams and wet lines of his own red blood.

The bicycle rumbled over pitted roads and lulled baby Klaus to
sleep. Four-year-old Brunhilde knew this trip was no game. She
watched her mother's tired face and whined about her legs hurting as they pressed against the metal ribs of the bicycle basket.
Friedchen wadded a blanket, folding and refolding it, making a

cushion to soothe Brunhilde. Friedchen pushed heavily against the bicycle's pedals with all of her weight. It would be days yet before they reached Lina's family in Thüringen, if they got there at all.

I know this trip of over three hundred kilometers on bicycle had been Lina's idea. A blistering air raid had shattered the CWH plant, and Recklinghausen was heavily hit. The last round of bombs decimated their block, leaving an endless expanse of stone rubble and twisted, smoking trees, although the Buschmann house had escaped destruction. But after firestorms in Hamburg and Dresden, the stories of people cooked in streetcars and turning to ash in their backyards, it seemed only a matter of days before bombs found the family. Posters went up in Marl and Recklinghausen to inform women and children of the two cities that the local authorities could no longer guarantee their safety. Else thought the train lines would be taken next and that bicycles were the only way.

"I don't know whether we're heading east or south—I hope the directions from that woman were right," said Else, who continued her stream-of-consciousness narration of their entire trip. "I wonder whether Marl is still standing."

Friedchen wanted to slap her. To be fair, Else didn't have children, didn't understand how much they heard, and didn't quite grasp that spewing fear didn't help any of them cope. Inge had started out with a smile as if the trip were a bold adventure, but she was now sullen and silent, riding meters ahead of them, sobbing to herself. Friedchen sighed and focused on the road, which seemed to spool so slowly under her tires. It was a desperate gamble, three women and two children out alone in the German countryside, waiting for the advancing line of whatever army caught them first.

Aside from the exhaustion, the filth, and the loneliness, the

worst part was the children's fear. They'd been lucky the first
two nights in begging for places to sleep. Last night they'd
been threatened and chased, so they decided to sleep in a dry
but dirty shed. Brunhilde curled next to her mother on an automobile tarp, looked up at her with huge blue eyes and asked,
"Does Daddy know where we are right now?" It was enough to
make Friedchen weep, but she kept her face calm, told Brunhilde
they'd see Papa again soon. As the hours passed on the roadway,
Friedchen imagined Heina's troops had been scattered on the
eastern front. Maybe he, too, would make his way to Kahla.

"Oh, shit," said Else, rolling to a stop.

"What is it?" Friedchen asked.

"Flat tire. I hope I brought that patch kit." Else threw the bike
on the roadside, and Friedchen had to stifle another cry of frustration. Else treated the bicycle like she was riding to the store
instead of to save her life.

Friedchen grabbed Brunhilde under the arms and lifted her
out of the bicycle basket, then lifted Klaus from the rear bike car-
rier. Brunhilde rubbed her eyes, coughed, and began to whine.
"Why are we stopping again?" she asked.

"It will only be for a few minutes," Friedchen snapped. "You
said you wanted out of the basket anyhow." Brunhilde pursed
her lips and squinted, her face flushed. Friedchen reached over
to rub dirt from Brunhilde's cheek, and as her fingers touched
the child's skin, she felt the blazing heat of fever.

The front dissolved, and Hitler ordered the destruction of Germany's railroads and bridges to leave nothing for the victors. Whole
units imploded, and men ran into the woods, heading north or
east or south based on rumors of safety. Maybe Heina fled from a
military hospital, limping with a bullet wound in his thigh, then
headed down a road lined with birches, the white scraps of bark

littering the ground. You don't plan your own death, Papa would have said. You don't think about it because that makes you weak. That's the first shackle.

In a hilly part of what might have been southeastern Poland, Heina followed dirt roads out far from a city, thinking there might be a better chance of finding food near a farm. The road branched to a vacant village. Cups and pots were strewn in the doorways, with a shawl draped like a flag across the gravel of the main road. Heina swept a glance along the wall of a hut and saw a mound of black fabric. He knew that shape: a pile of bodies. He turned and walked slowly in the opposite direction, breathing deeply with hiccups of pain.

After two hours he stopped. Something about that empty house up there, the dark sheltered area of the porch, a musty smell in the air, called Marl to mind. For a moment he felt a tingle on his skin, as if he were a civil servant, coasting on his bicycle into the backyard, seeing Inge kicking a soccer ball against the wall, sweet-faced and moody blond Brunhilde in her mother's arms beneath the cherry tree. And the third child, the one that must have been born by now if it had survived. Heina shuddered, a twinge like a sewing needle into his guts. What was it? A bad omen, something about the abandoned house, the trampled garden and overturned water cans and cracked flowerpots.

That heart twinge might have happened on April 4, the moment that four-year-old Brunhilde's lungs filled with fluid as she suffocated. Heina might have been only a few hundred kilometers away from Friedchen, who came into a borrowed bedroom to smooth the blanket over her sick daughter. I imagine she froze in the doorway, watching and watching for minutes to see the covers rise over her daughter's chest. No movement. Then came the temporary madness, the flashes of dark and disbelief. Friedchen somehow buried her daughter alone in that town, a place that would later be swallowed behind the Iron Curtain. Klaus, my mother, and Inge would make pilgrimages to visit their dead sister so far from home, decades after the curtain parted.

At the moment Brunhilde faded, Heina might have stood in the remains of the small village. The doors of the brown brick church had been pulled off. The front of the building was a gaping lipless mouth. Heina smelled vegetable refuse and found an alley and the heavy square container of a farmhouse waste bin. He propped the lid and dug with a stick. He took a breath through his mouth, reached down to stir greasy paper, flush with maggots doing their work, flipped aside a soiled dress, excrement in a white cloth, stems.

He found a bone of pork almost greenish with rot. Beneath it he saw the familiar brown head of a crumpled potato. He grabbed the potato and stirred deeper with the bone to search for anything remotely edible. He found a cabbage leaf and wiped it on the grass, still wet with dew. The cabbage was briny and tough as rubber, unchewable, and reeked of the trash bin, so he swallowed it in large chunks. He knew the potato was poison in the green parts but just foul in the purple. Potatoes absorb scents and juices like a sponge, but beneath the ash taste was a hint of true raw potato, chalky but with a memory of sweetness.

The potato made Heina sick, and he heaved up bile and white froth. He lay on the ground beside a path and slept in the daylight behind a tree, a stupid thing to do. But it was better to wait this out than to stumble around and tempt a fever. He closed his eyes and woke with the hazy afternoon light, an eerie gray, and a mist of sweat on his skin. He felt small and surreal, as if something beyond his control had turned for the worse.

Heina ate out of the garbage; this might have been the first thing I heard about my grandfather when I was a child, well before I understood the Second World War. As a child I imagined him striding across a map, finding garbage to eat as a sort of Easter-egg hunt along a board-game map with squares blocked out to mark his progress. He and his iron stomach returned. He fathered my mother, and then he died, and then I was born to imagine him eating those curled ribbons, to fear the malignancy of half-turned potatoes.

Before I was born my mother was a child with my face. She learned to eat: a slice of bread spread thick with lard was a delicacy, and even more so if it glistened with dark bits of cooked fat. At this strange table of her stories, no one ate until the father picked up his spoon. Bones were grabbed and sucked clean of marrow, and a soup was made from the blood of a goose that was stuck in the skull with a knitting needle and drained. The fatty gristle on a piece of meat was chewed like a luscious wad of bubblegum. That was the table where one's value as a kitchen goddess was proven by her skill at wielding a knife, the ability to slice bread so thin that sunlight showed through its porous surface. After the war Mom remembers that Heina once went to the trash heap to rescue a jar of rotten pears. Alarmed at the waste, compelled, he peeled off the mold with a knife and ate them, risking bacteria and death to appease the god of hunger.

I tasted history first through the way my mother ate: attacking the shiny leavings of meat on our plates, frying every bit of spare egg-and-flour breading after the pork chops were cooked, treasuring the burnt *schmaltz* that remained in the frying pan after the meat and potatoes were served. I didn't like rubbery fat. I gagged on the gristle of steak, repulsed at the way tough meat dragged against my tongue, determined to outlast any attack, to rake its fingers inside me, to survive intact. "Why do you *eat* like that?" I asked Mom, and she invoked the praise song of meat ends and discarded bits.

My mother, transplanted from Europe, will drive an hour through the maze of shiny midwestern strip malls to buy a decent loaf of bread, the kind with a surface lined and creased like a face. When she pays for a dense loaf, she holds it in her arms as if it were a child, cradling it, feeling the living heft of it. It can't have ever been touched by plastic, she says, because that suffocates the dough.

"Bread is my religion," she says.

Rolf Abrahamson knew another side to this faith. After surviving the circuit through the Nazi death camps, he arrived in Bochum in the fall of 1944. He was assigned to work in a grenade factory in the same waning months as Heina limped in the east, as Friedchen and her children pedaled eastward. After the bombs lit the air of the Ruhr, the Nazis forced Rolf and the other prisoners to find the undetonated bombs. He poked through dusty rubble with a broomstick. When he discovered a bomb's metallic hull, he nudged it. If the world did not vanish in a flash of hot light, he earned a piece of bread.

10

My Mother Remembers Roses

Soldiers and refugees from the Russian zone packed the open train compartment. Low voices spiraled and eddied, breaking into a shout, a nightmare, an argument. Heina burrowed his face into his jacket to sleep. He woke in darkness, believing he was shipping off to the front. Flashes of light from the gray landscape illuminated the train car: a bare scalp riddled with badly healed cuts, squinting hooded eyes. Under the rose light of dawn in the east windows, a soldier picked the Reichswehr patches from his uniform with a pocketknife, and the blade glinted as the man worried the thread. I imagine the train car that carried Heina home was filled with the static anxiety of expectation and dread. How could one build a new world with the dregs of bombed-out skin and flesh in this train car?

Heina scanned the horizon for church steeples, mine tipples, or smokestacks. The train lurched around a curve. Up ahead jutted an outcropping of ghostly pale rock. I imagine the rock had been Heina's marker for home since he was a boy. Unbelievable.

He passed the gateway back into his former life. He grabbed the strap of his knapsack and tightened his hands.

A broad-backed soldier pushed up the crowded aisle and stopped near Heina's seat, straining forward as if he could see his home through the smudged train window. "Auguste Viktoria has been blown to bits, man," said the soldier, studying Heina with bloodshot eyes. "Your family's nowhere near the mine, are they?"

Heina suddenly hated this man. "Shaft 1," he said. "But Marl got off easy, that's what I heard."

"The CWH is gone, man. Major target," said the soldier pitilessly.

Heina broke off eye contact with the man and focused on the sound of the train whistle as the locomotive rolled to a stop. Pushing through the sea of shoulders, tears, and shouts, Heina jumped from the train and walked near the tracks, then cut across the platform.

He walked up the hill to Viktoriastraße. The half-healed bullet wound pulled in his thigh and made him limp. The view from the top of the hill wasn't right. A space of blue sky loomed eerily over the road. One tall tipple was gone, its spindly legs and the hoisting wheel vanished. The mine building's tall façade had been crushed. Piles of rubble blocked the central entrance, and construction pits and temporary wood buildings fractured the mine's front yard. Heina turned the corner onto Scharnhoff Straße and stopped short. One house was perfectly preserved down to the shaped hedges, and the next yard was a crater. And there: number 159, still standing. A bit of white fabric flapped in the breeze, the hemmed edge of a white curtain blowing from an upstairs window.

Heina climbed the five stairs and knocked. The unfamiliar face of an older woman appeared at the open door.

"Guten Tag," the woman said slowly, with an edge of suspicion in her eyes, and introduced herself: "Frau Lux."

Heina struggled to move his tongue.

"Who are you looking for?" the woman asked. She explained that her family had been settled in the building because of the housing shortage. "Who do you want? The Buschmanns?" Heina could not find words. He raised a hand. "Knock on the inside door. I think she's at home."

The inner door opened, and there she was: hollow-eyed, roughened skin, her hair half-escaped from her braid, a spoon in her hand. He wrapped his arms around her, her warm skin beneath her clothes, her smell—the fabulous smell of home, the laundry soap, the sweat on her neck, her skin on his lips. She clung to him. He pulled away to look at her face, but she held tighter and began to tremble, as if she'd held herself in check for three years and was only now feeling what had happened. He smoothed her cheeks, ran his thumb over her jaw. "You're well," he said. "Did you get my letter?"

She shook her head. "Nothing. We heard nothing." She twisted her fingers into the rough fabric of his uniform, her shoulders shaking. A blond boy with fat cheeks peeked around the edge of the door, shyly, looking up with wide eyes, and made a slight whimpering sound.

"Es ist Papa!" said Friedchen, holding out her hand toward him. The boy, frightened by the sight of tears on his mother's cheeks, started to cry and ran back into the house.

Heina laughed, grabbed onto Friedchen's hand. "And Brunhilde?" he asked. "Where is my sunshine?"

Friedchen wrapped her arms around him and tucked her head into his chest.

"Where is she? What happened?"

"She's in Jena," Friedchen said, the sound of her voice vibrating into his chest.

Heina pulled back. The sense of foreboding hardened into an ache the weight and size of Brunhilde, curling against his body, tiny hands grasping his fingers.

"She sleeps, Heina."

Heina capped his fountain pen and stretched. He had only answered half of the questions on the form from the British Zone authorities. All employees who had held posts in the Nazi civil administration were now being investigated, and he had no guarantee of getting a position. He had risked his job and more when he refused to join the party, but the postwar government in the British Zone now suspected anyone who had not been fired by the Nazis.

He pushed back from the desk and went through the kitchen into the garden to stand under the cool shade of the back overhang. Somewhere nearby a saw buzzed amid the summer sounds of reconstruction. Rabbits, the family's best guarantee for food, rustled in the straw inside the new hutches. Klaus crouched next to Friedchen in the back vegetable garden, chewing on a pea pod, and Friedchen dropped string beans into a colander. Inge pumped up the tire on her bicycle. Sixteen and already engaged to Günther, she was thrilled with American music and ready to leap into her own life. When she heard Heina's footsteps, she looked up warily.

"Where are you off to?" Heina asked.

"I've already helped Mama with Klaus this morning," she said.

Heina bit his tongue, trying to choose words carefully. "I didn't mean you couldn't go." She stalked around the edges of his vision, seeming to blame him, maybe, for being gone or for Brunhilde's death, for all of the loss she'd had to endure.

She smoothed back her hair. "I'm going to meet Günther. The Brits are making the city administrators fix the roads. We're going to watch." This was her excitement nowadays, riding off with her friends to see the former Nazi mayor on a work crew led by British soldiers. According to postwar Marl history the top Nazi officials in the area administration were held temporarily in a camp on Kampstraße to await their trials. Within a year most of them would get off with minimal sentences and be absorbed back into the government. But for now many in Marl were satisfied to see their former Nazi leaders behind the camp fences.

Heina grabbed a broom and dustpan and swept pieces of crushed stucco and concrete from the slate path. The back wall of the house and part of the yard had been hit with rubble when the neighbor's house was bombed, and the stairwell and inner door could be seen through the ragged hole in the thick wall. The damage had forced Jupp and Else to find another apartment, and they never lived again under the Buschmann roof. This hole in the wall would be fixed before baby Gerhild, my mother, was born in 1946. She swears, however, that she remembers the glint of sunlight through the broken wall, as if the repetition or inheritance of the story created the memory.

Now everything needed to be fixed. How could one not be overwhelmed, first with gratitude for being alive, and then with the details? Heina itched to do something productive, to get back to work. The effort to rebuild the SPD kept him sane.

A shattering crash boomed across the yard. Heina's knees buckled. He saw black and crouched to shield his head with his hands. He was back on the front, southeast in the Crimea, waiting for the Russian troops to rise above the hills and swarm down over their unit. Time stretched and the seconds yawned apart.

Years later, it seemed, Friedchen's warm hand cupped his

shoulder. "Heina," she said softly. "The neighbors are knocking down their wall. They are breaking stone. That's all."

He looked down at his hands, sunk in the brown, cool earth, his clean hands. There was grass here and the remains of the garden wall. The rushing sound in his ears was the buzzing of summer insects and the tapping of a hammer on stone. He pressed a hand to his chest, relieved that it was so easy to get home again, and terrified that the battlefield was apparently also so nearby.

"We should plant a tree here, for Brunhilde," he said, patting the earth.

Heina's thick personnel file reveals that within a month a battle erupted over his job in the city administration. For reasons I don't understand, Heina requested a transfer from the main Reckling-hausen office to Marl. Maybe he wanted to be close to his family, to work at the office a few blocks from his home. Maybe he was mindful of the strain politics placed on his personal life and hoped to correct that by being nearby and more accessible. Or maybe political trouble had reared in his former office and he'd made enemies through his work with the SPD. The transfer to the Marl office was promised in one letter, then retracted in another, with vague references to an unclear conflict. In September 1945 a hiring committee wondered whether Heina had enough antifascist credentials. To prove his membership in any formal resistance groups during the war, he needed two signatures to attest to that fact. He left the form blank. Later the same month a superior wondered if Heina was qualified for the new position, and in October someone opposed him because he didn't take the proper qualification exam. Another letter stated that Heina couldn't transfer to Marl because it would have departed from the normal job promotion path. The writers of these letters don't seem to have a unified argument, and I sense a political battle beneath the surface, a swell of resistance from the left or the right.

Information to round out the picture of Heina's political work after the war reached me through coincidences and haphazard Internet searches. When I first started to learn about Heina, I found a Web archive for the German workers' youth movement. After corresponding with Herr Eppe, archivist for this national center, I realized he was based in the back rooms of a youth hostel in Oer-Erkenschwick, a ten-minute drive from Marl.

The archive was my first destination when I arrived in Germany in 2003. Uncle Klaus dropped me off outside the building, which was covered with a huge colorful mural depicting the work of Chilean socialist leader Salvador Allende. In the lobby a group of teenagers smoked cigarettes and shot pool. They shrugged and barely looked up when I asked for the archive. I asked directions from four or five other teens as I wandered through the halls.

I wanted to absorb every inch of the place, from the cigarette butts in the front shrubs and children's bright paintings taped to a window to the row of classrooms where a group of teens clustered in an intense meeting. It was Heina's dream made real: a youth home. It was the same feeling I had at the SPD political archives in Bonn, when I incredulously opened a locker and hung my coat in the quiet coatroom beneath SPD campaign posters. *They let me in the door,* I wanted to say with quiet glee. *I'm allowed here.*

Past a glass case with ancient SPD buttons and embroidered banners, I took another hallway to find the archives. Herr Eppe's desk and the entire library were blanketed with tall stacks of papers. He shook my hand and led me into the main room, stocked with bound volumes of old youth movement newspapers, photos, and correspondence. He poured me a cup of coffee and launched into an hour-long lecture on the political importance of the socialist youth. "My major project is a database, which will

prove how vital this small group—including your grandfather—
was in rebuilding Germany," he said.

I trembled, either from the strong coffee or the unexpected
moment in this tiny, tucked-away room. Herr Eppe brought
stacks of old newspapers from the years that Heina would have
been active in the SAJ. I inhaled the scent of the paper, and after a
half an hour, ran across my first treasure, an article in a publication for area leaders signed "H. Buschmann."

Later that day Herr Eppe asked if I'd scheduled any interviews
with people who knew Heina, and I said I'd made dozens of calls
to wrong numbers, people who didn't know Heina or were de-
ceased. "There has to be someone," he said, flipping through his
address book. Then he looked up. "Of course—Gustav Hackenberg."

Friedchen avoided Heina's eyes as she put bread and cheese on
the table. The air in the kitchen was thick with her worry. She'd
asked twice yesterday for the latest news from the city administration. Everything depended on Heina getting his job back.
What would they do otherwise? The military newspapers ran ads
urging all unemployed men to go into the mines. The only other
work available was road construction.

"I have to go see Gustav Hackenberg," Heina said, wiping his
mouth and putting down his napkin. "He's going to help me re-
organize the youth groups."

Friedchen brushed crumbs from the table and turned her head
to see whether Klaus was awake. "We need to get another set of
rabbits, Heina. Will you go out to the farms in the afternoon and
try for two?" she asked.

It was an innocent question about baby rabbits, asked with the
lilt of forced levity. He knew her too well and heard in the sentence her bottomless fear. Asking about the rabbits meant, *Why*

are you bothering with politics now? If you don't figure out something soon, we won't have anything to eat.

"The party work is important," he said. "Rhode will help get me my job back."

She raised her eyebrows in mock surprise. "What? I didn't say anything about the party."

He sighed. "I'll get the rabbits on my way home."

When Heina knocked on the Hackenbergs' door, he was still winded from a fast ride up the hill into Herten. Frau Hackenberg showed him into the living room. Heina shook hands and then launched into his pitch. "The party needs you both. You know how important the youth work is, how vital it was to us when we were young. You remember, don't you?"

Frau Hackenberg, a small woman with her hair swept up in a bun, nodded and smiled fondly. "It was where we each fell in love! It was the world, wasn't it?"

Gustav smoothed aside the shock of hair that fell forward over his forehead. "It's important, Heina, and I know you'll find someone with a lot of energy—a younger person—to do it," he said. "I was harassed so badly by the Nazis. My health isn't what it used to be. My energy isn't there anymore. You need a young person to run after crazy kids!"

Heina glanced down at the swirls in the threadbare oriental rug beneath his feet, searching for another line of argument. He looked back up to meet Gustav's eyes. "No," Heina said. "We need our links with the past, the memories of how things were done. Kids today have only known the Nazis' Reich. You're the one."

Gustav smiled and coughed nervously, then stood. "I'm sorry, Heina. It's just my health—I can't do it. You're such a good organizer, I know you'll find someone even better than this old man."

Standing at the door, Gustav shook Heina's hand and said, "I hear the antifascist United Front doesn't look so good these days. Rudi said there's no way he's working with the communists."

Heina scowled. "No, he proposed a United Front with the communists in the organizing meeting, and everyone just glared at him. That's what Hermann told me."

All around Heina, old comrades shied away from the work, and at the same time the movement split again and again from within. The atomic bomb had exploded last week on the city of Hiroshima, an earth-shattering death knell, and these old comrades wanted to sit in their living rooms and wait for the future to be written for them.

Gustav Hackenberg eventually relented under Heina's pressure, though Gustav told me it took Heina two more visits to wear him down. Gustav laughed, shaking his head, and the laughter faded to a wracking cough. He smoothed his hands across his round belly. I set my tape recorder gingerly on the table after checking the machine for the third time. Herr Eppe had driven me here in a heavy snow.

Gustav's voice rumbled. "Nach dem Krieg hat der Heinrich Buschmann uns nicht in Ruhe gelassen . . .," he began slowly, his ninety-two-year-old voice scratching with the harsh Ruhr accent that turns consonants into coal-miner's picks. "After the war Heinrich Buschmann didn't leave us in peace. He wanted my wife and me to run the youth group, and we said no, and he visited us three times until we gave in." Gustav licked his lips and considered what else to tell me. "Well, then I didn't know how to begin, and Heina said, 'Make an invitation, and the children will come.' Heina, he was very enthusiastic. *Ein ganz prima Mensch war der Heina. Er könnte aber führen,*" Gustav said. A wonderful human being, Heina. Boy, could he lead.

Gustav dug for a handkerchief in his pocket and spat. His daughter-in-law came out of the kitchen. "Papa, you have to rest," she said. "You're getting yourself too excited." Gustav shook his hand at her, told her not to worry, and went to search in another room for newspaper clippings describing a postwar political event. He returned and sat down heavily, wiping his wet eyes with his handkerchief.

"Aber mir tut's nicht Leid. Das Heim ist da, wird benutzt," he said. "I don't have any regrets. The youth home is there, and it is still being used." He motioned toward the building next door, the neighborhood youth home he had built at Heina's urging.

Gustav showed us pictures and a medal from the government for his youth work. He patted the arm of the empty armchair next to him, his late wife's habitual seat, and told us about her. After drinking tea and worrying about the deep cough in Gustav's chest, I wanted to hug him, to be close to this stranger who had joked with and wrestled with Heina, whose life had changed direction because Heina was headstrong and persistent. We shook hands warmly, excused ourselves so Gustav could take a nap. I love the German handshake custom, which some see as prim and reserved. It brings you into skin-on-skin contact, makes people real.

I took the last photo of Gustav Hackenberg and made the last recording of his voice on my microcassette recorder. The next day began with another blasting snowstorm and a phone call. Herr Eppe called to tell me that Gustav had died the night before. I went back to bed blankly, crying to think that I'd put a strain on his energy. I listened to British Top 40 radio and buried my head under the covers. Gustav gave me his last bit of time so I could know Heina. My aunt Christa saw me cry, said warmly, "Your house is built too near the water." Then she added, humoring me with a story about fate that I half believed, "Gustav was waiting for you."

I imagine the postwar reunions of old comrades, described in political texts with an aching fondness. I smell bratwurst sizzling on two grills and imagine men and women, socialist and communist comrades, sitting in loose clusters on folding chairs in a garden. The shifting shadows cast by the oak trees mottled the faces of the crowd. I picture a man named Otto pointing to a red flag, embroidered ornately with the SPD-Hüls logo, now hanging on the garden fence. "This was buried out by the youth home!"

Hearing Otto, the men and women cheered and raised their fists. A voice sounded the opening notes to one of the old songs, and tears came to Heina's eyes. He began to sing and reached for Friedchen's hand. The vibration of the same song in all their throats was an electric current uniting the crowd into one body.

The communists among the crowd exchanged glances as they joined in, noting that the song was a generic revolutionary tune instead of one explicitly supporting the SPD. Every gesture was loaded these days. Schumacher of the SPD had refused to work with the Communist Party. To the east Soviet Russia tightened its grip on its own people and reached into Europe. From the west reached the splayed, alluring fingers of American capitalism, movies, music, and sock hops. Old friendships blistered and tore as alliances were strained by international politics.

I can't guess Heina's political impulses in these postwar years from the contradictory bits of paper in the scrapbook folder. We found two ballots from the first election on October 13, 1946, both with heavy Xs through the boxes for the communist candidates. Why save these, of all the ballots? In the opposite political direction, Heina also saved a letter dated August 6, 1947, from the SPD area leadership, printed in smudged type on rough rationed paper. In shrill cold war language, the letter warned of communists' attempts to take over the unions and urged ever-greater sacrifices: "The highest activity is now needed for this hour! Every tolerance is senseless. This isn't only an issue of a functioning union organization, but finally about protecting the freedom of mankind." The SPD struggled in these years to articulate a position for Germany's self-direction. As the SPD walked this fine balance between the West and the East, many saw the party as reactive and lost.

As the song's last note rang in the air, the men and women who had survived the camps and prison wiped their eyes. "To the new Germany!" someone yelled, raising a beer in the air.

Paul Rhode approached Heina. "Do you mind if I sit?" he asked, nodding toward Friedchen. She smiled, resigned. "I know," he said, shrugging. "Always business." Rhode reached into his jacket pocket and brought out a letter in support of Heina's job change, which he unfolded and handed to Heina. "I've included quite a threat. They'll have to take on the whole SPD if they keep up this charade."

Heina scanned the sentences below the official SPD letterhead. Heina read parts out loud. "I am requesting the appointment of Heinrich Buschmann to this position . . . It's not acceptable that we're being led around by the nose. We take this as an offense against the party . . . I want to prevent open conflict." He folded the letter and handed it back. "Very well said. Thank you, Paul." This letter would also end up in Heina's personnel file.

"You're one of our newly elected area leaders! They're spitting in our faces." Rhode folded the letter. "It will go in tomorrow's mail. Then we'll see what's what." He stood, smoothing his jacket. "Well, I'll leave you to your Sunday relaxation, Familie Buschmann."

Friedchen turned, searching the garden for their son Klaus. She sighed and leaned toward Heina. "Are you meeting tonight?" she asked. "Should I hold dinner for you?"

"We're going to meet, but it should be quick," he said. Ah, Heina, just admit the truth: there was no such thing as a short meeting.

A fork rang on a water glass, and conversation in the garden hushed. "Comrades," Gustav Hackenberg called out. "Let me introduce the next generation, our new SAJ group from Hüls!"

Eight young people filed up to the head table, holding the SAJ banner as flashbulbs snapped. Gustav looked pointedly toward Heina and said, "My wife and I are happy to lead the Falken group, and all it took was a little nagging." Gustav sang out the first few words of an old SAJ song, and the grayed heads in the crowd tipped back, joining their voices. The kids behind the banner looked at each other, mumbling and struggling to remember the words they'd learned just days before.

After months of letters and threats from the SPD, the stonewalling administration relented, and Heina became civil administrator and justice of the peace at a small city government office near his home in Hüls. In his thick personnel file I found the letter of congratulations and notification of the appointment. The next document in the file was a sort of recommendation letter, called a *Persilschein*, written by Heina. Persil was the name of a popular German dish-washing detergent, and Persilschein affidavits accumulated after World War II in Germany like mountains of suds as people attempted to have their reputations cleansed and verified. Each letter from a certified anti-Nazi or noncollaborator vouched for the anti-Nazi credentials of an associate. As soon as Heina's name was cleared and his position was secure, it seems he took the opportunity to vouch for a man named Herr Lanfermann, a former boss at city hall. And one sentence in a single letter, contained in a file that should have been destroyed, seems to hold a key to understanding Heina's wartime fate and the fate of my family.

In the letter Heina describes Herr Lanfermann as a nice, reliable guy who went into the SA in '33 in order to avoid undue discrimination at his job. I will never know whether Heina believed or half believed this to be an adequate excuse for joining the SA, and what thoughts he had about Jupp's choices as he typed those sentences in support of Lanfermann. In the next paragraph Heina follows the standard Persilschein format, attesting that he gives the reference willingly and that he has never been a member of the Nazi Party. Then Heina writes that Lanfermann knew of Heina's SPD membership and never discriminated against him. Instead Lanfermann intervened and helped Heina keep his job when dismissal on political grounds loomed during the first years of the Third Reich.

Herr Lanfermann, SA man, I don't know what you did to whom during the war. I don't know what meshing of personalities made you respect and value Heina enough to help save him. Maybe, in your eyes, Heina was dependable and accurate, always ready to take on extra work. Or maybe you were won over by his gentle laugh, his mild humor, or his ability to soothe tempers in a fractious team of civil administrators. You saved his job, if not his life. For those judged politically suspect, a red letter added to a file folder often easily led to prison. Lanfermann, were you thin or fat? Kind or irritable? Did you use a wristwatch or a pocket watch? The bricks and mortar of a dictatorship seem to be pieced together with the favors traded by well-placed people. But in this case I have to say thank you, Herr Lanfermann, for the favor.

Rolf Abrahamson, the Jewish boy from Recklinghausen who survived a tour of the death camps, settled again in Marl as a grown man after the war. His wartime memories, published in a thin booklet on Marl history, include a description of a postwar social event, the opening of Marl's new Adult Education Center

in 1947. Rolf might have scanned an invitation he received in the
mail. "It's going to be nice," he may have said to his wife. "We
don't go out enough. You can wear your new dress."

I fabricate the scene, imagine that his wife shrugged and wondered how and why Rolf kept his optimism. He'd come back
to Marl—the town where his father had been burned out of his
own shop, the place where he was loaded into a transport and
shipped east, the place where he was forced to build grenades
for the Nazis—only because he had no family left and nowhere
else to go.

On the streetcar Rolf's wife studied the closed, cold faces of
people on the sidewalk. Should she say anything? Leaning close,
she tucked a piece of stray hair behind her ear. "Rolf," she said,
"people still have the same brains in their heads. I don't think
it's such a new era here."

"I'm not dead yet," he said. "I didn't live through everything
just to sit in my house and read the newspaper for the rest of my
life."

The couple walked toward the Adult Education Center near a
man-made lake in the new city center. A string of small light-
bulbs hung in arcs from the tree branches and swayed in the
breeze. A string quartet tuned up near a stage, and the tables
were decked with white tablecloths and pink flowers.

"Look, the flowers match your dress," Rolf said. He led his
wife by the hand through the crowd toward a large, round table
with several empty seats.

"Sir," he said to the lone man seated at the table, "may we join
you?"

The man studied them, looking back and forth between Rolf
and his wife for several uncomfortable seconds. Rolf glanced
around, assuring himself that there were no jackets or sweaters
thrown over any of the chairs. The table was vacant.

"I'm sorry," said the man. "This table is taken."

Rolf stared into the man's blue eyes, wondering whether he was imagining the slight. What should he do—make a scene? Was it even anti-Semitism, or just random rudeness? Should he tell this fool this was the new Germany? Or was he being too sensitive? Maybe the man really was waiting for a group of ten to arrive.

Rolf's wife pulled at his arm. "Let's go," she said. "I'll ask the host to seat us." Rolf followed, baffled, wondering what he should have said, feeling as though an essential opportunity had been missed, as if he had let down not only himself and his wife but his whole family as well as scores of the dead.

The host nodded at their request and led them back to a small table near the food prep area, behind an oak tree, where they were bumped all night by waiters and overcome with the steam and smell from the cooking food. This happened to Rolf Abrahamson in the new Germany.

Friedchen counted the ration cards that seemed to shake and dissolve before her eyes. Her son had been crying for days from hunger. She gave him an extra roll for lunch and tried to make do for herself with chamomile tea. Her infant daughter, Gerhild, whined and wrapped her arms around Friedchen's neck, clawing and nuzzling.

Klaus came into the kitchen. "Mama, Oma wants you."

"Hush, Heinz," Friedchen said, rubbing her eyes. "I'll go up to her."

"I'm not Heinz," he whispered, "I'm Klaus."

Lina banged on the door, then walked into the kitchen. "Friedchen! I have no onions or any kind of meat. And it's no wonder the children are crying. Even with no food, you could still keep the place clean." She ran her hand along the counter, then crossed

her arms and shuddered, maybe imagining herself somewhere
she felt she deserved, a lovely home far away from any stress.
Friedchen numbly boiled water for tea and rocked Gerhild to
sleep, hoping the baby could not feel her rage.

An hour later Heina opened the door to the dark kitchen,
where Friedchen sat with her head resting on her arms on the
table. "*Schatz*, I have a meeting, I'm sorry," he whispered. "Let
me just grab a roll for dinner. We've got a big controversy about
the general miners' strike, the round-the-clock shifts for coal
reparations."

"There are no rolls," she said, crying into her arms. "And your
mother is a demon. I wish we could leave here. I wish she would
die."

He patted her shoulder. "She's fierce sometimes," he said.
"But you're strong. She's all hot air." He stood, rubbing her
back. "There's a huge fight in the SAJ, I tell you. I don't know
what to do about it. Half the kids are saying there's no commitment anymore to real socialism . . ." Friedchen felt tears wetting
her sleeve, and she hated the sound of her husband's voice, the
way he droned on, wanting freedom for strangers but oblivious
to what was happening in his own house.

Heina leaned a flat package against the wall and removed his
shoes. He tried to move quietly on the creaking floorboards in
case the children were already in bed. Klaus ran from the kitchen,
carrying a stuffed dog.

"What's that, *Vati*?" asked Klaus, reaching for the wrapped
package. "Is it a picture?"

Heina's mind had buzzed furiously all day, and now he was exhausted. Schumacher and the regional SPD Party had announced
a scandal: a secret document showing a Soviet plan to take over
German labor unions. "It's for the party, Klaus," Heina said. He

reached down and tore the brown paper off the stack of placards. The top one read, "Neither Russian Control or World Capitalism! The Ruhr: Coal and Iron of the Working People—SPD!"

Klaus scanned the red graphics and tall white letters. His face
fell. "Oh," he said.

Heina sat down on the bench and reached for his slippers.
"It's about us getting to control our own lives," Heina said.

Friedchen stepped from the kitchen into the hall, drying her
hands on a dishtowel. "Klaus, leave your father alone," she said.
"Heina, I don't think he needs to learn about the communist-so-
cialist labor rift before bedtime." She turned, her braid swinging
on her shoulder.

Heina followed her into the kitchen and unfolded a sheaf of
papers eagerly, with fingers trembling. He had big news that just
might relight the fire of politics in her eyes. "Friedchen, I'd like
you to read the draft of my pamphlet, if you have time. It's for the
Bochum union council. They're printing thousands," he said, allowing himself a slight smile. Papa Heinrich would have been
thrilled.

Gerhild sat on the floor, whining, and Friedchen stooped to
lift the child onto her hip. "We need a vacation, Heina. Like Jupp
and Else. Why don't we take the kids somewhere this summer?"

Heina put down his pencil, feeling the pleasure of the pamphlet drain away. "You want a life like Jupp and Else's?" He
stopped himself. Friedchen looked exhausted, the skin around
her mouth drawn tight into the hard-bitten German woman's
scowl. Forty-one and still chasing babies.

She leaned against the sideboard and twisted to look out the
darkened window, avoiding his eyes. "I just listen to your mother
yell at me all day. We don't have money to do anything nice with
the kids. That's what she tells me, that we're raising our kids like
beggars." She reached down to tug at a hole in her ripped stock-

ing. Family friends and neighbors reported this detail decades later, the holes in Friedchen's stockings.

Heina stood up. "I'm going to talk to Mama right now." This was their dance, the feints and parries. Even as he stood, he waited for Friedchen to stop him. What would he say to his mother, the Dragon? *Be sweet, be kind, lose your bitter heart.* Could he ask her to move out? Impossible. And they couldn't afford to leave, either.

Friedchen shook her head. "Just leave it alone, Heina. There's no use arguing with her." This resigned sentence is one of Mom's only memories of her mother: "Lass et doch, Heina." Let it alone.

Heina sat down and leaned back against the kitchen bench, in the same kitchen where his father once proudly oversaw the family. They weren't beggars. They owned a house! The kitchen faucet dripped, and Gerhild lay in her mother's arms, chewing on her tiny hand. Heina catalogued the list of wants: Gerhild's little dress was split and mended at the seams, a hand-me-down once worn by a child now dead. Friedchen's slippers were ten years old, embroidered flowers shredded and gray. Papa had started from nothing, every bit of security an accomplishment, and from that Mama Lina had drawn only want and denial. He should say something to Mama, but if it came to outright war, Mama would always win. And Friedchen would be the one to suffer.

The subjunctive case expresses what might have, could have, should have been, and the German tense for rue and regret is marked with separate spellings to chart the complex imaginary landscape of alternate possibilities. Over coffee in the family kitchen, my aunt Christa described Heina with a head shake and a twist of the mouth: "Wann er wüste . . ." This sentence imagines a parallel universe in which Heina could have known the effects of his choices. I saw the anger in her face, felt her judgment first, and my heart rushed to Heina's defense as I silently listed his political contributions.

Weeks later, as I rode a train from Berlin back to Marl, my thoughts flitted randomly from English to German as I looked out at the overcast sky. I saw Aunt Christa's face again, saying those words: *Wann er wüste* . . . I heard the whole sentence: If he had known or understood, he would have done something different. Heina was oblivious to the pain at home, Christa said. But at the same time she almost gave him the benefit of the doubt, the potential for action: if he had seen, he *would have* made different choices. He would not have let Friedchen suffer.

The train passed an abandoned station at Gelsenkirchen Buer-Nord, an old brick building with smashed windows, half swallowed with the remains of ivy and weeds. Empty beer bottles glinted on the gravel, and a spray-painted slogan splashed a brick wall: *Nazis Raus, Kampf der Scheiße System*—Nazi Skinheads, Get Out. Fight This Shitty System. The train pulled through Bottrop-Boy past the Prosper-Haniel mine, winding around massive mountains of slag and mine tailings, some black as night and others seeded with grass and trees. The cwh stacks trailed thin streams of smoke, and another mine in the distance was ringed by a slag heap so tall and wide that it dwarfed houses and cars, made the evidence of human life look like tiny toys.

The energy generated by Heina's politics left immovable mountains of bitterness as a side effect of sacrifice, a woman processed and turned into mine tailings. As Friedchen's energy drained, the beating heart of political change pulled Heina farther away. I cannot barter my grandmother, set a price on what she suffered, and yet I wanted her suffering to be worth something. So it is a twisted comfort that the energy Heina took from his family went directly into his country.

At the very beginning of my search for Heina, I found an on-line archive of German socialist history. I typed "Heinrich Bus-chmann" in the search field, and an entry emerged, delivered in-stantaneously from a continent and an ocean away. I clicked on the link to find a postwar pamphlet from Münster in the Ruhr— author Heinrich Buschmann.

After I had learned more of Germany's postwar history, I set about unsnarling the spider web of sentences in that pamphlet. The author demanded economic democracy and called for la-bor unions to play a role in planning Germany's new economy. With a rush of pride and pleasure, I inhabited Heina's work-ing mind to appreciate the logic of the argument, the rhetorical flourishes, the challenging of assumptions, and the explanation of demands. It took a long time to fathom what this electric ci-pher whispered to me: that the man described by his family as "nobody" somehow found the energy not only to be somebody after the war, but to push to the forefront of change and work to rebuild a demolished nation. The cadence of the pamphlet's language, its phrasing and words, occupied a part of my brain reserved for the songs and stories I might have heard from the grandparents I would have known.

A year later I sat in the International Institute of Social History in Amsterdam, requesting every file I could find on the postwar Ruhr. Without really understanding the Dutch instructions for the online catalogue, I managed to fill out a pile of requests cor-rectly, along with an equal number of requests that left the an-noyed archivists baffled. My shrugs and apologies of "Sorry, I'm American" seemed only to make the situation worse. Nonethe-less I got my stacks of old books and boxes about postwar Ger-man labor unions. I had two days to photocopy and skim any-thing I could collect, so my method was haphazard at best.

I flipped through a book on postwar German labor unions in

the Ruhr, skimming the index by habit. No "Buschmann" listed. But in the appendix I noticed something familiar on the heading of a document: the title and structure of Heina's pamphlet. A shortened version of his original sentences followed below the title, with the same phrases and language, though without his name. The political maelstrom had apparently approved of Heina's offering and had absorbed the text into the nameless, authorless storm of conversation. According to the book the pamphlet had been edited and then distributed broadly throughout the British Zone. Now it rested peacefully in a hardback book, evidence of union growth in the postwar Ruhr. Politics takes what it wants from you, what it needs, what will serve.

"Shut the door behind you, Buschmann," the county administrator said.

Heina sat on the edge of a leather upholstered chair. The steward of the administrative union looked up and nodded at Heina to reassure him. Heina's supervisor at the Marl office sat to the left of the director and flipped through papers in a file folder, some of which survived and came into my hands, though I have filled in the details using bits of family stories.

"We have a complaint here, Buschmann," said the administrator, "and I see you haven't been able to resolve it with the Marl office."

The supervisor, Eichhorn, smacked his palm against a sheet of paper on the desk. "Sir, here's the list: seven days in which he took a long lunch or an afternoon off and then was listed in newspaper articles as a speaker at a political rally. Four instances of talking politics with coworkers or handing out literature. And here—" he said with relish, pulling out a pamphlet, "is the Wanne-Eickel labor statement with his name all over it."

Heina cleared his throat. "I worked evenings to make up for

the lost time," he said. "Those absences were all cleared in advance."

Eichhorn's steel-gray eyebrows bristled above his glasses, and
his eyes blazed. "How, I ask you, can a client feel comfortable
coming to Herr Buschmann for city services? Our job is to run
the city. We leave the politics to the city council and candidates!"
The union steward rolled his eyes.

The line between work and politics had blurred—that much
was true, and the party demanded hours, Heina's evenings and
weekends. The previous summer the U.S. government had wiped
out the old currency and handed everyone 60 crisp new deutsche
marks. Overnight the rush for the latest American music and
clothes was on. The Soviets feared Germany's tilt toward the
West and shuttered access to Berlin, and the United States began
airlifts in response. Germany was being torn like a paper doll,
and Heina could only too easily summon the doubt and regret of
the pre-Hitler days to ask himself whether one more action now
might make a difference. Each of those frantic evenings Heina
had run into the house to grab a sandwich. The children barely
even looked up when he came home, but they would thank him
later, he imagined, when Germany was safe and free.

"Buschmann has an impeccable record," said the union steward, drawing documents from his own file folder and handing
them to the administrator. "Commendations, awards, a history
of raises, letters of support from other clerks. And the union
contract specifically prohibits retribution based on political—"

Eichhorn broke in. "Sir, we've had several complaints about
him wearing the SPD pin on his lapel!" The detail about the SPD
pin is preserved like another insect in amber, a glinting treasure
in family lore.

In the midst of the raised voices, Heina's thoughts flitted to
Papa Heinrich. He imagined Papa standing in a corner looking

on, arms crossed over his round stomach, eyes gleaming, smile veiled by his white handlebar mustache. Papa would find this setting familiar, and he would approve.

The buzz of words continued to flow across the administrator's desk, the noises of bureaucratic warfare. "This is unacceptable," said the administrator. Then there was silence. "Buschmann, the union can fight us, but this kind of behavior isn't within your rights."

The other men in the room turned to stare at Heina. No proletarian army massed and roared on the street below in support of Heina's cause. No crowd of miners waved pickaxes at the front door of this building, and no line of red flags flowed in the wind outside the window. A streetcar's bell clanged. And out beyond this silence, Friedchen was pregnant again. If he got fired it would be the end of them; they'd have to sell the house and move. His options were to apologize and beg, or to gamble that he was too valuable for the administration to lose.

As subtle and clear as the flash on a knife blade, he touched in his soul the knowledge that he was Papa's son, despite the absence of a raving crowd to urge him on. A wave of indignation surged through his chest. "I'll quit, if that's what you want." He paused, waiting for his words to sink in. This offer to resign would be followed with a written letter expressing the same sentiment. "And the union will fight," he said.

The administrator sighed and removed his tiny eyeglasses. "There must be another solution," he said. "We'll have to schedule a hearing. I'd hoped it wouldn't come to this."

Chairs scraped against the wood floor. The union steward leaned in and whispered, "We'll get the mayor involved."

Heina, I always think of my actions as tiny compared to yours, but I do have a scrap of newspaper to add to your musty file folder. Deep in German research and seven months pregnant with Ivan, I found myself standing behind a podium at the university as the cameras whirred and snapped. Graduate students trying to organize a union had gathered to launch a healthcare campaign. Instead of playing my normal role as the organizer, I had offered myself as a case study. I couldn't afford the university health insurance, so I had to apply for state public assistance for the baby that would soon arrive. I had marched for fair wages countless times, but standing up to reveal my own checkbook balance made me flush with shame. My voice shook with the knowledge that my body, the round belly, made the emotional argument for equity. My words were secondary to that obvious statement.

My husband came home from the grocery store that afternoon and said, "I heard you on the radio, the whole speech." I felt exposed, even though the goal was to embarrass decision makers into action. And I used my tiny son—even before birth—as an instrument of propaganda. I made a cold decision as an organizer rather than as a mother, knowing that a pregnant woman's swollen body would make for a great visual on the news.

The next morning I flipped through the paper, heart in my throat, wondering what I'd done and hoping the article had not been written. But there I was, huge, on the last page of the Metro section, the stern, long-nosed face, eyes downcast, pregnant belly above a cardboard sign. My expression of sad concern seemed like such a cliché. I hoped no one in Columbus would see it. I mulled over the practical consequences: at least one of my four current employers in Columbus would notice the story. I wondered if my local journalism work would dry up mysteriously, as had happened in the past when I was seen as too political to be an objective reporter. I had talked myself into the action, and now I berated myself as a bad mother-to-be. But a few days later, after the embarrassment passed, I clipped the photo and taped it in a scrapbook that my son might someday wonder or ask me about.

My mom has only a few memories and images of Friedchen, a few moments from which to draw a lifetime of nurturing and love. One begins in darkness. The cries of the youngest boy, Werner, had awakened Gerhild, then four years old. She crept down the hall to the kitchen and saw a bar of golden light underneath the kitchen door. She pushed, and the door swung open to reveal Friedchen rocking Werner back and forth in the baby carriage. Friedchen's worried face, the early hour, the pinched cries of the red-faced baby, all meant the baby was sick. Gerhild might have been shushed, or maybe she stood there in her nightgown, watching.

Where was Heina? Maybe he crept in to see Friedchen, smoothed her hair, felt helpless, and then went back to the bedroom. He might have pulled a party bulletin out of a stack of papers and made a few notes. He and Dr. Ernst Immel, future mayor of Marl, would go door-to-door in the neighborhood later that day to hand out leaflets against Germany's remilitarization. An hour passed, and blue-green daylight showed beneath the window shade. Heina got up and dressed. As he slid his arm into his overcoat, he felt a pair of eyes on him. Gerhild stood in the doorway, her brown hair tangled on her shoulders. She shifted her weight from foot to foot.

"Where are your house shoes?" he asked. "Why aren't you in bed?"

She glanced toward the kitchen door. "I was watching Mama and Werner, but they're both asleep in the kitchen." She clasped her hands in front of her. "Are you leaving?"

He smiled and unfolded a pamphlet, holding it toward her. He didn't want to overwhelm the children with politics. He'd heard it day and night when he was a child, and Friedchen wanted to let them be children before they started worrying about the world economy and World War III. He leaned toward her. "It says, '*Ohne Mich!*—Without Me!'" said Heina. "Adenauer wants Germany to have weapons again, and we are going to a big rally today. We will tell Adenauer we don't want a Germany that wants to fight."

"Like Mama and Oma, yelling all the time?"

Heina folded the pamphlet. "They don't fight all the time. Oma is old, and that's why she has a bad temper."

Gerhild took in a breath, not wanting to disagree with her father. But they *did* fight all the time—he didn't hear how they yelled! He didn't see the way Mama had whacked a wooden spoon on the sink and broken it! Gerhild turned and went back to her bedroom, forgetting to say good-bye to the man who was always going away.

Heina, I will ask you directly: would it have been so difficult to bundle up that child and take her with you to the meeting? I know firsthand how embarrassing and awkward it can be to spread baby toys on a conference table, to watch as a toddler pulls the agendas into a spit-strewn pile. I've tried to breast-feed in conference halls, had a screaming infant scared out of his wits at the crashing shouts of a demonstration. But Heina, you were raised in a movement where children were included. What happened? Maybe, after the war, you realized or believed that politics was a wind tunnel of death, no place at all for children, only a place where hearts got crushed. But no, that can't be right . . . You supervised camping trips of the Falken socialist youth and left your own children at home. Did you change with your middle-class job, become squeamish at the thought of your kids mixing with the sons and daughters of miners? Or were you afraid to sacrifice your own to the movement?

"Have you figured out why he was like that?" Mom asked. "Why he believed politics was more important than his family?" Tears welled in her eyes.

A book on the Marl SPD lay facedown on the table. She'd been helping me with translation, and we whispered back and forth, trying not to wake Ivan, who slept on her shoulder, exhausted from a bout of colic. We'd taken turns crying all morning when we couldn't calm my screaming son. That helpless stress seemed to aggravate all kind of old hurts. Mom was here for me, but her own mother was long dead.

In a sleep-deprived fog I listed the theories I'd gathered from books: the die-hard culture of the SPD, the pressures of political office and postwar reconstruction. I wanted to say: see him as more complex than evil. Know the good that he did. But none of the reasons sounded believable or satisfying, not compared to the need of a living baby now or a living child then.

Ivan stirred, and Mom shifted him to the other shoulder. "I think my mother must have been an emotional cripple by the time I was born," Mom said with a raw edge of anger and confusion. "And my dad didn't do anything to stand up to his mother. He was so *weak*. I want to read what you're writing, because I want to understand him better."

I wanted to fill up that need, the need I grew up with, Heina's absence as a presence, one layer of Mom's massive well of hurt. I hoped it was a book-shaped hole but knew it was much larger.

Friedchen ran into the bedroom, slamming the door behind her. Lina's voice rasped down the hall, "If you don't care enough about me to even cook anything decent, that's just fine, but you should know that you're starving the children . . ."

The room seemed to tip, and Friedchen's face looked flushed in the mirror. Her back ached high up beneath her ribs. She was getting sick again—female trouble. She knew the cure was to drink plenty of water, but she hadn't had the presence of mind to do it today. Or something told her not to, some seed of hatred that made her neglect her body. She buried her face in the covers. Minutes later Heina came in and sat on the edge of the bed, waiting. He'd been so kind yesterday; they'd made love for the first time in a month, and she felt sure that he cared enough to do something, to stand up to the Dragon. Friedchen pushed her hair out of her eyes. Heina stared out the window, lost in thought over something far removed from this evening's drama.

Friedchen put her hand on his knee. "I'm sorry," she said. "But your mother—"

He didn't wait for her to finish. "What do you want me to do, throw her out?" He couldn't see a solution, so any mention of the problem brought frustration.

In the hallway a door slammed, followed by the sounds of Lina shuffling into her apartment. "I know," Friedchen said. "I know there's nothing to be done."

"I'll put the children to bed," he said, getting up. He sighed. He'd fallen in love with Friedchen because she was so strong, such an independent woman. How did she get so beaten down? Where was her spirit?

"Heina," she said, "can you feel my forehead? I feel so warm."

He reached over, placed his cool palm for a moment on her cheek. "No, *Schatz*, you're fine. It's July, after all—it's just too warm in here." He parted the curtains and opened a window.

She drew in a breath, waited for a swoon to pass. Her body felt filled with lead. "I don't feel well," she said. "I think we should call the doctor."

He rubbed her cheek. "Just get some sleep."

"Try to sleep," Mom told me.

My skin blazed with fever, yet I hoped I was on the mend after a urinary tract infection. I didn't have time to be sick. That spring of 2000 I'd spent the previous day driving from Ohio to Illinois to interview union organizers for a research project on working conditions in the mental health industry. The six-hour drive took eight because I stopped every half hour to pee and drink water. I knew this pattern, after all: years of travel, late nights and weeks like wind sprints, one after another, years of saying yes to any request from any comrade, friend, or coworker. I was young, I told myself, and I was in shape. The more you push yourself, the more you're capable of. I was just a little worn out, that was all.

The socialist youth conference held in Columbus the week before had been exhausting, and I'd tried to cram it in along with classes, work, and activist meetings. Then a guy from the conference slept on my couch for four nights until I fronted him money for a bus ticket. Then I made the drive to Chicago, shivering and sweating, and spent the day ticking tasks off my list, pressing "play" on my tape recorder, taking notes on legal pads, touring mental health facilities. I could not get warm. That night, back at my parents' house, I was half delirious and waiting for the fever to break.

I tried to sleep it off, but when I woke I couldn't walk a straight line. I agreed to go to the ER, where I was hooked to an IV for three days to flush out the bacteria that had bloomed inside me. The nurses took my temperature almost every hour to monitor the fevers, which spiked to 105 degrees. The nurses laid me on an ice blanket hooked up to a big pump that ran chilled water through a plastic mattress.

"We don't understand how a healthy woman would get such a severe infection," one doctor said. They gave me an HIV test and wondered aloud about leukemia. "Your immune system is completely suppressed. This infection is in your kidneys. If it goes into your blood, there is nothing we can do."

I kept asking the nurses if I was going to die. They kept telling me the fever was a good thing, that it meant my body was fighting the infection. Then I heard them talking to each other in the hall, saying, "It's at 105," their voices turned down at the edges and flat. I was so thankful for lime Jell-O and red juice, amazed at the photo of pink flowers hanging on the wall at the foot of my bed, crying in feverish ecstasy over that beautiful photo.

My parents, my sister, brother, and sister-in-law appeared in a rotating parade, and they told me all the family near-death stories. We laughed about each one, which seems kind of strange now, but at the time it was comforting, as if this would be another funny story with a happy ending. On the third day, thanks to bags and bags of premium antibiotics, the fever began to cool. I shuffled into the bathroom, dragging the IV stand. My face in the mirror looked like a corpse's, my skin the weird yellow-gray of a pre-tornado sky. Upper layers of my personality reasserted themselves: guilt for causing my family all this trouble and worry about whether my health insurance would cover the expense. I was irrationally irritable. I sat with the phone and my legal pad, running through a list of phone calls and to-do lists, canceling and rescheduling appointments, apologizing. At the time Mom and I didn't know this was the same condition that had killed her mother.

"Your mama is sick," Tante Hedwig said, smoothing a lock of Gerhild's dark hair behind her ear. "Why don't you go pick her some flowers?"

It was July 25, 1952. My mother-to-be, Gerhild, was five and a half. She shut the door behind her, purposeful, biting her lip carefully as she crossed the street. She knew the perfect spot to gather flowers. In the vacant lot half a chimney rose up into the blue sky, a ragged finger of brick. Chunks of cement and rock peppered the wild garden of flowers, nettles, and spindly weeds. Those nettles burned your skin if you touched them. Papa said never to go onto the old foundation because it might collapse. Bees and gnats buzzed, and a cloud passed in front of the sky.

She found a patch of irises, their purple flowers nosing firmly up out of the weeds. Their stems were tough, and she used her fingernail to cut into the stalks, which left a green juice on her finger. Flower-blood, but they were for Mama, would help her get better. Next came chamomile, the green-yellow heavy heads that looked like daisies. You could make a tea with them that was good for your stomach. And another white flower. All together, the flowers looked special. The closer she held them, the more real they became. Back in the dark hallway of the house, Gerhild carried the flowers in front of her, their color glowing strangely. Gerhild pushed open the door to Mama and Papa's room and saw Mama's tangle of hair. Tante Hedwig held Friedchen under the arms, draped in a gray blanket, above a chamber pot. This picture of Friedchen's vulnerability and helplessness is frozen in my mother's mind.

Tante Hedwig turned toward the door with a cross look. Oma Klejdzinski rushed Gerhild out of the room. In the hallway Oma Klejdzinski reached for the flowers with her gnarled fingers, shifting their careful arrangement.

"We'll put the flowers in a vase," Oma Klejdzinski said. "Mama will like them."

The doctor came that night and took Mama away to get better.

Heina, Inge, and Günther rode their bicycles home from the hospital in silence. They rolled into the yard, and Heina turned the corner. Mom remembers that he fell like deadweight from the bicycle and landed on the stone path. The bicycle wheels spun slowly in the air. Inge ran into the house, her distorted screams echoing in the stairwell.

What is it to lose a wife, a mother? Heina closed his eyes and saw Friedchen's flushed face, her dry lips moving, still parted and alive with breath. They'd known each other an instant. If he kept his eyes closed, she would be here, and they would start again in that tent in the woods. The path's stone edge pushed into his ribs. He opened his eyes and scraped his palms on the stones. Time continued, carrying him farther and farther away from the last minutes with her.

He found his children in the kitchen, put his arms around them, and said, "Wir bleiben immer zusammen." We will stay together always. My mom held these words close and repeated them to me solemnly. I imagine Gerhild and tiny Werner breathing in the scent of their father, his wool jacket and the smell of soap and sweat. It was warm here in his arms, only a little tight because of the way he held them. They tried to stay still, to make their father happy, to be good. They might have known that when people say "always," it means they're scared about losing you, about everyone going away. The children were sent to their rooms, told to be very quiet, and Inge brought them lunch to eat in their beds. Werner started to cry as he ate, knowing with a three-year-old's intuition that the murmurs and ringing of the phone meant something very bad. An uncle came to collect the boy, and Friedchen's sister, Tante Hedwig, came by later and told Gerhild to get a toy to bring with her.

I imagine Mom, the child Gerhild, grabbing a stuffed bear and taking Tante Hedwig's hand. They walked outside, and Gerhild leaned over the edge of the railing. In the back garden Tante Else and a neighbor moved systematically along the line of rosebushes and cut off every red and pink bloom. With each snip a flower's head fell heavily into a waiting pillowcase.

Heina ran up the porch stairs as Hedwig opened the door. He reached for Gerhild, and Hedwig clenched her arm tightly against the girl. "I should take this child and not bring her back," Hedwig said. "I'd give her a better life than you will. God knows you made Friedchen's life miserable. Forty-eight years old!"

After the children were gone Friedchen's body was delivered and carried into the house, where she was laid out on the dining room table. It wasn't her but a collection of features, hair, worn hands. The house filled with bunches of flowers, the sweet, damp smell of them wilting in the July heat. Coffee was made, and cakes were delivered and set with stacks of plates and forks on the kitchen table. Heina had not washed his face or changed his clothes since the day before, and someone steered him to the bedroom washstand, sternly commanded him to clean up in respect for his wife's memory. He splashed water on his face and looked into the mirror. There was the mouth that said, "Just wait. You're not sick. You'll be fine." The mouth that uttered the death sentence, the murderer's mouth, or so Friedchen's family and his own daughter Inge said. Or had he killed her with stress and his small paychecks? All her waiting and abiding for nothing now.

Strands of Friedchen's hair curled near a hair band on the bureau. The sheets were wrinkled and pressed in the shape of her body, the covers thrown back. He wanted to lie there and breathe her in. The door opened and someone called for him. Frau and Herr Klejdzinski, both ashen and stooped, stood at the end of the hall. Herr Klejdzinski curled his lips inward as if trying not to spit. Heina stepped forward to hug Friedchen's mother, wanting comfort, wanting her to tell him it would be somehow all right. She turned her face and pulled back. A button popped on her black crepe blouse as she wrenched free of his grip. "This is what you did to my daughter," she said.

Mom tells me that the coffin was lined inside with the heads of those thick roses, sweet fists, and that someone's fingers pulled apart Friedchen's stiff grip to insert Gerhild's iris and wildflower bouquet. The *Leichenwagen* came with its glass sides and black horses to take her away. The phone in the kitchen rang and rang, the shrill sound of a tiny clapper against the bell like a scream. Family friends called to offer support and condolences. Heina grabbed the black phone and ripped it from the wall. My mother remembers the roses. She remembers that afterward, they never had phone service to the house for as long as she lived there.

Lina Buschmann, the Dragon, outspoken activist and rebel, most likely suffered from mental illness. She slowly erased Friedchen's will, whittled her soul down to a sliver. Then Inge erased Friedchen a second time by refusing to tell any of the stories. Inge had twenty-three years with Friedchen but told my mother, "That's done with now. Let's not talk about it." I have watched Mom sit at a table with my aunt Inge, crying, asking desperately, "Did she love us?" Inge shook her head, pressed her lips together, kept Friedchen's stories in her mouth.

So I write fiction for selfish reasons. I imagine Friedchen spitting in Lina's soup. I imagine her looking in her mirror and hating her Polish profile, or maybe in a moment of pride loving the sexy slant of her Polish eyes. I imagine her longing for Heina and fighting with him in whispers. I have Friedchen's eastern look, my mother says, with the rough nose and almond eyes, the answer to my non-Aryan riddle. I have her face, and the only other shred to work with is my imagination and a few years of research. Whether or not I am allowed to, I extrapolate back, conjure her out of thin air:

I grew up, she tells me, in the tenements of the old neighborhood where the Polish miners lived. My mom, a German girl, always resented living in those narrow streets. I got spit on walking to school. Kids, of course, they're just stupid kids, but it does something to your soul when an old woman spits at you from a window, leaning with her meaty German elbows on the sill, casually letting a drop of spittle hang from her lip, releasing it so it hits your scalp. I felt the stink of that woman's acrid spit in my hair all day as I sat at my desk doing sums on my chalkboard. On the way home I walked near the woods and found some waxy yellow flowers to rub hard into my hair. Polish women in the shops always spoke to me in Polish, and I felt guilty that I didn't understand them. I shook my head, and they wagged their fingers at me like I was trying to trick them.

I lost two babies, then a third, and Lina blamed me for it, implied that I didn't know how to feed a child, warm a child, hold a child, that my milk was poisoned. It's the air inside and outside of this house that's bad. The world is starting to feel like a long gray tunnel through a mountainside, with no light, plenty of places to fall, and an enormous pressure bearing down on us. How could a baby get born and live when its mother has no hope?

I have never fit in anywhere except for the SAJ, except with Heina. We were bad for each other because we really believed, both of us, that if we just stepped sideways we would shrink into the grain of the wallboards and become invisible. We were not able to encourage each other to stand up for ourselves, be selfish, because we didn't know the first thing about it. We were both the type to take the longest list of tasks home from the meetings, the ones who wanted to see work get done, never mind being appreciated for it or occasionally saying no. Maybe it served us well. Being invisible was, for years, the single most important skill in Germany.

That last night I had in our home, I knew something was wrong. Heina said, well, let's wait until the morning and see how you feel.

I woke up in a sweat and realized I was too sick, and the ache near my kidneys was bigger than my body. Do I blame Heina for that? He didn't want to believe I was sick because sick in those days meant death, even after the war. So I shrugged that night, gave in, wanted to believe that it would be better with the sunlight.

Why did I do that? Why am I like that? Heina was my strength, but maybe if I had lived longer, gotten to come out more fully into the light of peace, I would have turned a corner. Maybe I would have shaken myself off and decided, no, I'm going to argue with my husband. He is my light and my life. Maybe if I had lived, I would have started to see that a union of souls can be even stronger when one person or the other occasionally says, "*Schatz*, I love you, but I think you're dead wrong."

I imagine the chaos after Friedchen's death. Inge may have leveled her finger at Klaus's face after Klaus threw a toy car at Werner, who was crying on the floor. "You leave your brother alone!" she yelled. Her pregnant belly poked straight out in front of her, ballooning her white apron like a dirigible.

Heina leaned over and pulled Werner up to a sitting position. "Be a good boy for Inge," he said. "I'll just be a few hours." He stood up. "Where's Gerhild?"

Inge narrowed her eyes. "She's in bed, crying for Mama. But I only have two hands, the potatoes are burnt, and I don't have a second to haul her out and get her dressed."

Günther stepped through the back landing into the kitchen and stood with his arms crossed. "Inge," he said quietly, "Das geht einfach nicht." This will not do. "You're going to upset yourself and the baby. Our baby."

Lina, sensing conflict, strode into the kitchen. "Is it nothing but chaos around here?" she said. "Heina, a fool could see that Inge can't handle this. You need to hire someone to help out."

Inge whirled. "I can handle it," she said, untying the apron. "But I don't want it. I'm not taking what Mama took. This is not my problem." She balled up her apron and threw it in the sink.

"Inge, just for a few hours," Heina said. "I *have* hired someone. Many. Oma keeps firing them."

Inge set her mouth in a line and shook her head. "I'll watch them for today. But this is it. I've taken care of them my whole life, all of your kids. It's enough."

Now, hours later, Heina sipped a glass of seltzer water and tried to calm himself. How did one make these things work? Friedchen had held it all together, a stunning, Herculean task, he saw now. Lina and Inge wanted to kill each other, and the children were wild. He was being punished for a sin he could not put his finger on, and there were too many sins. He couldn't figure out which one was the source of all this pain and acrimony.

At the SAJ reunion dinner Heina searched the crowd with restless anxiety. All the old faces, Gustav's laugh, Rudi's smile—every gesture made him feel and long for Friedchen's presence. She was here, just out of reach. Willi Seifert, an old comrade now in charge of the youth work in Marl, came up and stuck out his hand. "Heina, how are you?"

"Good," Heina said quickly. Willi peered over his glass. Heina hated those searching looks, as if even close friends wouldn't be satisfied until they saw him break down and admit his life was awful. "I'm keeping busy," Heina said. "Lots of work with the SPD-Hüls, we've got our campaign plan to put together . . ." Heina felt his mouth take over as he slid into an almost automatic account of the political work. His list of tasks helped the world make sense, and the days ran together faster because there was always one more appointment or rally.

Easy, loud laughter rang across the garden; Jupp had arrived. Heina turned slightly, still listening to Willi talk about the youth camps planned for this summer. In a crowd of people at the gate Jupp shook hands, patted backs, making a big show of his arrival. Was Heina only imagining it, or did comrades stiffen as Jupp approached? Did Jupp receive a few uneasy glances from older SAJ members who knew or guessed what he had done to get through the war?

Willi turned his head. "There's your brother," he said tonelessly.

Heina wondered why he'd been born the eldest. He got the house, yes, but with it he got his mother, who poisoned the mornings with her sighs and the afternoons with her disapproval. The house was packed, with the Schlingermanns on the second floor along with the widow Lux and her daughter in the side room. The Dier family on the third floor beside the apartment that needed repair, and Heina, three children, and Lina on the first floor. Jupp, meanwhile, had slipped out into what seemed to be a carefree existence.

Heina chatted with a few comrades, shielding his eyes from the sun, waiting for Jupp to approach. With a slap on the shoulder and a warm nod, Jupp asked how everything was at home. Heina shrugged. "We're doing well. I'm busy with party work." This was also meant to be a dig at Jupp, who seemed to feel little obligation toward political activity these days. "But the children are having a difficult time. Naturally."

"It's a shame you can't take the kids on a vacation," Jupp said. He smoothed the lapel of his well-cut suit and threaded his arm through Else's. "Na, *Schatz*? It's good to get away every once in awhile." Else caught Heina's eye, and her cheeks reddened. She was brash and chatty, but Jupp had embarrassed her with his competitive, provocative comment. Family stories tell me that Jupp had used connections, maybe even those made during the war, to get a prime appointment at Marl's central administration, with much better pay than Heina received. Through the shield of his glasses, Jupp's restless eyes glanced lightly off Heina's face. Papa would have been mortified to see that a lifetime of political work and training had produced a braggart whose main passion was skiing. Heina inched away from Jupp.

A large SAJ sign was propped against a chair, and a group milled around near a photographer who arranged people in rows for a portrait. The photographer grabbed Heina and placed him in front near the sign, with the other short folks. A comrade with a guitar lay on the ground and strummed, and someone hummed a few bars of an old hiking song. "Move closer, now! I want to get you all in the picture," said the photographer.

I study this photograph, see women on both sides of Heina jostling closer. I imagine that small and slight Heina felt momentarily held and supported by his old comrades. If he were to fall back they would catch him, the way it used to be. He smiled, and the flashbulb popped, catching his hesitating, gentle face in a moment of lightness and laughter.

Gerhild and Klaus ran into the house, swinging their book bags. My mama-to-be remembers a lighthearted game of pitching her bag through the hallway and into the kitchen, where it arced brilliantly and slid under the table against the far wall. "Perfect 10!" yelled Klaus. Gerhild raised her fists in the air, striking a mock-Olympic pose. Klaus's broad smile fell as he looked over Gerhild's shoulder. Gerhild turned.

"Is this the way you always come home from school?" asked a squat woman with ice-pale eyes. "Go to your rooms."

Gerhild opened her mouth in a half circle, a combination of sarcasm and shock. Who had ever been sent to their rooms by a complete stranger? Papa later introduced them to Anni Schminiski, the newest housekeeper, a bitter and stunned woman whose

husband had died three weeks after their wedding and whose
family was lost somewhere in East Prussia. She was hard as flint
and here to whip the house into shape.

Within a year Heina married her. Of all the outrages imaginable, Heina married Anni. To Heina this move of desperation was
not so inconceivable. Anni seemed to have a sweet side, at least
in the first few months, and the children needed someone who
would put the Dragon in her place, fight fire with fire. Inge was
busy with her baby and her own life. Gerhild was barely passing
school, and Werner cried and cried. What was necessary, above
all, was order, a strong woman to take charge.

Sunday morning before it was daylight, Heina opened his eyes,
eager to move and get out of the house. He dressed without waking Anni, who scowled even in her sleep. She was not kind and
quiet like Friedchen; her expectations had quickly grown to ex-
ceed the size of the house, his paycheck, and their current situation. Her sharp gaze and the dissatisfied twist of her mouth
made him miss Friedchen in every moment. Heina shined the
children's shoes as he stood by the kitchen stove, then spread
butter and soft pink *Mettwurst* on rolls for lunch. The children
woke and dressed for their weekly Sunday ride in the forest. The
click of their kickstands, the swing of the gate's hinges, made
Heina's heart expand. It had rained last night, and the bicycle
tires made a sizzling sound against the pavement as they rode
through Marl and toward the trailhead.

"We should get a car like Uncle Jupp," Klaus said as they
waited to cross a busy street. He was fascinated by the new vws
and American cars and wanted to be a mechanic. All three children wanted to be rich. Heina hesitated to lecture them about
wealth and power, not sure he could compete against James
Dean movies and American pop songs. If he began his tired political speeches, they might reject him as a silly antique.

On the path Heina pumped his pedals and waited for the children to catch up. Early morning mist still blanketed the pine forest, and the sun broke through in patches, lighting the ferns that covered the forest floor. Heina stopped and turned. Klaus sped up and rode ahead, Gerhild pedaled along behind looking annoyed, and Werner struggled to catch up. "You ride too fast!" Werner whined, delicate and moody. The children needed their mother. Heina had to look away, seeing too much of Friedchen's soft frown on Werner's round face.

Later as they rode, Gerhild asked, "Why don't we go to church on Sundays? Everyone in my class goes."

"We don't need to," Heina said. "God is here, in the forest." He didn't know he was leaving breadcrumbs for her, a trail to unwind, clues about an old Teutonic nature lover and his secrets of communing with the planet.

They rode for fifteen minutes, and Heina didn't say a word. He silently rehearsed a speech for a large celebration planned at the youth home the next week, where an area youth conference would kick off the next year's youth work. He wanted to express the clear hope that these young people would revitalize the SPD, make it their own . . .

Klaus started singing one of their favorite hiking songs: "Oh, wie drückt mich, mein Cylinder!" Oh, how my hat squeezes my head!

"Gerhild, have you practiced the poem you'll read at the reception next week?" Heina asked. She nodded, focusing intently on the path, barely looking at him. Heina tried to smile, to be unaffected by their moods. But this business of raising children was baffling and more complex than he'd ever imagined, and he hadn't even appreciated the work Friedchen did until it was too late. How had she dealt with all of their tempers, all of the questions and the different demands that they seemed to have at every age and every hour of the day? It made him feel completely inadequate. Hours later, when they rolled toward the house, Gerhild winced. The sound of irate female voices, Lina and Anni screaming at each other, echoed from the backyard.

Lina pounded on the dining room table with her fist. "I can't believe you would sell the back garden," she said to Heina. "That Prussian housekeeper just wants our money!" Since Papa's death Lina had withdrawn from politics, sealing off the only escape valve for her prodigious, critical energy.

Anni stood upright and narrowed her eyes, her face bright red. She grabbed a china coffee cup in her fist and smashed it down in front of Lina on the table, shattering it. Lina stood, knocking over a chair. I am guessing about the nature of these comments, but something sparked the conflagration that follows, a story I heard many times.

"This is how you treat your mother-in-law? This is how you treat me?" Lina sputtered. "It's because Heina has no taste in women!" The children sat with mouths open in shock. Werner ran crying into the kitchen, and Gerhild ran after him.

Heina's expected role was to look away, to hush the screaming women. But something—a headache, the wasteful shock of a smashed coffee cup—made his temper flare. This was the very room where Friedchen had been laid after death, and the sniping never ceased.

"Get out of this house!" Heina yelled at Lina.

Lina glared and crossed her arms, then turned to walk through the doorway to her apartment. "You can't evict me," she said. "This house is mine."

Heina got up and ran down the kitchen steps and into the shed near the rabbit hutch. He dug in the waste bin for scrap boards and grabbed nails and a hammer. Clutching the armload he strode to the doorway of the dining room that connected to his mother's apartment.

Inside her apartment Lina ranted to herself about Anni and Heina. Heina pulled the door closed and braced it with boards, holding a nail firm and hammering it into the smooth ridged wood of the door frame. The old wood opened into tiny vertical cracks along the grain. He focused the heat in his heart on that nail head, and the next, and the next, hating himself for not seeing the truth until now, decades late. This was not a problem to be solved with patience and gritting his teeth or asking Friedchen, Anni—any woman—to grit hers.

The volume of shouting rose behind the door. His mother realized that the only exit from her room was now through the opposite door, which led out into the hallway of the apartment building. She got up and lunged for the doorknob, rattled it like a shaking fist. Her mouth moved closer to the door, and Heina could feel the vibrations of her screams through the wood.

Heina focused years of violent visions and thoughts—rage that he had barely survived walking back from the Crimea, rage at the unspeakable murder and destruction during the war (visions of red, black crosses, boiling death), horror at the death of three children—onto the target of that shiny nail head. He lost his compassion for Lina. If Papa were alive this would not have happened. If he himself were a real man, he would have learned how to contain his mother.

He finished and tossed the hammer on the floor, then left the house.

The children tiptoed through the rooms that afternoon, whispering, turning their dark eyes to the corners, then escaped to play in the street or neighbors' yards. I'm sure they remembered the scary force of their father's wrath because their memories shaped this afternoon into another inscrutable inheritance for me. Those rough crosspieces in their careful and modest living room were signs of something ruptured and broken, a whole set of possibilities, exits and entrances, cut off. But nothing was discussed, so the children probably did not understand that those pieces of wood were a sort of furious and too-belated valentine to their mother.

Heina took militant action much too late, erecting a dividing wall between his family and his mother a few years before the Soviets walled off half of Germany in 1961. When the concrete slabs and barbed wire of the Iron Curtain rose, when the watchtowers were manned and lit, Brunhilde's grave was trapped on the other side in Kahla. SPD posters and pronouncements bristled with war rhetoric, intoning the need for a new German era oriented toward self-defense and the free market economy. I don't know whether Heina saw this stance as an abandonment of a dream or as a necessary adaptation for survival.

Locally, his own political work continued at a steady pace. In the Bonn SPD archive I found an invitation for the 1960 opening celebration of a modern-looking renovated youth home. The glossy image of the building on the invitation's front is tilted at an angle, highlighting the boxy Bauhaus-style architecture and the rows of staggered windows. Heina's signature graces the invitation, which lists a program that includes the People's Choir of Marl performing "Morgenrot," "The Red of Morning," an old SPD favorite, followed by a few Beethoven pieces from a string quartet, then comments from Heina, Mayor Rudi Heiland, and other speakers.

At a pause in the program Gerhild stood before the crowd in her pressed dress and shined shoes. She cleared her throat and enunciated the words of a poem about the working class, her voice floating above the audience, filling the air of that youth home, the place that was once a wood cabin, once a Nazi hide-out, now reclaimed. The room erupted into applause.

"Genau wie Lina, die Gerhild," said the old women, shaking their heads: Gerhild is the spitting image of Lina. Holding a glass of punch, Gerhild felt a shiver up her spine, either from the cold fruit juice or fear. People were always doing this, telling her she was a replica of Lina or Inge. She did not want to be either of those women. It made her feel trapped, as if she had no choice but to become them. It made her want to run as far as she could and not look back. And Papa looked so proud. "Töchterchen," he called her, his pet name, littlest daughter.

I imagine the youth center celebration as a public escape for Heina, a bright spot of joy. At home Heina opened the door every evening to tension barely contained. Lina lost her mind in the months before her death and occasionally stripped herself naked to run into the street. Gerhild helped Heina to wrestle Lina back into her clothes, and their hands slid over her wrinkled, loose skin as she fought them. She refused to eat, and they kept her alive by giving her a daily cup of coffee with a raw egg broken into it. An eye infection had led to the removal of one eyeball, and the glass eye stood in a water tumbler on her nightstand, staring at Gerhild when she came in to collect Lina's dishes or the chamber pot. Best not to mention these things. One could be ashamed, but best not to let on.

The slick invitation and the ceremony were better proof of a life's work. The renovated youth home attested to the fact that Heina's efforts in the 1920s had borne fruit forty years later, that his work as a young man had remained relevant. The glossy program saddens me, too, with its stiff agenda of Beethoven and presentations by aging notable public figures, makes me wonder how many young people were in the audience, and whether the faces arrayed in that hall showed the shrinking numbers of the SPD's youth movement. The opening ceremony also marked Heina's last major public contribution to politics.

Heina's American second cousin, Henry Freise, mouthed his cigar. "Unions in the states are a whole different ballgame, Heina," he said, his German words stretched by an American accent. "We run St. Louis." Henry had flown in for an international labor conference in Düsseldorf and came up to Marl to visit. He'd taken Anni and Heina out twice for dinner, all the while persistently urging sixteen-year-old Gerhild to come with him to the States.

Gerhild finished her ice cream, and Heina reached for his wallet. "Oh, I'll get it," Henry said, laughing as he shifted his weight and struggled to reach into his pocket. He pulled out a wad of cash fastened with a clip and unfurled the stack of bills. "I know I've got some German cash in here somewhere . . . There it is." He threw money on the table and noticed Gerhild's eyes widen. "That's how it is in the States, sweetheart. Money to be made."

"Has the Meatcutters' Union run any candidates for office?" Heina asked.

Henry didn't seem to hear him as he leaned across the table toward Gerhild. "We'll throw you a coming-out party at the Meatcutters' Hall. You'll be a debutante," Henry said. "We've got a big house and a heated pool!" Then he turned to Heina, his face serious. "You send her to us, we'll send her to an American college."

As she walked back from the ice cream parlor, Gerhild's dark eyes fastened on her father's. "I want to go," she said. It was her chance to escape from Anni, from this boring quiet town, her chance to see America. And she deserved to have something good. She'd lost her mother, then spent years fighting with Lina and Anni until Lina's death last year.

"How would we ever afford a ticket?" Anni asked. "We don't have that kind of money, especially not on your father's retirement." Anni turned away, mouth tight.

Heina looked down at the sidewalk, unable to respond to the urgent look on Gerhild's face. "If you want to go, we can mortgage the house," he said.

Anni sighed, her hands tightening on her purse. "Did you forget that we've already borrowed against the deed?" Since Heina had had a mild stroke last year, his thoughts seemed to sometimes swim in his head. He waited for the words to cohere. "Oh, you've got no brains left, old man," Anni said.

Heina looked into a neat, gated yard as they walked up the street. That was how you hoped life would be, peaceful, measured, and scenic like a little landscaped garden. But sometimes it didn't grow into nice right angles. "We can take out a second mortgage," he said to Gerhild, "if this is what you want." He did this, reaching with all that he had, sending his youngest daughter away so she could follow her dream and get an education.

Red bunting, draped with swathes of somber black, hung from the second-floor balcony of the Marl courthouse. The mayor, Dr. Ernst Immel, stood at the podium and spoke to the crowd of more than a thousand people gathered in the light rain. Ernst listed Rudi Heiland's many political accomplishments, then described Rudi the person: headstrong, always laughing, ready to stand up and howl at you in a meeting for your traitorous abandonment of working-class politics and then smile disarmingly a second later. Flickers of white handkerchiefs appeared in the crowd as people dried their eyes and blew their noses.

Heina put his hand out to steady a heavy flower wreath on the stage that wobbled on its stand. Images flashed before his eyes: Rudi, the round-faced spark plug, running across the soccer field near the youth home, demanding to be put on a team, as his father Guido punted the ball high in the air toward the far goal. Rudi, the stubborn rebel, showing up at Heina's apartment after quitting the SPD, eyes blazing, delivering a challenge Heina couldn't rise to. Rudi waiting in a Nazi jail cell for two years, then emerging to become mayor. Too many memories.

A line of city and party officials wearing black armbands for mourning stretched on either side of the podium. It was good to see that so many people had turned out for the funeral, despite the disgrace of Rudi's later career, the bad investments he'd made with Marl city money as he tried to replace the cash flow from the postwar boom. Was each old man up on the stage thinking about his own future funeral? No, each old man was thinking that Rudi had died too young, and that they themselves would cheat death, live into their eighties or nineties, and see before they died a hint of the SPD's resurgence.

Despite the trouble at home, despite the fog in his head, the chest pains, and the numbness in his hands, Heina was glad to feel the mist on his face. We are old, Heina thought. He remembered each of the men and women on the stage when they were eighteen or nineteen, with enough energy to argue day and night and plan for the revolution that was so near it seemed to shimmer on the horizon. Now the SPD had abandoned its socialist roots, had bought into the free market ideology of . . . Heina stopped himself. There was time, for today, to see the red of the flags and the flowers and not argue with himself about the government.

The procession to the cemetery took over an hour. Rudi's coffin, borne by relatives, floated and swayed at the head of the crowd. Behind the coffin Heina walked in a double line of SPD members who held aloft the flag of SPD-Hüls, taking slow, measured steps. After the coffin was lowered, the city hall hosted a coffee reception and memorial exhibit with photos from Rudi's life. Anni had stayed home, claiming she had a cold, and Heina moved through the crowd with more energy than usual, starting conversations, smiling at people. He felt free here to enjoy the quiet.

Willi Seifert approached and handed Heina a cup of coffee. "How's your daughter doing in America?" he asked.

"She's getting married. I'm hoping to go over for her wedding in July," Heina said. He hadn't bought a ticket yet, and he wouldn't. There was no money to buy it. In any case his doctor had forbidden him to make the trip because the strain might cause another stroke. But Willi didn't need to hear these complaints. He and Willi walked through the exhibit, smiling at photos and finding black-and-white images of people they knew, laughing at the long hair, the smooth faces, the ancient-looking baggy clothes. Then Heina stopped in front of a photo: the SAJ Hüls at a summer campground gathering, kids posing with their sign, their guitars, arms around each other. Rudi stood at the front, beaming. And there she was, Friedchen, with a group of girls off to the side, a secret and shy smile hiding all of her hopes for a wonderful, happy life. At the back, looking headstrong and wild, stood Heina.

A year after Rudi's funeral Heina had another stroke. My mother got the phone call and strained to hear the truth about her father's condition through the static on the trans-Atlantic line and the vague phrases from Klaus and Inge. The house was mortgaged a third time to pay for her ticket home.

When she arrived at the hospital she stood for a moment at the door of his darkened room. Thankfully the room was quiet. Anni must have gone downstairs for food. Her father lay on the bed, his head turned to the side, his skin pale and yellowish. She took a silent step into the room, and he turned his head. "How are you?" he asked. His eyes looked a bit clouded, but alert. His voice had a catch to it, as if his throat were sore.

"The flight was fine," she said. She smiled awkwardly. His eyes drifted down to the wedding ring on her finger. "Stan says hello. We just found an apartment in St. Louis last week," she said, sitting on the edge of the bed. "There's a really small kitchen, but we're fixing it up. The neighborhood is pretty busy, and there's a German couple two buildings down that I met before I left . . ."

He smiled, enjoying her bright energy but struggling to connect the meaning of the words to things he remembered. Unless he strained hard to concentrate, the syllables were just sounds. He tried to pick out one word every few seconds and identify it. It exhausted him. He closed his eyes to fight off this splitting headache. A moment later, it seemed, he heard a sharp rustling of paper.

"He's been asleep for an hour," Gerhild said.

Heina opened his eyes. Klaus shrugged off his coat, and Klaus's wife, Christa, cleared a place on the bedside table for a vase of carnations and fern fronds.

"You're looking better already, Papa," Klaus said. "How are you feeling?"

Heina shrugged and smiled. Anni walked in, her heels clicking on the linoleum, her sharp blue-gray eyes surveying the room. "You look exhausted, Heina. You need to rest." She fussed with a flower arrangement, picking off dead blooms. "Has the lawyer come by yet?" she asked.

He closed his eyes and looked away. This was something stressful, though he didn't remember the details.

"Heina," Anni said sharply, "you have to sign the will. I want to stay in that house. I don't want to be kicked out!" She had pushed Heina to leave the house to sixteen-year-old Werner, unmarried and easy to manipulate. Heina had given in, and in the process disinherited his oldest son, Klaus, to appease Anni's fears. He put a huge burden on Werner, who would later crack under the pressure and run away to Australia.

"For God's sake!" Klaus yelled. "You have no respect! Leave him alone."

Heina rolled over on the bed and turned away, heaving his body and curling into himself. My mother remembers this last gesture, his struggling to turn away. He was so tired. Couldn't Anni see that he had just a tiny flicker of energy left? He had to rest. The house was what she wanted—

And then he was there, standing in the front hallway, smelling the wood and damp stone, working in the backyard, fixing the corner stairwell after the war. The goldfish pond, the rabbit hutch, the side storage room for the garden tools, the yard where he'd played with Brunhilde, Heinz, Karl-Heinz, every precious inch. The house, a castle his father believed would protect the family, the castle his mother wouldn't leave, the square of private property Anni now wanted.

He was about to go back there. He was about to get up and go on a hike. He was ready to leave for a trip with Friedchen and Jupp and the SAJ, ready to grab his backpack and be out under the canopy of trees, breathing in the smell of earth and ferns. He was about to board a train and head east, into a horrible battle with pits of the dead on either side. He was taking off on his bicycle, speeding down a rough hill, with dangerous secret cargo in the basket. He was rushing through the air, exhausted by the pace, hungering after all this movement for space to be still.

Heina, thank you for your advice the other day. I haven't solved the problem by any means, because a girl's got to make a living. But knowing you were there to ask—that helped while I was limping in tight shoes around downtown Columbus, late to an interview at the labor union's headquarters.

I found the union president's office, and he launched into the job description of the work they needed me to do. I was taken, I tell you, full of love and the sense of being needed. I nodded and made comments, able to finish his sentences. It was clear, laid out in front of me—the work, the press releases to write, the contract fights looming, the policy issues. I felt an itching in my fingers to be at the keyboard, to start on the list of slogans. I felt that sharpness of focus and concentration around my eyes.

"Well, it sounds like you understand what we're about," the union president said, smiling. I liked him; he seemed honest, worn by his work. "What other questions do you have?"

"You mentioned in the ad that this could be a contract position," I said. "I have a six-month-old son, and I don't have good daycare. I'm not sure I could do full-time work right now."

He leaned back in the black leather chair. "I'm not going to shade the truth here," he said, his smile fading like shutters crashing down, replaced with the union tight-lipped bargaining face. "This is more than a full-time job. It's probably about three full-time jobs." In my chest, desire caught and spun, a bicycle gear without the chain, a withering sense that I could promise my life away effortlessly in this free fall. "I know how hard it is to find good childcare," he said. "When my daughter was little we were lucky enough to have an Indian couple looking after her. They cooked every day, and when our daughter came home each evening, she smelled delicious."

He smiled again, flashing his teeth through a white beard. "Of course her first word was *Mammam*, and my wife—well, my ex-wife now—thought she said, *Mama*. But it was mammam she was asking for, a lentil dish. Very tasty, by the way." I laughed, smiled, felt the edges of my eyes crinkle in false amusement and dread. Oh, god. "But back to the job," he said. "This is a bargaining unit position. The benefits are excellent, the pay is pretty good . . ." He pushed the pay scale worksheet across the table toward me. I saw a column of figures and dollar signs. The first pay grade was more than I'd ever made, and beyond that, incredible raises.

We shook hands again. I shuffled my papers together and grabbed the pay scale worksheet. At a stoplight I put my hair up in a ponytail and dug through my bag for the worksheet, dumping my portfolio of press clips onto the floor as I accelerated. I was greedy to touch that piece of paper, to see that row of numbers, to imagine each paycheck. All that money. I drove down Broad Street toward the highway and passed an old stone church. On the low wall near the road was a Day-Glo printed sign: "Childcare for Infants and Toddlers—Open Enrollment Now!" And I could pay for daycare. And we'd have good benefits. And that might be the most loving sacrifice I could make.

Trust your gut, I told myself. But I didn't have a gut feeling—I was just sad. My brain wanted to make it work, to take the childcare sign, the good vibe from the office and the interview, the fat paycheck, as a list of neon arrows pointing in the right direction. The fresh blisters on my feet stung, and I kicked off my shoes, finding the gas pedal with my bare toes.

I tried to imagine the taste of an Indian dish on my tongue, the curry, the sweet and pungent spices. I tried to imagine the second or third day of work in the union office, the to-do lists creeping down the legal pads. Neither of these choices—stay-at-home mom or union warrior—made sense for me right now. I looked in the rearview mirror and merged into speeding traffic.

"Don't give me guilt about the movement," I said—to someone, a reflexive voice in my head. "The movement will still be here in two or three years." Who was that voice? It wasn't Heina goading me on. Heina had little compassion for himself, but he would look at me with aching eyes and want, for me, moments of rest. That is what he would have wanted, if he had known. I imagined the bottomless, bitter hunger in Lina's eyes, the desire for both justice and safety. And I imagined you, Heina, baby boy in a carriage, advancing toward a line of policemen and scabs on a picket line. So that's what I have, for right now, a sinking sense that even though my gut wants the rush of a fight, I can't lay down my baby boy for this job, for this good cause. And tomorrow it starts all over again. Heina, I'm going to try to do this right, but you have to help me. Help me do this right.

Buschmann Family Tree

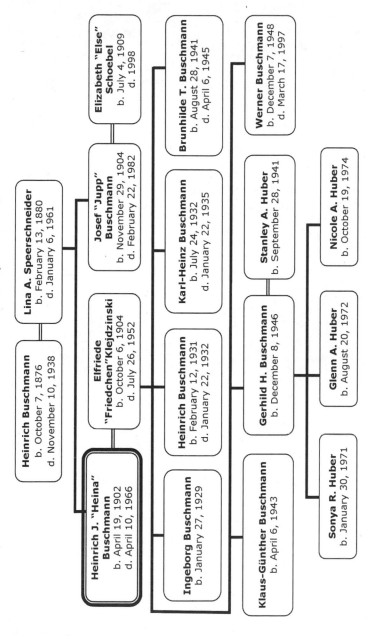

Political and Family Chronology

1902

April 19: Heinrich Johann "Heina" Buschmann born to Heinrich Buschmann Sr., coal miner, and Lina Buschmann.

1903

Heinrich Buschmann Sr. joins the SPD.

1904

Max Peters, a sixteen-year-old apprentice in Berlin, founds the Union of Apprentices and Young Workers.

October 6: Elfriede "Friedchen" Klejdzinski born.

November 29: Josef "Jupp" Buschmann born.

1905

More than two hundred thousand miners strike in Ruhr-area mines as the unions struggle with internal tensions and discrimination against Polish workers.

Failed Russian Revolution.

1907

January 8: Heinrich Buschmann Sr. excommunicated from the Catholic Church by the court in Rhade due to union activity; now lists his religion as "God-Believer."

September 30: Heinrich Buschmann Sr. opens "Sweet Heinrich" candy store on Bahnhof Straße in Kahla in Thüringen area of southeast Germany (Prussia); he also works as a baker.

1908

Youth group organizes under SPD, with a newspaper called *Arbeiter-Jugend*, or Worker-Youth.

"Gag" act passed to restrict use of foreign languages at public meetings, targeting Polish workers.

1909

July 4: Heinrich Buschmann Sr. granted citizenship in Kingdom of Prussia.

1910

Heina Buschmann misses thirty-two days of school due to lung infection.

1912

Local branch of SPD founded in Marl.

Stenographers' Union founded in Bochum, which begins the Bochum youth movement.

SPD's success in Reichstag elections leads to antisocialist hysteria.

1913

Buschmann family returns to Marl.

The growing SPD wins five seats in Marl City Council.

1914

June 28: Archduke Ferdinand assassinated in Sarajevo, and Austro-Hungary prepares to attack Serbia.

August: Germany sees itself in a stranglehold and declares preemptive war on France and Russia.

August 2: Heinrich Buschmann Sr. mobilized with Battalion Five, will see battle in Verdun and Somme.

1915

December 15: General Ludendorff makes comments about need to acquire racial "breeding grounds" in the east.

1916

Germany attacks Verdun, resulting in three hundred thousand German casualties.

Heinrich Buschmann Sr. released from active military service.

SPD purges independent activists from its ranks; Sozialdemokratische Arbeitsgemeinschaft, an independent socialist group to the left of the SPD, is founded.

Karl Liebknecht, an independent socialist member of parliament, is arrested at a May Day antiwar rally in Berlin. Universal conscription for all men between seventeen and sixty.

September 30: Heina Buschmann graduates from Handelsschule Pyra in Recklinghausen.

1917

"Turnip Winter," food shortages and miners' strikes.

February: Heina begins as apprentice at Recklinghausen county administration.

March: Russian Revolution begins.

April 6: As a result of Germany's U-boat campaign, United States declares war on Germany.

The Independent Social Democratic Party of Germany, or Unabhängige Sozialdemokratische Partei Deutschlands (USPD), is founded to protest the SPD's position of support for the war, and one hundred thousand leave the SPD to join the USPD.

November: Bolshevik Revolution in Russia.

1918

November 6–8: Workers' and Soldiers' Councils take power in Hamburg, Bremen, Lübeck, Dresden, Leipzig, Chemnitz, Magdeburg, Brunswick, Frankfurt, Köln, Stuttgart, Nuremberg, and Munich.

November 9: Revolution forces the abdication of the Kaiser. The newspaper *Tägliche Rundschau* (*Daily Observer*) briefly becomes *Die Rote Fahne* (*The Red Flag*).

November 10: German provisional revolutionary government established.

The Freikorps, the conservative militia, begins organizing.

When naval officers protest lack of pay, Friedrich Ebert of the SPD orders the SPD to crush the strike. To protest this use of violence, the USPD leaves the Ebert government.

1919

Communists occupy newspaper building in Berlin. Many area Workers' and Soldiers' Councils lean toward the conservative Freikorps as Germany erupts in civil war. Freikorps spreads anti-Bolshevik hysteria and demands federal takeover of Workers' and Soldiers' Councils.

January 15: Rosa Luxemburg and Karl Liebknecht murdered.

February 14: Bloody invasion of Dorsten by the government, which spreads the next day to Recklinghausen.

April: A soviet republic declared in Bavaria.

May 1: Munich retaken by federal troops, one thousand killed.

June 28: Treaty of Versailles signed.

November 18: Hindenburg testifies that Germany lost the war because it was "stabbed in the back" by Jews and Marxists.

1920

March 13–20: Kapp Putsch put down by a general strike. Ruhr workers then face a takeover attempt from the Freikorps and Reichswehr. The Red Army builds to fifty thousand in the Ruhr, and the Reichswehr retaliates with tanks.

April 1: The Freikorps invades the Ruhr and Marl is occupied. Leaders of the USPD are sentenced to death.

The USPD splits the following month, with half joining the Soviet-led Comintern and a minority going back into the SPD.

August 28: First Worker-Youth fest in Weimar; youth organization has seventy-five thousand members. Right-wing youth groups formed, including the Bismarck League and the German National Youth Association, whose members carry truncheons and harass Jews.

1921

Heina Buschmann joins SPD.

1922

Most strikes (4,338) in German history, with 1.6 million workers involved. Industrialists push for a ten-hour day for workers without additional pay; many workers at starvation level.

June 24: Walther Rathenau, a charismatic Jewish foreign minister, assassinated.

October 29: The SPJ and the Verband der Arbeiterjugendvereine come together to form the SAJ.

1923

Astronomical inflation; French occupy the Ruhr.

National Socialist (Nazi) Party introduces propaganda emphasizing cleansing towns of the "Red Terror."

November 8–9: Hitler's failed Beer Hall Putsch in Munich.

November 20: Communist Party temporarily outlawed.

December: Approximately 1.5 million Germans are unemployed, including one-fourth of union members; almost half of those with jobs are only half-time.

1924

Socialist youth home opens in Marl.

1925

February 28: Friedrich Ebert, SPD leader of German government, dies.

April 25: General Hindenburg elected with support of SPD.

October: Left opposition expelled from SAJ.

1926

Heinrich Buschmann Sr. and Lina Buschmann run for city council.

1927

Heinrich Buschmann Sr. is head of coal miners' co-op store and working as an overseer in coal mine. Buschmann family builds a house.

1928

August 10: SPD votes in favor of funding Germany's military rearmament.

October 21: Heinrich Buschmann Sr. honored for twenty-five years of activity in SPD.

November 24: Heina Buschmann and Friedchen Klejdzinski are married.

1929

All Quiet on the Western Front published.

January 27: Heina and Friedchen's daughter Inge born.

Industrialists and right-wingers attack unemployment insurance, and SPD withdraws support for government coalition.

October 24: Wall Street crash in United States, bringing sudden end of U.S. loans to Germany.

1930

Heina elected to county-level leadership in SAJ.

A "poor kitchen" run out of the youth home.

March: Chancellor Müller cuts unemployment benefits to save money; SPD pulls out of the government to protest this move.

July: Reichstag is dissolved.

September 14: Nazi Party gains ninety-five seats in Reichstag.

December: Leadership of SPD sends Reichsbanner to break up meetings of Rote Kämpfer, a left-wing youth group.

sphere exists in the streets, with many deaths at the hands of the SA. Nazis and communists involved in a physical fight in Reichstag, throwing ashtrays, spittoons, desk tops, and phones. Circle of advisors around Hindenburg promotes Hitler as next leader.

33

January 30: Hitler appointed chancellor.

January 31: Heina Buschmann's house searched.

February 28: Reichstag is burned, and Nazis blame communists, launching waves of repression.

March 23: Hitler asks Reichstag for four years without parliamentary control to reform the country.

May 10: Nazis occupy SPD offices, and most leaders emigrate.

May 17: Hitler gives Reichstag speech about his peaceful intentions.

June 8: Heina has to fill out a form attesting to Aryan descent.

June 22: Hitler outlaws all SPD activity.

September 15: Heina has to fill out a second form attesting to Aryan descent and whether a relative served in World War I.

September 30: Heina has to fill out a questionnaire listing his former political affiliations.

December 1: Heina joins NS Volkswohlfahrt (NSV), a Nazi Party welfare organization.

34

January 1: Heina joins Reichsbunds Deutscher Beamten (RDB), a company union of government officials.

June 30: SA purge, called "Night of the Long Knives."

35

January 22: Heina and Friedchen's son Karl-Heinz, age two and a half, dies.

1931

February 12: Heina and Friedchen's son He

Sozialistische Arbeiterpartei founded.

September 29: SPD expels left-wing leader

October: SPD leaders create the Iron Fro
against Fascism. Iron Front campaigns for
bol is three white downward-pointing ar
resistance to Nazism, to communism, and

October 10: Hindenburg interviews Hitler
cellor, finds him unfit.

November: Boxheim Papers leaked, which
after seizure of power. Government does n

1932

Heina joins the Reichsbanner and Iron Fro

January 22: Heina and Friedchen's son
months, dies.

February 2: SPD supports Hindenburg (its
election.

April: Nazi SA and SS banned due to press
ing Prussia.

May: Right-wing German government ho
zis by giving them power, and aims to crus
SPD.

July 20: German government takes over SP
ernment, and SPD does not mobilize to re

July 24: Heina and Friedchen's son Karl-H

July 31: Nazi Party wins 230 seats in Parlia
munists win more votes than socialists
izes. Communists declare the SPD to be
Nazis.

One in three Germans is on public assis
man suicide rate is triple that of Britain

January 28: Recklinghausen-area SA defaces graves of communist activists.

March 9–May 6: Heina enlists in Arbeitsdienst, the work-service corps. He gets a raise at work, joins Reichsluftschutzbundes (RLB), a neighborhood air raid watch group.

May 1: Mass arrest during illegal May Day celebration in Essen.

September 15: Nuremberg racial laws announced.

1936

Second search of Buschmann home. Youth home is closed.

January 7: Heina has to sign a form pledging allegiance to Adolf Hitler.

March 8–May 9: Heina sent to military service in Stettin with the "Pionier," or Pioneer Company 5.

September 18: An officer sends a letter to Heina's boss inquiring about Heina's criminal record; reply says no crimes have been committed.

November: Heina joins Reichskolonialbund, a Nazi organization devoted to the "recovery" of German colonies in Africa.

November 13: Heina has to fill out a long questionnaire about his past political work.

November 24: A memo is sent to the county office of the Nazi Party asking for a confidential report about Heina's political activities.

December 9: The official Nazi union verifies that Heina is not politically questionable. Heina helps with welfare collections.

1937

January 11: Heina is given notice of a three-month probationary period leading to position as Beamte, or county administrator.

January: Heina joins Verein für das Deutschtum im Auslande

(VDA), a state organization devoted to "uniting" Germans worldwide.

February 8: Heina passes a medical exam as part of his probationary requirement, with good health except for his lower-left lung.

May 7: Heina is sent another questionnaire about membership in the Nazi Party, and he replies "Nein."

1938

March 15: Heina is sent another questionnaire about membership in the Nazi Party, and he replies "Nein." He responds also that he is a member of Kraft durch Freude, a workers' leisure organization run through the Nazi Party official labor organization.

June 4–August 9: Wave of repression against homosexuals in Köln.

November 9–10: *Kristallnacht*, or "Night of Broken Glass," coordinated attacks on Jews across Germany.

November 10: Heinrich Buschmann Sr. dies of black lung disease.

1939

March 15: Germany occupies Czechoslovakia.

September 1: Germany invades Poland.

September 3: Britain and France declare war.

September 28: Heina sent to military service as a medic with Pioneer Company 5.

1940

March 1: Heina promoted to *Gefreiten*, or private first class.

April 9: Germany invades Denmark and Norway.

May 10: Germany invades Belgium, Holland, Luxembourg, and France.

October 16: Heina on leave from military service.

1941

April: Germany invades Yugoslavia and Greece.

June 22: Germany invades Russia.

Summer: "Final Solution" leading to Holocaust launched.

August 28: Heina and Friedchen's daughter Brunhilde Trauhild born.

December 7: Japan attacks Pearl Harbor.

December 11: Germany declares war on United States.

1942

January 20: Wannsee Conference, which details plans to carry out Final Solution.

April 1: Heina promoted to *Kreisobersekretär*, or county head secretary.

June 29: Heina drafted into military service.

September 3: Heina receives a card telling him that through an order from the Sixth Battalion of Münster, he's assigned to Feldtruppe Einheit, Feldpostnummer 2 44 21.

Fall: Battle of Stalingrad begins.

1943

January: Sixth Army surrenders at Stalingrad.

February: Goebbels calls for Total War.

April 6: Heina and Friedchen's son Klaus-Günther is born.

June: Hüls Bunawerk factory bombed, 850 dead.

1944

June 6: D-Day in Normandy.

June 20: Unsuccessful attempt to assassinate Hitler.

1945

Friedchen, Else, Inge, Klaus, and Brunhilde flee on bicycles to Thüringen.

April 6: Heina and Friedchen's daughter Brunhilde, age three years, dies.

April 30: Hitler commits suicide.

May 7–9: Germany surrenders.

July 8: Heina sent home from war with bullet wound in left thigh.

July 30: Heina has to fill out a form about his political history (in German and English); he reports that he was not a member of resistance groups and did not have his freedom restricted by the Nazis.

October 21: First postwar meeting of Hüls village-area SPD.

November 4: SPD reformed in Marl, and Heina elected a part of first area leadership.

1946

January 1: Heina leaves position at Recklinghausen county office to move to Marl office.

April 23: Meeting in Frankfurt to plan socialist youth conference.

July 26–28: Youth conference in Nuremberg.

December 8: Heina and Friedchen's daughter Gerhild Heidi born.

1947

February 12: Area socialist youth meet in youth home.

December: Heina's pamphlet calling for union participation in economic planning is published.

1948

May 6–9: Youth conference in Herne, with much conflict about whether the organization should be pedagogical or revolutionary.

December 7: Heina and Friedchen's son Werner born.

1949

Heina Buschmann is promoted to *Verwaltungsdirektor*, or office director.

1952

July 26: Elfriede "Friedchen" Buschmann, age forty-seven, dies of kidney infection/failure.

1953

SPD suffers huge loss in elections.

1954

Heina delivers opening speech at a youth celebration hosted at youth home.

1956

February: Khrushchev's speech on crimes of Stalin.

1960

Youth home renovated.

1961

January 6: Lina Buschmann dies.

August 13: Berlin Wall built.

1962

March: Heina suffers first stroke.

1963

August 1: Heina retires.

1965

May 12: Rudi Heiland's funeral; fifteen hundred in attendance.

1966

April 10: Heina Buschmann, age sixty-three, dies.

Bibliography

I consulted many sources to learn about German history, but I have included in this list mainly the works that provided detail on Marl or Ruhr-area history. Many of these are transcriptions of interviews conducted and published by nonprofit organizations, small archives, or individuals, and I felt it important to acknowledge this grassroots historical research to spread awareness about these resources.

Adler, Hannelore, et al. *Neuer Aufbruch zu altern Ufern? Über die Wiedergründung der Sozialdemokratischen Partei Deutschlands im Bezirk Westliches Westfalen nach 1945.* Dortmund: SPD Bezirk Westliches Westfalen, 1992.

Bauke, Dieter. *SAJ-Erinnerungen 1928, Nach Dortmund und dem Rhein: Das Tagebuch von Alfred Rosenkranz.* Oer-Erkenschwick: Archiv der Arbeiterjugendbewegung, 1998.

Bogdal, Hermann. *Rote Fahne im Vest,* Vol. 1, *Novembertage 1918 in Recklinghausen.* Essen: Klartext Verlag, 1984.

―――. *Rote Fahne im Vest,* Vol. 2, *Die Niederschlag des Kapp-Putsches.* Essen: Klartext Verlag, 1984.

Brack, Ulrich, ed. *Herrshaft und Verfolgung: Marl im Nationalsozialismus.* Essen: Klartext Verlag, 1987.

Brack, Ulrich, and Klaus Mohr. *Neubeginn und Wiederaufbau: Marl in der Nachkriegzeit 1945-1949.* Essen: Klartext Verlag, 1994.

Dunke, Gert Dieter, and Wolfgang Gottschalk. *Paul Rhode: Ein Leben für die sozialdemokratie, Leben und Wirken Eines Recklinghäuser Sozialdemokraten.* Recklinghausen: Sozialistische Bildungsgemeinschaft Recklinghausen e.V., 1986.

Gröschel, Roland. *Zwischen Tradition und Neubeginn: Sozialistische Jugend im Nachkriegsdeutschland.* Hamburg: Ergebnisse Verlag, 1986.

Hansen, Werner. "Der Kampf der Gewerkschaften im Hinblick auf die Neuordnung der Wirtschaft: Rede des Landesbezirksvorsitzenden des DGB Nordrhein Westfalen." Düsseldorf: DGB Nordrhein Westfalen, 1950.

Kleßmann, Christoph, and Peter Friedemann. Streiks und Hungermärsche im Ruhrgebiet, 1946–1948. New York: Campus Verlag.

Kulczycki, John J. The Foreign Worker and the German Labor Movement: Xenophobia and Solidarity in the Coal Fields of the Ruhr, 1871-1914. Providence: Berg, 1994.

Niethammer, Lutz, ed. "Hinterher merkt man, daß es richtig war, daß es schiefgegangen ist": Nachkriegs-Erfahrungen im Ruhrgebiet. Lebensgeschichte und Sozialkultur im Ruhrgebiet 1930 bis 1960, Band 2. Berlin: Verlag J. H. W. Dietz, 1983.

Peukert, Detlev. Ruhrarbeiter Gegen den Faschismus: Dokumentation über den Widerstand im Ruhrgebiet, 1933–1945. Frankfurt: Roderberg-Verlag, 1976.

Porck, Friedhelm. SPD: Unsere Arbeit, Unser Weg in Neuen Revier. Unterbezirk Recklinghausen, 1945–1955. Gladbeck: Unterbezirk Recklinghausen SPD, 1955.

Rüter, Stefan, and Sonja Böcker. Marl in der NS-Zeit: Was man nicht verdrängen sollte. Marl: Marler Stadtmagazins News, 1997.

Seebacher-Brandt, Brigitte. Biedermann und Patriot: Erich Ollenhauer—Ein Sozialdemokratisches Leben. PhD diss., Frei Universitäts Berlin, Rheinbreitbach, 1984.

In the American Lives series

UNIVERSITY OF NEBRASKA PRESS

Also of Interest in the American Lives series:

Bigger than Life
A Murder, a Memoir
By Dinah Lenney

Bigger than Life is a compellingly edgy memoir describing how Dinah Lenney navigated her life amid the complex feelings that surfaced after she learned her father had been murdered by three teenagers during a botched kidnapping and robbery.

ISBN: 978-0-8032-2976-1 (cloth)

Turning Bones
By Lee Martin

Farmers and pragmatists, hardworking people who made their way west from Kentucky through Ohio and Indiana to settle in southern Illinois, Lee Martin's ancestors left no diaries or letters; apart from birth certificates and gravestones, they left little written record of their lives. Turning Bones is the moving account of a family's migration over two hundred years and through six generations, imagined, reconstructed, and made to speak to the author, and to readers, of a lost world.

ISBN: 978-0-8032-3231-0 (cloth)

The Fortune Teller's Kiss
By Brenda Serotte

Shortly before her eighth birthday, in the fall of 1954, Brenda Serotte came down with polio—painfully singled out in a world already marked by differences. Her bout with the dreaded disease is at the heart of this poignant and heartbreakingly hilarious memoir of growing up a Sephardic Jew among Ashkenazi neighbors in the Bronx.

ISBN: 978-0-8032-4326-2 (cloth)

Order online at www.nebraskapress.unl.edu or call
1-800-755-1105. Mention the code "BOFOX" to receive a 20% discount.